The Environment of Disability Income Policy:

Programs, People, History and Context

Jerry L. Mashaw

and

Virginia P. Reno

Editors

Disability Policy Panel Interim Report
Washington, D.C.
1996

NATIONAL
ACADEMY
OF·SOCIAL
INSURANCE

The National Academy of Social Insurance is a nonprofit, nonpartisan organization made up of the nation's leading experts on social insurance. Its mission is to conduct research, enhance public understanding, develop new leaders and provide a nonpartisan forum for exchange of ideas on important issues in the field of social insurance. Social insurance, both in the United States and abroad, encompasses broad-based systems for insuring workers and their families against economic insecurity caused by loss of income from work and protecting individuals against the cost of personal health care services. The Academy's research covers social insurance systems, such as Social Security, unemployment insurance, workers' compensation and Medicare, and related social assistance and private employee benefits.

The Academy convenes study panels that are charged with conducting research, issuing findings and, in some cases, reaching recommendations based on their analyses. Panel members are selected for their recognized expertise and with due consideration for the balance of disciplines and perspectives appropriate to the project. The findings and any recommendations remain those of study panels and do not represent an official position of the Academy or its funders.

In accordance with procedures of the Academy, study panel reports are reviewed by a committee of the Board for completeness, accuracy, clarity and objectivity. The findings and recommendations in this report are those of the Disability Policy Panel.

The project received financial support from The Pew Charitable Trusts, The Robert Wood Johnson Foundation and corporate members of the Health Insurance Association of America that offer long-term disability insurance.

© 1996 National Academy of Social Insurance

Library of Congress Catalog Card Number: 96-70001
ISBN 1-884902-05-7

The Disability Policy Panel

Jerry L. Mashaw, Chair, Sterling Professor of Law
Institute of Social and Policy Studies
Yale University Law School, New Haven, CT

Monroe Berkowitz, Professor of Economics, Emeritus
Rutgers University, New Brunswick, NJ

Richard V. Burkhauser, Professor of Economics
Center for Policy Research Maxwell School
Syracuse University, Syracuse, NY

Gerben DeJong, Director
National Rehabilitation Hospital-Research Center
Washington, DC

James N. Ellenberger, Assistant Director
Department of Occupational Safety and Health
AFL-CIO, Washington, DC

Lex Frieden, Senior Vice President
The Institute for Rehabilitation and Research
Houston, TX

Howard H. Goldman, M.D., Professor of Psychiatry
University of Maryland School of Medicine
Baltimore, MD

Arthur E. Hess, Consultant
Former Deputy Commissioner of Social Security
Charlottesville, VA

Thomas C. Joe, Director
Center for the Study of Social Policy, Washington, DC

Charles Jones, President
National Council of Disability Determination
Directors, Lansing, MI

Mitchell P. LaPlante, Associate Adjunct Professor
Institute for Health and Aging
University of California, San Francisco, CA

Douglas A. Martin, Special Assistant to the Chancellor
University of California, Los Angeles, CA

David Mechanic, Director
Institute for Health, Health Care Policy
    and Aging Research
Rutgers University, New Brunswick, NJ

Patricia M. Owens, President
Integrated Disability Management
UNUM America, Brooklyn, NY

James M. Perrin, M.D., Associate Professor of Pediatrics
Harvard Medical School
Massachusetts General Hospital, Boston, MA

Donald L. Shumway, Co-director
RWJ Project on Developmental Disabilities
Institute on Disabilities
University of New Hampshire, Concord, NH

Susan S. Suter, President
World Institute on Disability, Oakland, CA

Eileen P. Sweeney, Director of Government Affairs
Children's Defense Fund, Washington, DC

Preface

The Disability Policy Project of the National Academy of Social Insurance began with a request from the Chairmen of the Committee on Ways and Means of the U. S. House of Representatives and its Social Security Subcommittee in the 102nd Congress. The Academy was asked to undertake a comprehensive review of the Social Security disability programs, with a particular emphasis on improving work outcomes for applicants, beneficiaries and denied applicants for disability benefits. The letter of request is at appendix A.

To conduct the study, the Academy assembled a panel of leading experts on disability policy from varied disciplines and very different perspectives on disability policy. As we began our work, we found that it was it imperative to step back from the details of policy proposals to articulate our goals and perspective on disability policy and to undertake a broad review of the context of disability income policy in the United States. This report presents those findings after the first year of our work.
In chapter 1 we present our perspective on disability policy. We believe that the primary goal of disability policy is the integration of persons with disabilities into mainstream society. Further, we agree that disability is not just an attribute of individuals. Rather it reflects the relationship between individuals who have impairments and the broader environment. This report explores that broader environment.

In chapter 2, we find that the two federal programs that are the focus of our study — Social Security disability insurance (DI) and Supplemental Security Income (SSI) — each have distinct purposes and they are only part of the network of disability income programs in the United States. While their coverage is broad, they are strictly and frugally designed to provide only modest levels of income support to persons who meet a very strict test of work disability. The state-administered workers' compensation system provides cash benefits to workers injured on the job. Unlike DI and SSI, workers' compensation is paid for temporary work incapacity and for partial work disability. And workers' compensation pays for medical care and rehabilitation as well as cash benefits.

Workers whose illness or injuries are not caused on the job may be eligible for paid sick leave or short-term disability insurance. But this coverage is spotty. While five states have mandatory programs of temporary disability insurance, in other jurisdictions coverage of short-term sickness or of the early months of longer-term disability is available at the discretion of employers or is negotiated by unions. Fully 30 percent of private sector workers have neither paid sick leave nor short-term disability insurance. Another 26 percent have only sick leave, which often does not last long enough to cover the early months of longer-term disabilities. While short-term disability benefits offer an opportunity for early intervention and return to work initiatives by employers and insurers, gaps in this protection are problematic as we consider ways to promote work among those who ultimately turn to the federal benefit programs.

In chapter 3 we find that the working-age population with any sort of disability is much larger than the number who have met the strict test of eligibility for DI or SSI benefits. DI beneficiaries tend to be older workers — more than half are over the age of 50 — and they often are ill or have impairments associated with aging. SSI beneficiaries tend to be younger. Mental retardation or mental illness is the primary diagnosis for more half of the beneficiaries. About 3 in 10 SSI beneficiaries have impairments such that they need a representative payee to manage their benefit checks. Our review of the research literature on applicants who had been denied DI benefits from the 1960s through the 1980s finds that fewer than half had succeeded in returning to work within a few years after being denied benefits. The economic status of those who were not working was poor, and their self-reported health status was not appreciably better than that of persons allowed benefits.

Chapter 4 traces the wide fluctuations in DI benefit awards that have occurred over the last quarter of a century. Cyclical changes in the availability of jobs in the economy appear to influence disability benefit claims. But as detailed in chapter 5, both subtle and not-so-subtle changes in law, administrative practices and the adequacy of administrative resources in relation to workloads can have a profound effect on disability benefit awards. This sobering finding impressed upon us the importance of formulating changes in the disability benefit programs carefully with due regard for the long-term consequences of even relatively modest changes.

Finally, in chapter 6 we explore how changes in the broader environment beyond the DI and SSI programs affect opportunities and constraints for workers with disabilities and how this broader environment affects demands placed on the DI and SSI programs. First, structural shifts in the labor market appear to be a two-edged sword. Declining demand for workers with limited skills places an added burden on workers doubly disadvantaged by limited skills and physical or mental impairments. On the other hand, technological advances and the public accommodation features of the Americans with Disabilities Act of 1990 open up opportunities for workers with significant physical impairments who also have high aptitude and advanced educations.

Second, a host of other public or private policy interventions can be viewed as alternatives to income support through DI or SSI for some subset of applicants. Consequently, developments in vocational rehabilitation, job subsidies, unemployment insurance, private pensions, employment-based health insurance and generalized assistance programs affect demands placed on federal disability income programs. Third, severe mental illness is an important cause of work disability. Changes in treatment of mental illness have increased the likelihood that individuals with severe mental illness live in the community, rather than in institutions, and therefore need and qualify for income support in order to cover daily needs for food, clothing and shelter. Finally, state and local governments, employers, insurers and health care providers have recognized cost savings to their systems by ensuring that SSI and DI serve as first payer of benefits for individuals who have severe and persistent disabilities. A sophisticated cadre of experts has become available to claimants or alternative payers to help file claims for the federal disability income programs. All of these environmental factors have a role in influencing demands placed on the DI and SSI programs.

In this report, the Panel issued findings on three topics related to disability income policy: the importance of health care coverage; the need for adequate resources to administer disability benefits; and the gaps in knowledge that can only be filled by an on-going commitment to research on disability populations and programs.

This report was prepared under the direction of the Disability Policy Panel by Virginia P. Reno, Director of the Disability Policy Project. Mary L. Ross contributed to many sections of the report and prepared the appendices on the legislative development of the DI and SSI programs. Ronald L. Davis prepared the review of the research literature on persons who had been denied DI benefits. Suzanne Payne provided research assistance to the project and invaluable support to all project activities including the completion of this report.

The Panel and staff received assistance from many individuals and agencies, including the Department of Labor, the Department of Health and Human Services and the Social Security Administration, all of which responded promptly and fully to requests for information. We particularly wish to acknowledge those components of the Social Security Administration that have provided data for this report — the Office of the Actuary, the Office of Disability, the Office of Hearings and Appeals, the Office of Research and Statistics and the Office of Supplemental Security Income.

This report was issued in preliminary form in March 1994 as a way to invite public comment and suggestions for proposals for the Panel's consideration as we developed our recommendations. This report also formed the groundwork for the analyses that culminated in the recommendations in our final report, *Balancing Security and Opportunity: The Challenge of Disability Income Policy,* issued in 1996. Whether or not readers embrace our policy recommendations, I trust that this report will remain a valuable resource for scholars, advocates and policy makers as they consider the future of disability income policy in the United States.

Jerry L. Mashaw
Chair, Disability Policy Panel
Sterling Professor of Law
Yale University

Contents

OVERVIEW 1

Chaper 1   **THE PANEL'S PERSPECTIVE** 11

Chapter 2   **DISABILITY INCOME PROGRAMS** 13
Social Security Disability Insurance 14
Supplemental Security Income 25
Compensation Programs 29
Private Short-Term Disability Benefits 34
Private Long-Term Disability Benefits and Pensions 37
Other Needs-Based Disability Cash Benefits 41

Chapter 3   **THE POPULATION WITH DISABILITIES** 45
Prevalence of Disability 45
Persons Receiving Social Security or Supplemental Security Incomes 47
Outcomes for Persons Denied Benefits 55

Chapter 4   **FLUCTUATIONS IN DISABILITY BENEFIT AWARDS** 61
Cyclical Changes in the Economy 61
The Beneficiary Rolls 62

Chapter 5   **HISTORY OF DISABILITY INCOME POLICY** 67
The Early 1970s: Growth in the Disability Rolls 67
1975-1980: Controlling Expansion 70
1981-1984: Retrenchment and Reaction 76
1985-1989: Economic Expansion, Agency Downsizing 79
The Early 1990s: Growth of the Disability Rolls 79
Summary 82

Chapter 6   **THE BROADER CONTEXT OF DISABILITY INCOME POLICY   85**
Structural Shifts in the Labor Market   85
Changes in Other Public and Private Support   88
Availability of Health Insurance   93
Changes in Treatment for Severe Mental Illness   94
Claimant Representation and Third Party Interest   97

Chapter 7   **PRELIMINARY FINDINGS   103**
Disability Benefits and Health Care   104
Effective Administration   105
Long-Term Research   108

APPENDICES   111
A. Letter of Request   111
B. Legislative Development of the Disability Insurance Program   113
C. Legislative Development of the Supplemental Security Income Program   131
D. Federal Programs Affecting Persons with Disabilities   147

PANEL BIOGRAPHIES   157
ABBREVIATIONS   161

Overview

The Disability Policy Panel of the National Academy of Social Insurance issued this report as a way to invite public comment and suggestions for specific policy proposals for the Panel's consideration in developing its policy recommendations.

The Panel was convened by the Academy in March 1993 in response to a request from the chairmen of the Committee on Ways and Means of the U. S. House of Representatives and of its Social Security Subcommittee. They asked the Academy to conduct a comprehensive review of disability income policy with a particular emphasis on ways to enable persons with disabilities to remain in or return to the work force as well as to better serve those who are denied benefits but do not find work. In its first year, the Panel engaged in fact finding and information gathering with regard to disability policy and the broad economic, social and political environment in which that policy operates. Preliminary results of that review are in this report.

THE PANEL'S PERSPECTIVE

Chapter 1 presents the Panel's perspective on disability policy. The Panel believes: that the primary goal of disability policy is the integration of persons with disabilities into mainstream society; that "disability" is not just an attribute of individuals, but instead represents the interaction between individuals — who may have physical or mental impairments — and the environment in which they live; that there is great diversity among persons with disabilities in terms of their abilities, capacities, needs and limitations; that the goals of economic self-sufficiency for persons with disabilities are not inconsistent with income security goals of disability income programs; that integration of and support for persons with disabilities are important to the productive capacity of the nation and require coordinated responses of the private sector as well as federal, state and local governments.

PRELIMINARY FINDINGS

In the last chapter of the report, the Panel outlines the topics of its future work and describes its current findings on three issues that have repeatedly been raised as problems by persons with disabilities and other experts the Panel has consulted.

Health Care and Disability Income Policy

Health care is important to all Americans. It is particularly important for persons with disabilities because they often have special health care needs, many are at risk of very high health care costs, and they often cannot gain adequate coverage in the private insurance market. The Panel has heard directly from individuals with disabilities that the fear of losing health care and related services is, for many, the major barrier that keeps them from maximizing their earning capacity. Many recipients of Social Security disability insurance (DI) and Supplemental Security Income (SSI) disability benefits have said that the risk of losing Medicare or Medicaid coverage that is linked to their cash benefits is a far greater work disincentive than is the loss of cash benefits. Earnings from work can compensate for the loss of cash benefits. But earnings, alone, cannot buy health care coverage when that coverage is simply not available to persons with severe chronic conditions.

The Panel finds that ensuring universal protection against health care costs would present a major breakthrough in national policy with regard to disability income and work. Such a guarantee of necessary health care — independent of work, disability, health or cash benefit status — would be a significant gain in:

- *alleviating fear and insecurity among the nation's citizens with disabilities who now rely on Medicaid and Medicare for the health care they need and who risk losing that coverage if they are found able to work;*

- *enabling persons with disabilities to maximize their independence by remaining in or returning to the paid work force as well as participating in other productive activities; and*

- *fostering cash benefit policies that provide security, while encouraging work among persons with disabilities who have the capacity to do so.*

Universal health care would also foster early intervention to prevent diseases or impairments from becoming permanent work disabilities. Improved access to uniform health care information will also improve the decision-making process for cash disability programs.

The Panel also emphasizes that certain health care benefits are particularly important for persons with disabilities, including children. These features include coverage for prescription drugs, durable medical equipment, personal assistance services and devices and rehabilitation services for congenital or chronic conditions, including mental illness.

The Panel is not prepared to take a position on the merits of particular health care reform proposals. There are many factors to be considered as that debate proceeds and they are not our primary focus. Nor do we, as a Panel, take the position that only a universal health care scheme can address the particular concerns that are the subject of our work. Rather, our purpose is to highlight that secure appropriate health care for persons with disabilities is an important underpinning for developing sound disability benefit policies that facilitate entry or return to paid employment for those with the capacity to do so.

Importance of Adequate Resources to Administer DI and SSI

In its review of the history of the DI and SSI programs over the last 25 years, the Panel has been struck by the volatility of disability benefit claims, allowances and terminations. Major factors in this volatility are cyclical changes in the economy and radical shifts in administrative and legislative policy. From this review of the tumultuous history of the disability programs over the last 25 years, the Panel sees several important lessons:

First, stable administration of DI and SSI is critically important to the economic security of the persons with severe disabilities who rely on these benefits as well as for public support and the fiscal integrity of the programs.

Second, cutbacks in administrative resources in the 1980s were accompanied by growing concerns that vulnerable populations are not being well-served. Problems were reported about provisions for assigning and monitoring representative payees for beneficiaries who need them, difficulties beneficiaries have in getting information about how particular changes in their work would affect their benefits, the need for outreach to enroll eligible persons in SSI, difficulties beneficiaries face in receiving prompt answers to their questions, and prompt adjustments in benefits as their circumstances change in order to minimize underpayments or overpayments.

Third, adequate staff and other resources to administer the programs are essential. The investment in making correct, timely initial disability decisions and documenting them fully should shorten delays in getting correct benefits to applicants, reduce appeals and avoid the cost of paying any incorrect allowances. If the required medical improvement standard for conducting continuing disability reviews is to be implemented properly, allowances must be sufficiently documented to support an assessment of whether there has been a change in the beneficiary's condition between the allowance and the review. And to be fair to the beneficiary, there must be adequate staff to assure that the record is fully developed at the time of review. For program integrity and public confidence in the programs, resources must be adequate both to decide and document initial claims promptly and correctly, and to conduct appropriate quality reviews and continuing disability reviews.

Fourth, changes in regulations that were called for in legislation and court decisions in the 1980s require greater emphasis on assessing claimants' functional capacity in conjunction with medical evidence. If properly conducted, these functional assessments are likely to be more time consuming than determinations based solely on medical evidence. This shift needs to be taken into account in resource allocations.

Finally, it is reasonable to expect some volatility in disability claims with cyclical changes in the economy. Disability claims have risen during every economic recession since the late 1960s — with the one exception of the early 1980s, when unprecedented retrenchment policies offset those effects. The majority of working-age persons with disabilities do, in fact, work. They have much better prospects for finding and keeping their jobs when jobs are plentiful. When they lose their jobs during recessions and exhaust other sources of support, it is reasonable to expect that they will apply for disability benefits. Flexibility in administrative resources is needed to accommodate cyclical changes in disability claims.

The Social Security Administration is now engaged in rethinking and reengineering its disability adjudication processes to ensure that available resources are used as efficiently as possible. At the same time, in the wake of reduced staff resources in the 1980s, the recent rapid growth in initial claims and backlogs, the growth in pending appeals, the fact that continuing disability reviews are not being done as called for in the law, and ongoing concerns that vulnerable populations have difficulty gaining the service they seek:

The Panel finds that staff and related resources are not now adequate to administer the DI and SSI programs. It believes that such resources must be set at a level that ensures stable, effective management of the disability programs. Specifically, resources must be adequate to: provide fair, accurate and prompt decisions on disability claims; provide the individualized service to disability beneficiaries that are contemplated under current law, including clear and accurate answers to individuals' questions about how changes in their work effort will affect their benefits; and conduct timely and predictable reviews of the continuing eligibility of those receiving disability benefits.

Importance of Long-Term Research

Long-term research is needed to better understand the size and attributes of the underlying population of persons with disabilities who could meet the program definition of disability if they were not working, as well as to make valid and reliable decisions of eligibility. Such research is needed in order to anticipate the consequences for disability claims and allowances: of cyclical changes in the economy, of outreach efforts to enroll eligible persons, or of other changes such as appropriate updates of the medical and other criteria for making disability determinations. Such research would also provide information about the circumstances that distinguish persons with disabilities who are successfully integrated into the work force from those who become unable to work because of their impairments. That information could help develop ways to expand opportunities for successful integration of beneficiaries into the world of work.

There has been a dearth of rigorous research on the disability benefit programs over the last 10-15 years. In the 1960s and 1970s, the Social Security Administration conducted periodic comprehensive surveys to measure the prevalence of work disability in the general population and to assess the role of the disability income programs in meeting the needs of persons with work disabilities. No comparable data have been collected since 1978.

A comprehensive program of long-range research is needed in order to provide basic information about the populations being served and the changing environment in which disability programs operate. The Panel is encouraged to find that thoughtful new research initiatives are planned and underway to rectify major gaps in information that is needed to evaluate and forecast disability income programs. Multi-year funding commitments are essential for long-range research. The Panel strongly supports the continued investment in such research initiatives.

The Panel's Further Work

In its remaining work, the Panel focussed on specific issues in disability income policy, and invited public comment and suggestions on specific policy proposals for its considerations in the following broad categories:
- the definition of disability for DI and SSI eligibility, and its assessment in functional, medical and vocational terms;
- work and other incentives and disincentives for DI and SSI applicants and beneficiaries;
- prospects for vocational rehabilitation and job placement for persons with significant disabilities;
- the coordination of health care and cash benefits for persons with disabilities;
- provisions for personal assistance services and assistive devices for persons with significant functional limitations;
- the coordination of short-term and long-term disability income protection;
- implementing and administering cash benefits and services for persons with disabilities;
- the relationship of disability and retirement policy, particularly in light of scheduled increases in the Social Security normal retirement age; and
- the special concerns of subgroups of persons with disabilities, including children and persons with severe mental illness.

The Panel's findings and recommendations are contained in its final report, *Balancing Security and Opportunity: The Challenge of Disability Income Policy*. Findings and recommendations about benefits for children with disabilities are in the report of its Committee on Childhood Disability, *Restructuring the SSI Disability Program for Children and Adolescents*.

DISABILITY INCOME PROGRAMS

Chapter 2 provides an overview of major employment-based public and private programs and means-tested public programs that provide monthly cash disability benefits. It begins with a review of Social Security DI and SSI disability provisions, which are the focus of the Panel's work. It also reviews coverage and provisions of compensation programs for workers who are injured on the job or veterans who are injured while on active duty in the armed forces. State temporary disability insurance and private sector short-term and long-term disability income plans also are covered. It finds that among private sector employees:
- Almost all are covered by Social Security DI, which provides earnings replacement benefits after a five-month waiting period for workers with severe long-term disabilities.
- About 30 percent of private sector employees have no short-term disability income protection. Another 26 percent have sick leave only, which typically replaces 100 percent of earnings for only a few weeks, rarely long enough to cover the full period until DI benefits begin. About 44 percent of private sector employees have some type of short-term disability insurance, which usually replaces about 50-67 percent of the worker's earnings for up to six months. This insurance includes mandatory social insurance programs in five states and union-negotiated and employer provided benefits in other states.
- Employer-provided long-term disability insurance, which is supplemental to Social Security disability insurance, covers about 25 percent of private sector employees, with upper status white collar workers much more likely than blue collar

workers to be covered. These benefits typically replace about 60 percent of prior earning and are offset $1 for $1 by Social Security. About another 17 percent of private sector employees are in defined benefit pension plans that provide immediate disability pensions if the worker meets the age and service requirements of the plan.

THE POPULATION WITH DISABILITIES

Chapter 3 provides information about the population of persons with disabilities, including estimates of the prevalence of disabilities in the total population, the attributes of DI and SSI beneficiaries, and what is known about outcomes for persons who have been denied DI benefits in the past.

Prevalence of Disability

There is great diversity among persons with chronic health conditions, or disabilities. For example, as many as half the total population (including children, the elderly and working-age adults) have some type of chronic health condition, but for most, the condition does not limit their ability to work, attend school, or engage in other daily activities.

Chronic health conditions can limit activities in a variety of ways. Among working age persons in 1990, 19.4 million people (12.8 percent) said they were limited in some way because of a chronic health condition, including: 6.7 million (4.4 percent) who reported they were unable to work; 7.4 million (4.9 percent) who were limited only in the kind or amount of work they could do; and 5.3 million (3.5 percent) who were limited only in non-work activities. A small portion of the working-age population report such significant functional limitations that they require assistance with activities of daily living. They include some individuals who report they are able to work, despite the need for assistance.

Persons Receiving Social Security or Supplemental Security Income

At the end of 1993, a total 6.7 million adults under age 65 were receiving Social Security or SSI benefits based on disability. To receive benefits, individuals must meet a strict test of work disability, due to a medically determinable physical or mental condition. In addition, children under 18 receive SSI based on a definition of disability for children comparable to that for adults.

There is great diversity among DI and SSI recipients. Those who receive DI as disabled workers must have had recent covered work in order to be insured for benefits. They tend to be older — most are in their 50s or early 60s — and their impairments frequently are associated with aging — such as musculoskeletal impairments including arthritis, or circulatory or respiratory diseases. Mental illness is a growing cause of disability among disabled worker beneficiaries, however, particularly those under age 50. It is the primary diagnosis for about 1 in 4 persons receiving disabled worker benefits.

SSI recipients tend to be much younger. Many have developmental disabilities and enter the rolls as children (if they live in low-income families) or when they reach adulthood, when their eligibility based on income and resources is considered independent of the financial status of their parents. For about 1 in 4 adult SSI recipients, the primary diagnosis is mental retardation; for another 1 in 4 adults, it is mental illness.

While adults who receive DI or SSI based on disability have severe work limitations, most beneficiaries are capable of managing their own affairs. When beneficiaries are not capable of managing, or directing the management of, their benefits, representative payees are assigned to manage the payments for the beneficiary's use and benefit. About 1 in 8 disabled worker beneficiaries and about 3 in 10 SSI recipients age 18-64 have representative payees to help them manage their benefits.

The SSI criteria for determining disability for children were modified following a 1990 Supreme Court decision in *Sullivan v. Zebley*. The number of children receiving SSI has grown rapidly since 1989 and was 770,000 at the end of 1993. Among children on the rolls at the end of 1992, mental retardation was the primary diagnosis for about 40 percent. Other mental disorders — including autism, Down syndrome, organic mental disorders, schizophrenia, mood disorder, attention deficit disorder, personality disorders, and developmental and emotional disorders for infants — together accounted for 16 percent. Another 16 percent of children on the SSI rolls had impairments of the nervous system or sensory system, such as vision or hearing impairments as their primary diagnosis.

Outcomes for Persons Denied Benefits

Five different studies over the years have examined outcomes for people who applied for but were denied DI benefits. These five studies, conducted between the mid-1960s and the late-1980s show many similarities in outcomes for persons who were denied benefits and who were still alive and not on the disability or retirement benefit rolls three to five years later.

- In each study, fewer than half the surviving denied applicants were working. Lower employment rates among denied applicants were associated with higher nationwide unemployment rates.
- The economic status of denied applicants who are not working is poor. Their main sources of income are earnings of other family members or assistance. Denied applicants who were working generally were better off.
- The self-reported health status of denied applicants who were not working is not much better than that of those who were allowed DI benefits. Denied applicants who were working generally reported fewer health problems.

TRENDS AND POLICY HISTORY

Chapters 4 and 5 describe the trends in DI and SSI benefit awards and terminations over the past 20-25 years and review how cyclical changes in the economy, new legislation and administrative policy affected the likelihood of disability benefit receipt. The tumultuous history of the disability programs supports the Panel's finding that adequate staff resources and stable administration are critical for protecting both the rights of individuals as well as public support for and the fiscal integrity of the disability programs.

The Early 1970s: Growth in the Disability Rolls

The early 1970s were characterized by rapid growth in the number of people awarded DI benefits as well as the large influx of SSI recipients when that program began in 1974. Economic recessions and high unemployment in 1969-70 and in 1973-75 and legislative expansions in DI before and during this period contributed to the growth. Under pressure to process new claims in an era of government-wide restrictions on personnel, staff resources were diverted from reviewing the accuracy of disability decisions and conducting continuing disability reviews of those on the rolls to processing new claims.

1975-1980: Controlling Expansion

The period after 1974 was characterized by growing concern about the rapid rise in the number of people receiving DI benefits, the escalating cost of benefits and the projected insolvency of the DI trust fund. Legislation reduced future disability benefits in 1977 and in 1980 and, in 1980, required in law that more quality reviews and continuing disability reviews (CDRs) be done. During the late 1970s, administrative initiatives tightened adjudicative standards, placing new emphasis on "medical" as opposed to "functional" criteria for assessing disability. Also, the review standards for CDRs were changed to permit benefit terminations without a finding that the beneficiary's condition had medically improved.

1981-1984: Retrenchment and Reaction

With administrative tightening that began in the late 1970s, and the 1980 legislative mandate in place, the new administration, which had promised to reduce the size and cost of government, sought through administrative initiatives to significantly reduce the cost of disability benefits. In the midst of a deep economic recession with unemployment rising to record levels in 1982-83, administrative initiatives to review the rolls and terminate benefits were implemented abruptly without adequate staff or training. In response to widespread dismay at the human suffering cause by the abrupt retrenchment, the courts, the states, the administration and the Congress all acted to rectify the situation.

By June of 1983, after two district courts had declared the Social Security Administration's (SSA) restrictive policy for assessing mental impairment claims to be illegal, the Secretary of Health and Human Services issued a moratorium on denying disability claims based on mental impairments until new guidelines were developed. In April 1984, the Secretary announced a nationwide moratorium on continuing disability reviews and pledged to work with Congress on reform. By that time nine states were operating under a court-ordered medical improvement standard for continuing reviews, and nine other states had suspended reviews pending implementation of a court-ordered medical improvement standard, or pending action by the circuit court. In 1984, Congress responded with reform legislation.

1985-1989: Economic Expansion, Agency Downsizing

As the nation enjoyed sustained economic growth and unemployment rates fell, disability claims leveled off. New adjudicative criteria called for in the 1984 legislation were put in place. It was generally agreed that deciding claims based on the new criteria for assessing disability based on mental impairments and for conducting disability reviews would be more labor intensive than the approaches that had been invalidated by the courts.

A major administrative initiative during this period was a decision to significantly reduce the number of SSA staff — from about 80,000 employees in FY 1985, to about 63,000 in 1989. Along with the agency downsizing, SSA leadership sought ways to streamline operations. In the process fewer field office personnel were available to provide individualized attention to vulnerable populations — such as SSI recipients. Meanwhile, Congress called for improvements in service to the public, including outreach to enroll eligible persons in SSI, more responsive representative payee services and improved response to individuals' questions and needs. Legislation also extended work incentives for SSI recipients and incremental changes improved access to SSI for persons with severe mental illness.

The Early 1990s: Growth in the Disability Rolls

The early 1990s, like the early 1970s, were characterized by rapid growth in the disability rolls, with particular growth in SSI claims. The growth coincided with an economic recession in 1990-1991. It also followed legislative, administrative and judicial actions that enhanced access to SSI — through SSI outreach activities and new standards for determining childhood disability. In the wake of agency downsizing during the 1980s, and increased workloads in the 1990s, agency resources are not allocated to conducting continuing disability reviews in order to process new claims. The agency is currently engaged in reassessing and reengineering its disability processes to ensure that available resources are used as efficiently as possible.

THE BROADER CONTEXT OF DISABILITY INCOME POLICY

Chapter 6 explores some of the broader environmental factors beyond the DI and SSI programs that influence the context in which disability benefits are claimed and decisions are made to allow or deny benefits. While these environmental factors affect the context of disability benefit programs, no attempt is made to precisely associate these factors with past or future trends in the disability benefit programs.

Structural Shifts in the Labor Market

Structural changes in the labor market have long-term effects on employment opportunities for particular subgroups of workers, including those with disabilities. On one hand, analysis of earnings level trends show a declining demand for workers with limited educations and job skills. To the extent that such workers have disabilities, they are likely to be doubly disadvantaged in the labor market. On the other hand, the shift from manufacturing to service sector jobs is projected to increase jobs for well-educated workers, which would mean that highly skilled workers with physical disabilities will have better opportunities to find work. At the same time, workers with cognitive limitations or mental illness may still have difficulty finding work.

Changes in Other Public and Private Support

All western European countries as well as the United States face the problem that large numbers of people lose their connection with the labor force before retirement age. It happens particularly during economic recessions, but occurs in normal times as well. The social welfare responses to this problem can be grouped as follows: work-based interventions, which provide rehabilitation or training or expand job opportunities; unemployment benefits, which provide income continuity to those actively seeking work; disability benefits, which provide income security to those severely limited in their ability to work; and assistance, which provides universal income guarantees or means-tested benefits for the poor.

The comparative research suggests that differences in the size of disability rolls across countries depend much more on the relative strength of these four social welfare responses than on differences in the underlying health of the population. The United States, in contrast with many other western countries, has relatively weak support systems other than for disability. For example, job creation, rehabilitation and training programs serve small numbers of persons relative to the numbers receiving disability benefits; unemployment benefits are paid to only about half of those seeking work and are limited in duration; federal funding for assistance, other than that based on disability, is available only to certain low-income families with children and those benefits have declined in value over the past two decades. The same analysis suggests that policies that seek to reduce reliance on one or more of these sources of support, are likely to increase reliance on others.

Availability of Health Insurance

In the absence of universal health care coverage, persons with disabilities face particular problems in gaining the coverage they need. If they are employed, they may be covered by employer-sponsored health insurance. But standard employment-based plans may not cover the services needed by persons with chronic conditions. Furthermore, coverage under employment-based insurance has been declining. Between 1988 and 1992, the number of persons under age 65 in the United States without any private or public health care coverage rose by nearly 5 million. The growth in the number without any coverage occurred despite significant growth in the proportion of that population who were covered by Medicaid. In the absence of universal health care protection, individuals who lack the coverage they need may turn to DI and SSI to gain coverage under Medicare or Medicaid, which accompanies entitlement to cash disability benefits.

Changes in Treatment for Severe Mental Illness

An important change in DI and SSI that occurred in the 1980s is an increase in the number of persons with severe mental illness who qualified for benefits. Contributing to this growth were changes in DI and SSI adjudicative policy in the early and mid-1980s, a longer-term trend away from state mental institutions to community-based care for persons with severe mental illness, and incremental changes during the later 1980s that were designed to increase access to SSI for persons with severe mental illness.

While changes in treatment of mental illness represent advances in the integration of persons with severe mental illness into the community, they also bring a shift in sources of support. Medicaid and SSI, as well as Medicare and DI, are important underpinnings of the community-based system. Effective treatment in the community still requires coordinated services that replicate what had previously been the responsibility of state mental hospitals — housing, some supervision, medical and psychiatric care and psychosocial rehabilitation. Because of the importance of SSI and Medicaid for their clients, many mental health practitioners now consider it part of their job to help their clients qualify for these programs.

Claimant Representation and Third Party Interest

Over the past 15-20 years, there has been a significant increase in the number of Social Security claims that are appealed after initially being denied, as well as an increase in the likelihood that benefits will be allowed on appeal. There has also been a significant increase in the size and sophistication of organizations of claimants' representatives and growing interest of third parties in helping individuals gain access to DI or SSI disability benefits. Recent legislation also expedited the process for approving fees that representatives may charge their clients when their appeals of denied benefits are successful.

Third party interests include groups other than the claimant, or the claimant's representative, who have a direct interest in having DI or SSI claims allowed to certain individuals. They include state and local governments with state financed assistance programs, which seek to ensure that SSI is first payor for low-income persons with disabilities. Employers and insurers that provide private disability insurance calculate premium and replacement rates based on Social Security DI being first payor of benefits to disabled workers. Consequently, they often encourage or require those claiming private benefits to also claim DI. In addition, hospitals, rehabilitation facilities or other providers of services may have a direct interest in helping patients qualify for SSI and therefore Medicaid, so that they can be reimbursed for their services. Without Medicaid coverage for their patients, the care they provide is likely to be uncompensated.

Chapter 1: The Panel's Perspective

The Disability Policy Panel believes that the primary goal of national disability policy should be the integration of people with disabilities into American society. The Panel endorses the statement of the Americans with Disabilities Act of 1990 (ADA): "The nation's proper goals regarding individuals with disabilities are to assure equality of opportunity, full participation, independent living, and economic self-sufficiency." In pursuing these ends, disability policy should provide resources to promote or maintain functioning and work for people with disabilities as well as income support for those who cannot work or whose ability to work is very limited. For some individuals with disabilities, there may be the need for both income support and other resources in order to enable them to return or enter the work force.

In proposing disability policy reforms affecting income and work, the Panel believes:

First, work in the marketplace is the principal source of income in all modern societies. While income security programs are necessary for those with disabilities who are severely limited in their ability to work, disability policy should strive wherever possible to maintain and integrate people with disabilities into mainstream employment.

Second, "disability" is not just a characteristic of individuals. Instead, it represents the interaction between individuals — who may have physical or mental impairments — and the environment in which they live. Consequently, interventions to foster independence and functioning for people with disabilities may require changes in policies affecting the economic, social and physical environment, not just direct provisions or accommodations for individuals with determinable impairments. In particular, improving the demand side of the labor market and reducing barriers to access to work which do not place an undue burden on business may be as important in promoting competitive employment by persons with disabilities as are the supportive activities and work incentives that operate on the supply side of the labor market equation.

Third, physical and mental impairments are widespread in the population, they are a natural part of the life process, and people with disabilities have extremely varied abilities, capacities, needs and limitations. In 1990, nearly 20 million working-age adults had disabilities that limited their ability to work or to carry out other life activities. In December 1993, 6.7 million had work limitations so severe that they receive Social Security or SSI benefits based on disability. A wide range exists in the severity of disabling conditions within the population as well as a wide variation in the effects of the same condition on different individuals in different circumstances. Indeed, even among those receiving DI or SSI based on disability, beneficiaries have significant differences in their ages, types of disabling conditions, educational backgrounds, past work experiences, capabilities and vulnerabilities. Disability policy must recognize and respond both to the breadth and the diversity of the population of persons with disabilities.

Fourth, the income security goals of Social Security disability insurance and Supplemental Security Income assistance are consistent with the goals of the ADA that we have endorsed. The cash benefits these programs provide, offer a crucial form of economic self-sufficiency for people who are significantly limited in their ability to work. At the same time, other individuals with disabilities are able to work, despite significant impairments. The challenge is to design, administer and coordinate programs for people with disabilities in ways that protect those unable to work, while both minimizing the disincentives to work inherent in any income security system and avoiding unrealistic expectations about the capacities of people to function without assistance in our less than barrier-free social and economic environment.

Fifth, disability policy is of the utmost importance to the welfare of the community as a whole. We need the fullest possible participation of all persons in the civic, economic and social life of the country. Particularly in times of constrained public resources we need to assure that the supports provided to persons with disabilities are consistent both with the nation's current ability to pay and with wise investment in its long-term social and economic well-being.

Finally, it is clear that the Federal Government does not now and should not in the future shoulder the full responsibility for developing, implementing or funding national disability policy. Instead, the private and non-profit sectors as well as local, state and federal agencies must assume their responsibility in funding benefit programs and in integrating persons with disabilities into society. Such a broad approach can provide persons with disabilities the levels of independence and self-sufficiency that are both their right and their responsibility.

Chapter 2 Disability Income Programs

This section provides an overview of major employment-based public and private programs and means-tested public programs that provide monthly cash disability benefits. Figure 2-1 summarizes the programs covered. They include two compensation programs for injury on the job: the state workers' compensation programs and the veterans' compensation program for those who are injured while on active duty in the armed forces.

Other work-based cash disability benefits for workers, regardless of whether the disabilities are caused on the job, include separate programs for short-term disability and long-term disability. The programs for short-term disability include mandatory social insurance programs for temporary disability insurance (TDI) in five states, and other private employer provisions for paid sick leave and for sickness and accident insurance in states that do not have mandatory TDI programs. The major long-term disability benefit program is the disability insurance (DI) portion of the OASDI (Old-Age, Survivors and Disability Insurance), or Social Security, system. Employers may supplement this protection with private long-term disability insurance. Private defined benefit pension plans also may provide disability retirement pensions.

Means-tested cash benefits, for low-income people with disabilities that are paid regardless of recent or current work connection, include the federal Supplemental Security Income (SSI) program and veterans' pensions paid to low-income disabled or elderly veterans who have had wartime service.

This section begins with a review of DI and SSI, which are the primary focus of the Panel's charge to review disability policy. It then reviews the compensation programs and other private work-based disability benefits.

This review does not cover public programs (other than for veterans), where the government essentially is filling the role of employer, such as federal, state and local government provisions for sick leave, long-term disability insurance or disability pensions. Nor does this section cover sources of private disability payments that are not job related, such as individually purchased long-term disability insurance, or indemnity payments that are compensation for automobile injuries or other types of personal injuries.[1]

The federal government provides funding for an extensive network of programs in addition to cash benefits that affect people with disabilities. An inventory of those programs is provided in an appendix. In addition, state and local governments have an important role in financing and delivering services to people with disabilities, particularly to those with severe mental illness or developmental

---

1. For a more comprehensive review of aggregate expenditures for disability payments, see Monroe Berkowitz and Carolyn Green, "Disability Expenditures," *American Rehabilitation,* Spring, 1989.

disabilities. These programs are not covered in this review, but will be considered in the Panel's future work.

The programs reviewed here indicate the following general findings about the extent of employment-based disability income protection:

- Almost all (95 percent) of workers are covered under Social Security disability insurance, which provides earnings-replacement benefits after a five-month waiting period for workers with severe, long-term disabilities.

- The vast majority (87 percent) of wage and salary workers are covered under workers' compensation, which pays for medical care and provides earnings-replacement benefits for workers injured on the job. Benefits are paid for temporary disability and for total or partial permanent disability. The benefits are coordinated with Social Security so that workers eligible under both programs generally have their combined benefits limited to not exceed 80 percent of their prior earnings.

- Some type of short-term disability protection that is not limited to job-related injuries covers 70 percent of private sector employees, including:
  - 26 percent with sick leave only, which usually replaces 100 percent of earnings for a few weeks;
  - 20 percent with short-term disability insurance only, which most often replaces 50 percent of prior earnings for up to six months; and
  - 24 percent have both sick leave and short-term disability insurance.

- Employers may provide long-term disability income to supplement Social Security disability benefits. Private sector workers with this protection include:
  - 25 percent who have long-term disability insurance, which is usually integrated with Social Security to pay combined benefits that replace about 60 percent of prior earnings; and
  - 17 percent who are in defined benefit plans that provide immediate disability retirement pensions if the worker meets the age and service requirements of the pension plan.

Other key features of these benefit plans are summarized in figure 2-1.

SOCIAL SECURITY DISABILITY INSURANCE

Social Security disability insurance is a major component of the Social Security program of Old-Age, Survivors, and Disability Insurance (OASDI). The basic principles underlying the OASDI program are that workers and their employers (and the self-employed) pay contributions from earnings during working years and, when earnings stop because of the retirement, disability, or death of the worker, benefits are paid to partially replace the earnings that have been lost. The benefits are paid as a matter of right, without a means test. Consequently, workers and their employers have a base on which to build supplemental earnings replacement protection — such as pensions, insurance or individual savings. Finally, OASDI is designed to meet social adequacy goals, in that benefits replace a higher proportion of earnings for low paid workers than for higher earners, and supplemental benefits are paid to family members of retired, disabled or deceased workers.

The DI portion of Social Security provides benefits that will replace, in part, the earnings that are lost when a person is no longer able to work because of disability. Benefits are paid to the disabled worker and to his or her child under age 18, aged spouse, or spouse of any age who is caring for an eligible child under age 16 or any age if disabled before age 22.

OASDI benefits based on disability are also payable to certain dependents or survivors of retired, disabled or deceased workers. Specifically, the adult child of a worker, if the disability began in childhood (before age 22) and the widow(er) aged 50-64 of a deceased insured worker may receive benefits.

As of December 1993, about 4.5 million individuals received Social Security benefits based on their own disability. They include 3.7 million disabled-worker beneficiaries about 147,000 persons who received benefits as disabled widow(er)s and 656,000 who receive benefits as adults disabled since childhood. About 936,000 disabled Social Security beneficiaries were also receiving SSI payments as a supplement to their DI benefit. An additional 1.5 million persons were receiving Social Security benefits as the children or spouses of disabled workers.

The DI program developed from modest beginnings in the 1950s, and expanded in scope and coverage during the 1960s. A history of the legislative development of the disability insurance program is in an appendix. Background on how legislative and administrative developments in the 1970s, 1980s and early 1990s contributed to fluctuations in the size of the DI program are in chapter 5 of this report.

Key features of the DI program today have their roots in the early DI legislation in the 1950s. These features include: a separate DI trust fund to ensure fiscal accountability for DI apart from OASI; strict work requirements for "insured status" to be eligible for DI benefits; a strict definition of disability based on inability to work; administrative arrangements that rely on the states to make disability determinations; and a concern for rehabilitation.

Financing

Social Security is financed largely by OASDI (or FICA)[2] taxes on earnings up to an annual ceiling, currently $60,600 in 1994. Of the OASDI tax rate — 6.2 percent each paid by employees and employers — 5.6 percent is allocated to the OASI trust fund and 0.6 percent is allocated to the DI trust fund, and is then used to pay DI benefits and administrative costs. The allocation to DI is now scheduled to increase to 0.71 percent in 2000. The DI tax rate is lower than it would have been at this time if part of the DI tax rate had not been reallocated to the OASI trust fund in 1983, when the DI fund was projected to be over-financed relative to the OASI fund.

The revenues and expenditures of the DI trust fund for 1993 were $32.2 billion and $35.6 billion, respectively. Thus, the fund declined from $12.3 billion at the end of 1992, to about $8.9 billion at the end of 1993. In the absence of remedial action, the DI trust fund is projected to be depleted late in 1995. A reallocation of part of the OASI rate back to the DI fund, however, could remedy the short-range financing problem for DI. The OASDI Trustees, in the outgoing Bush administration, had proposed a reallocation of part of the OASI rate to DI. The Clinton administration had a similar proposal, which would have raised the DI allocation from 0.6 to 0.875 effective in January 1993, and was estimated to produce sufficient funds to pay DI benefits until 2020 and OASI benefits until 2037. No such legislation has been enacted as of February 1994 when this report was prepared.

Coverage and Eligibility for Benefits

To qualify for DI benefits, a worker must not only be disabled, but must meet certain requirements such as working in jobs covered by Social Security. About 95 percent of all jobs in the United States are covered by Social Security. The main groups not covered are about 25 percent of state and local government employees, where the government entity did not choose to have its employees covered, but provides alternative benefits; federal employees hired before 1984 who have not opted for Social Security coverage and are covered under the civil service retirement system; railroad workers who are covered under the railroad retirement system which is coordinated with Social Security; household workers and farm workers whose earnings do not meet certain minimum requirements; and persons with very low net earnings from self-employment (generally less than $400 a year).

---

2. Taxes to finance Social Security are authorized under the Internal Revenue Code provisions originally included in the Federal Insurance Contributions Act (FICA) and the Self-Employment Contributions Act (SECA).

Figure 2-1. Selected Disability Benefit Programs in the United States, 1994

Type of benefit	People covered	Provides	Disability concept	Who pays	Rationale/philosophy
Compensation for injury on the job					
Workers' compensation	87% of wage and salary workers	Health care, rehabilitation, cash benefits for temporary, permanent or partial disability	Temporary or permanent total work disability and permanent partial disability	Employer	Employer liability for injury on the job; encourage safe work conditions; predictable and prompt compensation in lieu of employee tort litigation.
Veterans' compensation	All armed forces for injury on active duty.	Health care, rehabilitation, partial and total disability cash compensation (and education, housing, loan and other benefits as for non-disabled veterans)	Permanent disability ranging from partial to total (10% to 100%). Impairment based, not related to ability to work.	Federal government (as employer)	Government obligation to compensate those injured in national service. Underpins government authority to draft citizens into service and expose them to hazardous duty in national defense.
Other work-based cash benefits					
Sick leave	50% of private sector employees	100% of pay for several weeks	Unable to do own job	Employer	Union negotiated and employer provided benefit. Promotes income continuity for workers and work place health and safety.
Temporary or short-term disability insurance	44% of private sector employees	50-67% of pay, usually for 26 weeks (may have 1-7 day waiting period)	Unable to do own job	Employee; employer; or both	Mandatory social insurance in five states. Union negotiated or employer provided benefit in others. Rationale similar to sick leave, but for longer-term illness, injury or maternity.
Social Security disability insurance (DI)	95% of work force	After 5 month waiting period, earnings replacement ranging from about 55-60% for low-paid, 42% for average earner, to 25% for max-maxiimum earner ($60,600 in 1994).	Unable to work due to medically determinable physical or mental impairment expected to last 12 months or result in death.	Employee and employer each pay half	Universal mandatory social insurance. Contributory earnings-replacement protection against loss of income due to work disability before retirement.

Figure 2-1. Selected Disability Benefit Programs in the United States, 1994, continued

Type of benefit	People covered	Provides	Disability concept	Who pays	Rationale/philosophy
Other work-based cash benefits (continued)					
Private long-term disability insurance	25% of private sector employees	Usually 60% of past earnings, offset by DI	Often, unable to do usual occupation (for 2 years) then unable to do any occupation	Employer; or both employer and employee	Union negotiated and employer provided benefit.
Disability pensions in defined benefit plans	35% of private employees with defined benefit plans, about half offer immediate disability pensions	Pension, usually based on years service and earnings	Varies. Unable to do own occupation or DI test.	Employer, usually	Union negotiated and employer provided benefit.
Means-tested benefits					
Supplemental Security Income	Low-income aged, blind and disabled persons.	Federal income guarantee of $446 in 1994. States may supplement	(same as for DI)	Federal general revenues	Basic income guarantee to assure all aged, blind or disabled residents basic minimum income for food, shelter and clothing.
Veterans' pensions	Low-income veterans with wartime service	Basic income guarantee of $651.50 for an individual veteran in 1994.	Non-service connected permanent and total disability or 65 and older.	Federal government (as former employer)	Basic income guarantee for veterans with wartime service who are aged or become permanently and totally disabled after military service.

To qualify for disabled worker benefits, the worker must have worked under the program for about one-fourth of the time after age 21 and up to the year of disability and, in addition, must have recent covered work — equivalent to five of the preceding ten years (or alternatively, if under age 31, half the time since age 21). Of all persons age 25-64 in the population, about 85 percent of men and 68 percent of women had enough covered work experience to be insured for disabled worker benefits as of January 1993.

Also, there is a five-month "waiting period" after the onset of the disability before the monthly benefits can begin. This waiting period reflects the long-term disability character of the DI program and the expectation that short-term disabilities and the early part of long-term disability would be handled through private employer-based programs and state temporary disability insurance programs, which have not developed as broadly as may have been anticipated in the late 1950s and early 1960s.

Benefit Amounts

Benefits for disabled workers are based on the same formula used to determine retirement benefits for those who retire at the normal retirement age,

Table 2-1. Illustrative Social Security Disabled-Worker Benefits, 1993
Illustrative Benefits and Replacement Rates by Earnings Level

Earnings level[a]		Monthly benefit	
Annual	Monthly	Amount	Replacement rate (percent)
$ 6,000	$500	$392	78
12,000	1,000	552	55
18,000	1,500	712	47
24,000	2,000	872	44
30,000	2,500	1,018	41
36,000	3,000	1,093	36
42,000	3,500	1,168	33
48,000	4,000	1,243	31
54,000	4,500	1,318	29

a. Represents average past earnings that are indexed to reflect economy-wide earnings levels near the time of eligibility: technically, the average indexed monthly earnings (AIME) used in the Social Security benefit formula.

currently 65.[3] Workers' benefits are based on their average earnings in covered employment.[4] Table 2-1 illustrates how benefits relate to earnings under the formula in effect in 1993.

In general, the higher prior earnings have been, the higher the benefit will be. However, the benefit formula is weighted in favor of lower-paid persons so that benefits replace a larger proportion of earnings for lower-paid workers than for higher-paid workers.

---

3. The "normal retirement age" or age of first eligibility for unreduced retirement benefits is scheduled (under 1983 amendments to the Social Security Act) to increase gradually from age 65 for persons born before 1938 to age 67 for persons born in 1960 or later. Reduced benefits would continue to be available for workers at age 62, but the maximum early retirement reduction would be increased from 20 percent to 30 percent.
4. Earnings are averaged over the number of years between age 21 and the onset of disability (or attainment of age 62 if earlier) minus five years. Past earnings are indexed to reflect prevailing economy-wide earnings levels near the time the person becomes eligible for benefits.
5. The complete language of section 223(d) is included at the end of appendix B.

The average monthly benefit for all disabled workers receiving them in January 1994 was about $641. For a disabled worker with a wife and child it was $1,092. The benefits are adjusted each year to keep pace with increases in the consumer price index (CPI).

Benefits are paid in the spirit of an earned right, and without any means test, so workers may supplement their Social Security disability protection with additional private protection. For higher income beneficiaries, a portion of the benefits (that part of the benefits that cannot be attributed to the worker's own contributions) is included in taxable income for federal income tax purposes. Beginning with 1984, up to 50 percent of the benefits for persons with adjusted gross income plus certain non-taxable income, above specified thresholds, could be included in taxable income. Under the 1993 Omnibus Budget Reconciliation Act, the proportion of benefits that is potentially taxable was increased to 85 percent.

Definition of Disability

The definition of disability for the DI program has always required severe limitations in a person's ability to work for pay, based on a medically determinable impairment. Initially, the law required a finding of total and permanent disability. Today, section 223(d) of the Social Security Act includes the following requirements:[5]

'Disability' means inability to engage in any substantial gainful activity by reason of any medically determinable physical or mental impairment which can be expected to result in death or which has lasted or can be expected to last for a continuous period of not less than 12 months ...

An individual shall be determined to be under a disability only if his physical or mental impairment or impairments are of such severity that he is not only unable to do his previous work but cannot, considering his age, education, and work experience, engage in any other kind of substantial gainful work which exists in the national economy, regardless of whether such work exists in the immediate area in which he lives, or whether a specific job vacancy exists for him, or whether he would be hired if he applied for work. 'Work which exists in the national economy' means work which exists in significant numbers either in the region where such individual lives or in several regions of the country.

A special definition of disability applies to people who are blind. They meet the statutory definition of disability if their vision in the better eye is 20/200 or less, with correction, or their visual field is 20 degrees or less even with a corrective lens.

The law requires the Secretary to prescribe by regulations criteria for determining when an individual is engaging in substantial gainful activity (SGA). Effective for 1990 and later, earnings of $500 per month generally constitute SGA.

The method of making disability determinations is specified in regulations and is a multi-step sequential process, which is illustrated in figure 2-2. Figure 2-2 also shows the proportion of all initial decisions on DI claims that were decided at each step of the sequential process in FY 1991. In brief, the sequence of the disability determination is as follows:

1. Is the applicant engaging in substantial gainful activity? If so, the claim is denied.

2. Does the applicant have a severe impairment, one that significantly limits physical or mental capacity to do basic work? Is it expected to last 12 months or result in death? If not, the claim is denied.

3. Does the applicant's impairment(s) meet or equal the degree of severity specified in the "medical listings" in regulations? If so, the claim is allowed.

4. If not, can the person still perform his or her past work? This determination is based on an assessment of the person's "residual functional capacity." If the person is found able to do past work, the claim is denied.

5. Can the person do any other work that exists in the national economy? This determination is based on the person's residual functional capacity in conjunction with his or her age, education and prior work experience. If the person is found unable to do other work, the claim is allowed, otherwise it is denied.

Administration and Role of State Agencies

In general, the OASDI program is administered by the Social Security Administration (SSA) through a network of about 1,300 local offices throughout the United States. Funds to administer OASDI are appropriated by Congress and paid from the respective OASI and DI trust funds. In 1992, administrative costs amounted to 0.9 percent of total contributions to (or benefits paid from) the combined OASDI trust funds; these administrative costs were 0.7 percent for OASI and 2.8 percent for DI.

From the beginning of the DI program, the law provided for SSA to enter into agreements for disability determinations to be made by state agencies that were responsible for administering the state plan approved under title I of the Vocational Rehabilitation Act, or any other appropriate state agency. In the original law, SSA was authorized to review and reverse state agency findings to allow disability benefits, but could not reverse state agency denials. This provision reflected the congressional concern that SSA might be too lenient in making the disability determinations. The state agencies, with their emphasis on rehabilitation, were expected to be more cautious in allowing disability claims. Not until the 1980 amendments did SSA receive congressional authority to reverse state agency denials as well as allowances.

Appeals Process

The process for deciding and appealing disability claims has many layers. First, applications for disability benefits are filed at local Social Security district offices, which collect available evidence and determine whether DI applicants meet insured status requirements. Case files are then sent to the state

Figure 2-2. Social Security Disability Determinations: Sequential Decisionmaking Process and Distribution of Initial Decision on DI Claims, 1991

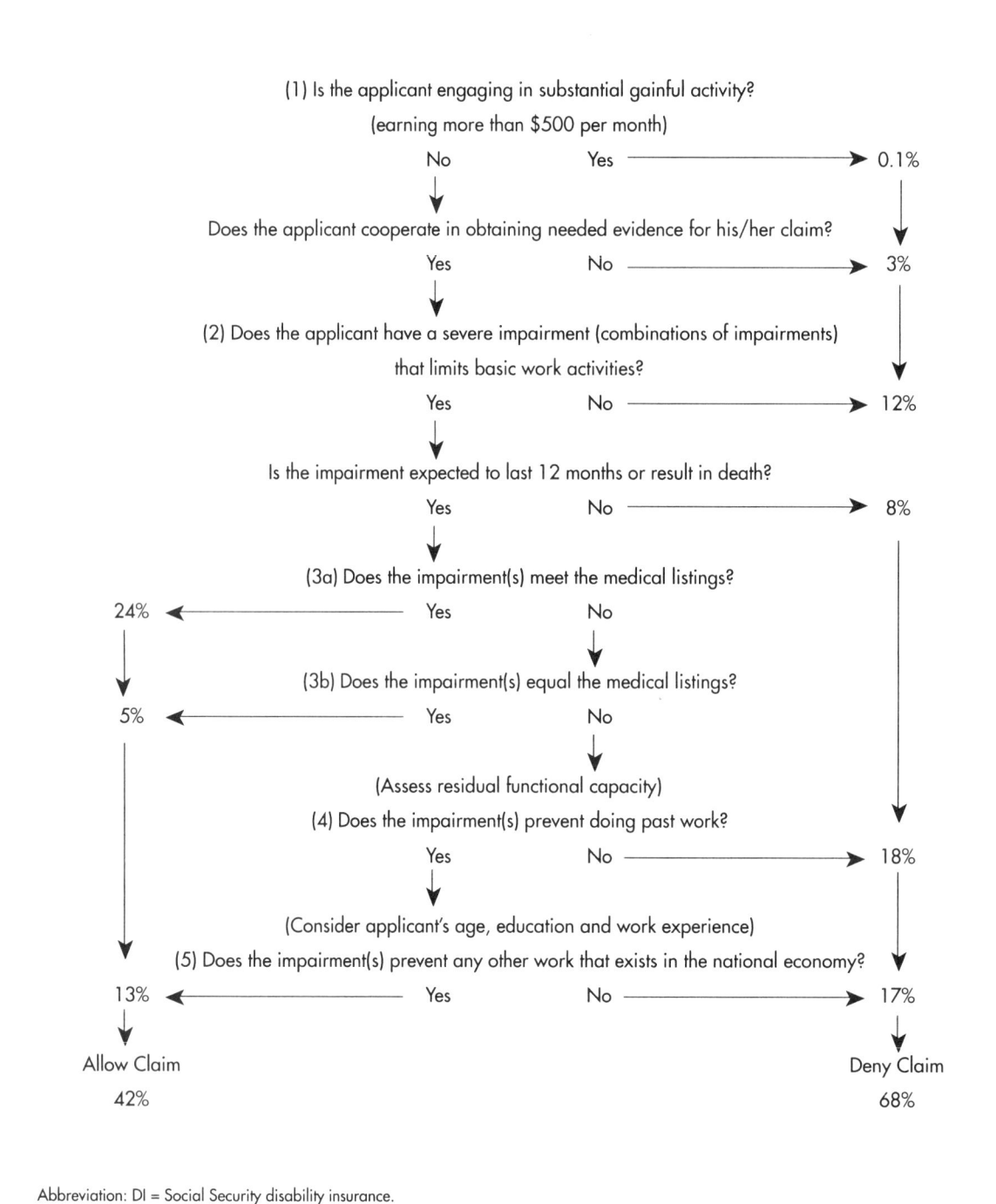

(1) Is the applicant engaging in substantial gainful activity?
(earning more than $500 per month)
- No ↓
- Yes → 0.1%

Does the applicant cooperate in obtaining needed evidence for his/her claim?
- Yes ↓
- No → 3%

(2) Does the applicant have a severe impairment (combinations of impairments) that limits basic work activities?
- Yes ↓
- No → 12%

Is the impairment expected to last 12 months or result in death?
- Yes ↓
- No → 8%

(3a) Does the impairment(s) meet the medical listings?
- 24% ← Yes
- No ↓

(3b) Does the impairment(s) equal the medical listings?
- 5% ← Yes
- No ↓

(Assess residual functional capacity)
(4) Does the impairment(s) prevent doing past work?
- Yes ↓
- No → 18%

(Consider applicant's age, education and work experience)
(5) Does the impairment(s) prevent any other work that exists in the national economy?
- 13% ← Yes
- No → 17%

Allow Claim: 42%
Deny Claim: 68%

Abbreviation: DI = Social Security disability insurance.

disability determination service (DDS) agencies, which gather additional medical evidence, if necessary, and assess the evidence to determine whether applicants meet the disability criteria for benefit entitlement. If a claim is denied, the applicant can request a reconsideration, which is done in the DDS by personnel other than those who made the initial denial. If the claim is again denied, the applicant can request a hearing before an administrative law judge (ALJ). If the ALJ denies the claim, the applicant can request a review of that decision by the Social Security Appeals Council. If the Appeals Council affirms the denial, the applicant can begin civil action in the U.S. district court. At each step in the process, individuals are informed of their right to appeal the decision to the next level. They are also told how to seek the help of an attorney or other representative.

In fiscal year 1992, the number and outcome of decisions on claims for OASDI or SSI disability benefits are illustrated in figure 2-3 and show:[6]

- Of 2.3 million initial DDS decisions, 43 percent allowed benefits and 57 percent denied the claim.

- Of 604,000 reconsiderations by DDS agencies, 17 percent were allowed and 83 percent were denied.

- Of 318,000 hearings before ALJs, 69 percent allowed the claim, 9 percent dismissed the case, and 22 percent denied the benefit claim.

- Of 56,600 decisions rendered by the Appeals Council, 4 percent allowed benefits, 32 percent of cases were remanded to the ALJ for further development and 64 percent denied the claim.[7]

- Of 4,800 cases decided by federal courts, 20 percent allowed benefits, 70 percent denied benefits and 10 percent dismissed the case or remanded it to SSA for further development. These decisions included appeals of benefit terminations as well as of denied claims.

Relation to Rehabilitation

Rehabilitation has been a major concern since the inception of the DI program, both among those who feared that the DI costs would soar because the rolls would swell with "malingerers," and among those whose primary concern was to enhance the quality of life for persons with disabilities. Although the statutory language has been modified to accommodate program changes, much of the present language of section 222 dates from the early 1950s:

> "It is hereby declared to be the policy of the Congress that disabled individuals applying for a determination of disability and disabled individuals who are entitled ... shall be promptly referred to the state agency or agencies administering or supervising the administration of the state plan approved under title I of the Rehabilitation Act ... to the end that the maximum number of such individuals may be rehabilitated into productive activity."

The law also provides for payment from the trust funds for successful rehabilitation and for the suspension of benefits to persons who, without good cause, refuse to accept available vocational rehabilitation services. As a practical matter, the actual referral is made by the state DDS which refers those cases which meet certain "screens" to the state agency which administers the vocational rehabilitation (VR) program. That state agency then decides which beneficiaries it will contact for further screening or evaluation for rehabilitation services.

---

6. U.S. House of Representatives, Committee on Ways and Means, *Overview of Entitlement Programs (1993 Green Book)*, WMCP: 103-18 (Washington, DC: U.S. Government Printing Office, 1993), p. 62. The data are for title II, title XVI and concurrent claims for disability benefits, including disabled workers, disabled widows and disabled adult children. All of the data, except for court decisions, are for initial claims only. They do not include decisions on cessations.
7. These include cases reviewed by the Appeals Council on it "own motion," (including allowances as well as denials by ALJs), as well as cases appealed by applicants.

Figure 2-3: Outcome of Decisions on OASDI and SSI Disability Claims and Reviews, Fiscal Year 1992
Tittle II, Title XVI and Concurrent Title II and XVI Decisions for Disability Claims by Workers, Widows, Widowers and Disabled Adult Children [a]

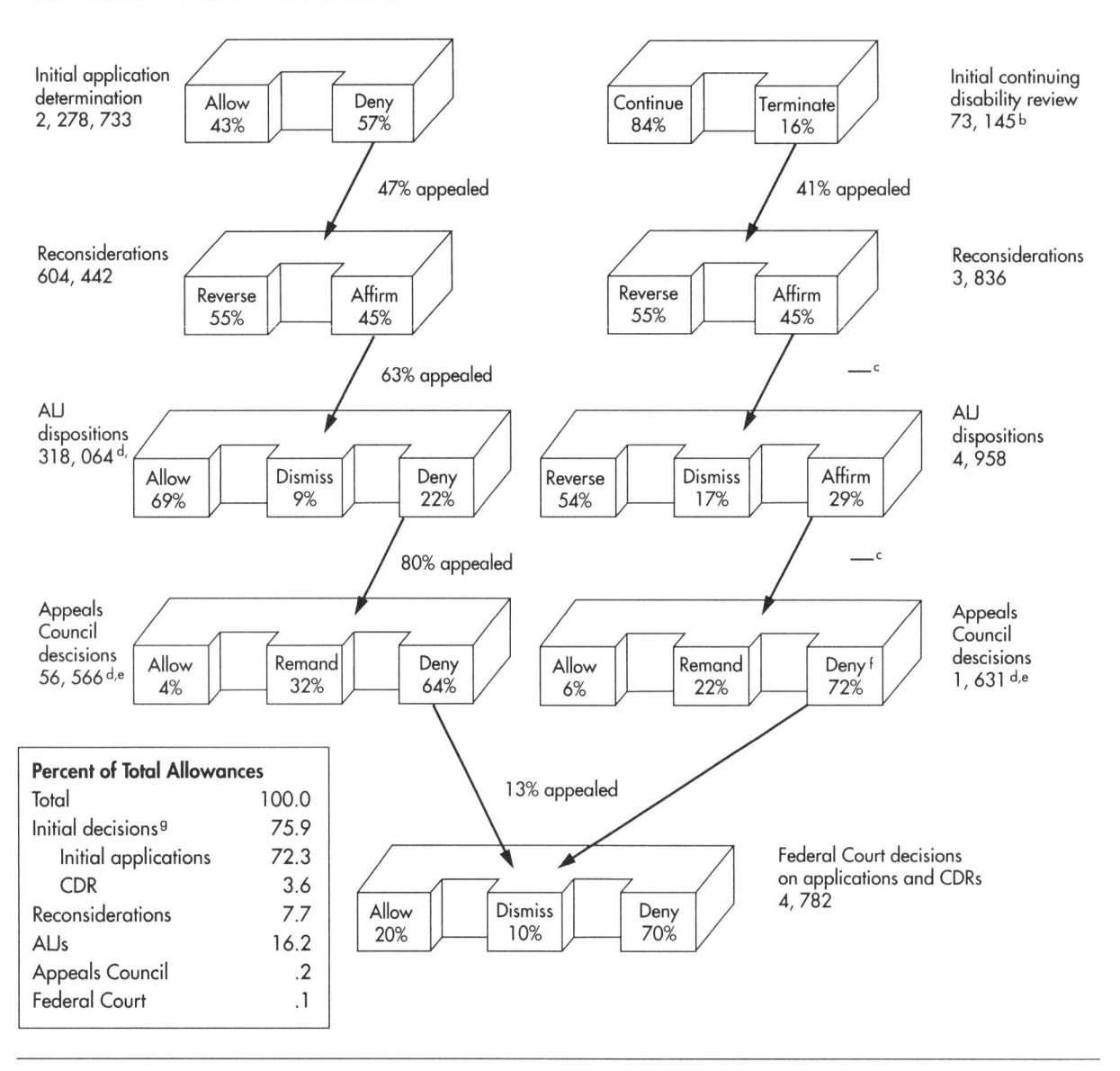

Initial application determination 2,278,733: Allow 43%, Deny 57%

47% appealed

Reconsiderations 604,442: Reverse 55%, Affirm 45%

63% appealed

ALJ dispositions 318,064 [d]: Allow 69%, Dismiss 9%, Deny 22%

80% appealed

Appeals Council descisions 56,566 [d,e]: Allow 4%, Remand 32%, Deny 64%

Initial continuing disability review 73,145 [b]: Continue 84%, Terminate 16%

41% appealed

Reconsiderations 3,836: Reverse 55%, Affirm 45%

—[c]

ALJ dispositions 4,958: Reverse 54%, Dismiss 17%, Affirm 29%

—[c]

Appeals Council descisions 1,631 [d,e]: Allow 6%, Remand 22%, Deny [f] 72%

13% appealed

Federal Court decisions on applications and CDRs 4,782: Allow 20%, Dismiss 10%, Deny 70%

Percent of Total Allowances	
Total	100.0
Initial decisions [g]	75.9
Initial applications	72.3
CDR	3.6
Reconsiderations	7.7
ALJs	16.2
Appeals Council	.2
Federal Court	.1

a. The data relate to workloads processed at various levels in fiscal year 1992, and therefore include some cases where the prior level of decision was made in a prior period. The data include determinations on initial applications as well as continuing disability reviews (both periodic reviews and medical diary cases).
b. Includes 15,300 CDRs where there was "no decision." The continuance and termination rates are computed without the "no decision" cases.
c. Many ALJ dispositions and Appeals Council decision are based on DDS determination from a previous year. Therefore, a percent appealed is not provided.
d. Preliminary data.
e. Includes ALJ decisions not appealed further by the claimant but reviewed by the Appeals Council on its "own motion" authority.
f. Includes requests for review, own motion and reopening cases.
g. Initial determinations plus CDRs.
Abbreviations: ALJ = administrative law judge, CDR = continuing disability review, DDS = disability determination service, OASDI = Old-Age, Survivors, and Disability Insurance, SSI = Supplemental Security Income.
Sources: Social Security Administration; and U.S. House of Representatives, Committee on Ways and Means, *Overview of Entitlement Programs (1993 Green Book)*, WMCP: 103-18 (Washington, DC: U.S. Government Printing Office, 1993), p. 62.

Table 2-2: Vocational Rehabilitation Experience of DI and SSI Beneficiaries, Fiscal Years 1992-1993

Type of claim	Persons referred	Persons rehabilitated Number	Persons rehabilitated Percent	Total (millions)	Average
		FY 1993			
Total	299,847	6,154	2.0	$ 64.4	$ 10,465
DI	45,248	2,068	4.6	20.2	9,768
Concurrent	67,773	1,928	2.8	22.0 [a]	11,410
SSI	186,826	2,158	1.2	22.2	10,287
		FY 1992			
Total	280,732	6,269	2.2	$63.6	$10,145
DI	44,954	1,801	4.0	17.4	9,661
Concurrent	63,020	1,634	2.6	18.0 [a]	11,016
SSI	172,758	2,834	1.6	28.3	9,986

a. 1993 includes $15.3 million for the DI share and $6.7 million for the SSI share. 1992 includes $12.7 million for the DI share and $5.3 million for the SSI share.
Abbreviations: DI = Social Security disability insurance, FY = fiscal year, SSI = Supplemental Security Income.
Sources: Social Security Administration, Office of the Actuary and Office of Legislative and Regulatory Policy.

The current provision for reimbursing states only for successful rehabilitation of disability beneficiaries was enacted in 1981, and is more restrictive than the prior policy which allowed a portion of DI trust funds (1.5 percent in 1974-1980) to be used to pay state VR agencies for services to beneficiaries, whether or not the beneficiary successfully returned to work and left the benefit rolls.

In FY 1992, when 2.3 million individuals had DI or SSI disability claims decided by state agencies, 280,730 persons, or 12 percent of those individuals, were referred to state vocational rehabilitation agencies. In the same year, 6,269 disabled individuals on the DI or SSI rolls were rehabilitated by the VR agencies, for which those agencies were paid $63.6 million, an average payment of just over $10,000 per case. The payments were made from the DI trust fund for DI beneficiaries, and from general revenues for SSI beneficiaries (table 2-2).

Medicare Coverage

In 1972, legislation extended Medicare coverage to persons receiving Social Security on the basis of their own disability. Coverage becomes available 24 months after benefit entitlement, or 29 months after the onset of disability.

Part A of Medicare, or Hospital Insurance (HI), is financed by FICA taxes, currently 1.45 percent, paid by both employees and employers on total earnings in 1994. HI covers inpatient hospital care, inpatient care in a skilled nursing facility following a hospital stay, home health care and hospice care. Once a beneficiary has paid the inpatient hospital deductible amount ($696 in 1994), all remaining costs of covered hospital services for the first 60 days in a benefit period are paid by Medicare. For stays longer than 60 days, the beneficiary is subject to additional cost sharing. For care in a skilled nursing or rehabilitation facility following a hospital stay of at least three days, Medicare pays the full cost of covered services for the first 20 days; for the 21st to the 100th day of skilled nursing care, the beneficiary is responsible for paying a daily coinsurance rate ($87 in 1994). Medicare does not cover more than 100 days of skilled inpatient care in a benefit period.

Part B of Medicare, or Supplementary Medical Insurance (SMI), covers services of physicians and other Medicare-approved practitioners, and services in outpatient settings. The beneficiary is responsible for paying for the first $100 of covered services in a year plus 20 percent of costs over that amount.

Medicare covers approved durable medical equipment for home use, such as oxygen equipment, wheelchairs, and prosthetic devices. Medicare generally does not cover prescriptions or over-the-counter medications or personal services for long-term care.

Work Incentives/Disincentives

It is, of course, recognized that work disincentives are inherent in any program that is designed to provide earnings replacement benefits to persons who are unable to work due to long-term severe mental or physical impairments. Several provisions of DI — such as the strict test of disability, the low level of the SGA screen, and the fact that earnings are only partially replaced by benefits — mitigate an inherent incentive to claim benefits.

In addition, provisions have been added to the DI program over the years to encourage beneficiaries to return to work. As a general rule, beneficiaries who are found to have medically recovered have their benefits and Medicare coverage terminated after a three-month grace period. For beneficiaries who have not medically recovered, however, special "work incentive" provisions are designed to ease the transition from benefit receipt to work. These include: a disregard of impairment related work expenses (IRWE) in determining whether a disabled beneficiary is able to engage in substantial gainful activity; a trial work period; a three-year "extended period of eligibility;" and an option to buy Medicare coverage after that coverage ends.

Impairment related work expenses (IRWE) can be subtracted from earnings to determine whether a person's earnings amount to SGA (now generally $500 a month). These may include expenditures for such items as: attendant care services performed at work or in preparing for work; the cost of modifications in a vehicle that is needed for transportation to work; medical devices and equipment; prostheses; or other work-related equipment. In each case, Social Security field office staff must make the individualized determination whether items can be deducted as IRWE, based on such criteria as: whether the expenses relate to work, are paid by the beneficiary and not reimbursed by another source, and are a reasonable cost for the goods or services provided.

The purpose of the **trial work period (TWP)** is to give DI beneficiaries an opportunity to test their capacity to work, during which time their earnings will not affect their benefits or count as SGA. A DI beneficiary is allowed nine months of such trial work in any five-year period. A month generally counts as a trial work month if the beneficiary earns $200 or more. After the trial work period, SSA reviews the person's work to determine if he or she is engaging in SGA. If the worker is not engaging in SGA, DI benefits continue. If the work constitutes SGA, benefits continue for three months and then stop. The person is then in the extended period of eligibility and Medicare continuation period described below.

The **extended period of eligibility (EPE)** allows persons to return to DI benefit payment status after the trial work period if, at any time in the next 36 months, they do not engage in SGA. During this EPE, benefits are not paid for any month in which the person engages in SGA, but are reinstated in any month the person does not engage in SGA. This provision was intended to ease the transition to benefit termination by removing, for a period of time, the concern that should the work effort fail, the person would have to start all over again with an initial application for benefits and a lengthy and new determination of his/her disability.

The **Medicare continuation** provision extends Medicare to former DI beneficiaries who return to work despite their impairments, and ultimately leave the benefit rolls after the extended period of eligibility. Disabled beneficiaries remain eligible for regular Medicare coverage through the end of the trial work period and this continues for at least 39 months after the trial work period. After regular Medicare continuation coverage ends, the former DI beneficiary can purchase Medicare coverage. The cost of Part A is the same premium the uninsured elderly pay, or $245 a month in 1994. The cost of Part B is the same premium paid by all persons enrolled in SMI, or $41.10 a month in 1994. States, through their Medicaid programs, are required to pay the Part A premium for such qualified working individuals if they meet certain income and resource criteria. Also, large employers which generally have health insurance plans for their employees and who hire former disabled Social Security beneficiaries, or persons with disabled beneficiaries in their families, are required to provide the same health care coverage for these workers (and families) as for other workers.

SUPPLEMENTAL SECURITY INCOME

The federal Supplemental Security Income program provides monthly cash assistance benefits to persons age 65 and older and to blind and disabled persons of any age who have limited income and resources. As of December 1993, there were about 3.7 million blind or disabled adults under age 65 and 770,000 blind or disabled children receiving SSI. Federal SSI expenditures for blind and disabled individuals for 1992 amounted to some $15 billion, with state supplementation amounting to another $2 to $3 billion. Expenditures include payments to blind and disabled recipients over age 65.

Eligibility and Benefit Amount

Basic Eligibility and Benefits. To be eligible for SSI, an aged, blind, or disabled person must have countable income of less than $446 per month ($5,352 per year) in 1994 and countable resources of less than $2,000. For couples, the amounts are 150 percent of those for individuals: countable monthly income of $669 ($8,028 per year) and $3,000 in resources. For persons with no countable income, the basic monthly federal benefit rate (FBR) of $446 ($669 for couples) in 1994 is payable. The FBR is automatically adjusted each January to account for increases in the CPI. The amount of the federal SSI payment decreases as countable income rises.

Citizenship and Other Requirements. To be eligible for SSI, a person must be a U.S. citizen or an alien who is lawfully admitted for permanent residence or allowed to remain in the U.S. and a resident of the U.S., including the District of Columbia and the Northern Mariana Islands. An exception to this residency requirement is provided for the child of a person in military service permanently assigned overseas.

There are several additional eligibility requirements. A person must agree to apply for other benefits for which he or she may be eligible, blind or disabled persons are required to accept available vocational rehabilitation, and alcoholics and drug addicts are required to accept appropriate treatment and to have representative payees.

State Supplementation. The federal SSI program is administered by the Social Security Administration in the 50 states, the District of Columbia, and the Northern Marianas. (The matching programs of old-age assistance, aid to the blind, and aid to the permanently and totally disabled remain in effect in Puerto Rico, Guam, and the Virgin Islands.) The federal SSI program is financed by annual appropriations from federal general revenues.

Forty-three states and the District of Columbia provide for optional supplementation, from state funds, of the federal SSI benefit.[8] In 17 states and the District of Columbia, these supplemental benefits are administered by SSA on behalf of the states and the federal government pays the cost of administering them.[9]

---

8. The states with no optional supplementation include: Arkansas, Georgia, Kansas, Mississippi, Tennessee, Texas, and West Virginia.
9. The 17 states with federally-administered supplements include: California, Delaware, Hawaii, Iowa, Maine, Massachusetts, Michigan, Montana, Nevada, New Jersey, New York, Pennsylvania, Rhode Island, Utah, Vermont, Washington and Wisconsin.

Medicaid and Other Benefits. States are generally required to cover recipients of SSI under Medicaid. However, states may use more restrictive eligibility standards for Medicaid than those for SSI if they were using those standards on January 1, 1972 (before the enactment of SSI). States that have chosen to apply at least one more restrictive standard are known as "section 209(b)" states, after the section of the Social Security Amendments of 1972 that established the option. These states may vary in their definition of disability, or in their standards related to income or resources. There are 12 such 209(b) states.[10]

In most states, persons who are eligible for SSI are also eligible for food stamps. Also, SSI recipients may be eligible for a range of services under state or local programs, including programs supported by Federal Social Services Block Grants under title XX of the Social Security Act.

Definitions of Blindness and Disability. The definitions of blindness and disability for SSI purposes are generally the same for adults as those used in the Social Security disability insurance program:

- Blindness is 20/200 vision in the better eye, with correction, or a visual field of 20 degrees or less even with a corrective lens; and

- Disability is the inability to engage in any substantial gainful activity (SGA) by reason of a medically determinable physical or mental impairment that has lasted or is expected to last at least 12 months or to result in death.

For disabled children — persons under age 18 or students age 18-22 — the law specifically prescribes use of a definition of "comparable severity." Following the 1990 Supreme Court decision in *Sullivan v. Zebley*, to be disabled for SSI purposes, a child must have substantially reduced ability to function independently, appropriately, and effectively in a manner that children of similar age would function, due to a physical or mental impairment(s) which has lasted or is expected to last for at least 12 months or to result in death.

The method for determining disability for SSI applicants is spelled out in regulations and follows the same five-step sequential decision-making process used for DI applicants. SSI benefit claims are filed in local district offices of the Social Security Administration and disability determinations are made by state disability determination service (DDS) agencies. The process for appealing the denial of SSI disability determinations is generally the same as that for DI.

Rehabilitation

Blind or disabled applicants for SSI are generally advised of the existence of state vocational rehabilitation (VR) programs, of the possibility that they may be referred for rehabilitation, and of their obligation to accept appropriate rehabilitation if offered.

Actual referrals to state VR agencies are made by the state disability determination services which make the initial disability determinations and which screen cases for possible VR referral. The state VR agency generally does further screening before deciding which cases will be contacted for further evaluation and possibly offered VR services. Under the present funding of the VR program, about 80 percent of VR expenditures represent federal funds, and the remainder is state matching monies. For SSI beneficiaries who are successfully rehabilitated — that is who, as a result of VR services, perform SGA for a continuous period of at least nine months — the Social Security Administration reimburses the states for the full cost. In FY 1992, 2,834 SSI recipients and 1,634 beneficiaries receiving SSI as supplements to DI benefits were successfully rehabilitated by state VR agencies (table 2-2).

---

10. The 209(b) states include: Connecticut, Hawaii, Illinois, Indiana, Minnesota, Missouri, New Hampshire, North Carolina, North Dakota, Ohio, Oklahoma, and Virginia.

Countable Resources and Income

In general, income and resources are evaluated on an individual basis except, where the parties live in the same household, an ineligible spouse's income may be "deemed" available to the other spouse and parental income may be deemed available to a child under age 18. Also, the income of an alien's sponsor may be deemed available to the alien for a period of three years.

Resources. Resources may include such things as cash, bank accounts, real and personal property and the like. However, certain items are not counted as resources for purposes of the SSI resources limits. Among these excluded items are: the home a person lives in and the land it is on; household goods and personal property worth not more than $2,000; one wedding and one engagement ring; burial funds valued at $1,500 or less and burial spaces; life insurance policies with a combined face value of $1,500 or less; lump-sum retroactive SSI or OASDI benefits are excluded, for up to six months; and a car, regardless of value, if it is necessary for employment, medical treatment, modified for use by a disabled person, or necessary to perform essential daily living activities.

Certain additional resource exclusions are designed to augment work incentive provisions or to avoid thwarting the purposes of other programs. Thus, additional exclusions from resources include: property essential to self-support; resources that a blind or disabled person needs for an approved plan for achieving self-support; and the body of a trust account set up according to state law to which the beneficiary does not have access. Similarly, certain types of payments that are not counted as income when received are excluded from resources if retained, such as: certain support and maintenance payments and home energy assistance; certain disaster relief assistance; and cash received for the purpose of replacing an excluded resource.

Income. Countable income includes both earned and unearned income and in-kind income in the form of food, clothing or shelter. However, there are numerous exclusions from countable income for purposes of determining SSI eligibility and monthly payment amounts, such as: the first $20 of monthly income; the first $65 of earned income and one-half of the remainder; up to $400 of earnings per month (but not more than $1,620 per year) for a student (a person under age 22 and attending school); grants and scholarships used to pay tuition and fees at an educational institution; the value of food stamps, home energy assistance and state or local assistance based on need; food, clothing or shelter based on need and provided by a private nonprofit agency; payments from a trust account for items other than food, clothing, shelter or payments made by others for expenses of the beneficiary for items other than food, clothing or shelter (such as the phone bill); income set aside under a plan for achieving self-support; earned income tax credits; airline or other commercial transportation tickets if used for that purpose; victim's compensation payments; and loans that the individual must repay, income tax refunds, and small amounts of income received irregularly or infrequently.

Living Arrangements

SSI benefit payments may vary depending upon an individual's living arrangements. For persons living in their own apartment, home, trailer, and so on, and homeless persons, the SSI payment is based on the full FBR of $446 per month for individuals and $669 for couples in 1994. For persons who live in the household of others and receive in-kind support and maintenance, benefits may be reduced by up to one-third.

Persons who live in nonmedical public institutions (such as prison) are not generally eligible for benefits. One exception is that persons living in public emergency shelters can receive regular SSI benefits for up to six-months in any nine-month period. Regular SSI payments can also be made to persons who live in publicly operated community residences which serve no more than 16 people. Finally, regular SSI payments can be made to persons who live in a public institution for the purpose of attending approved educational or job training.

Persons who reside in public or private medical institutions in which Medicaid is paying for half the cost of the individual's care can receive SSI payments on a reduced basis. The basic benefit rate for persons in this situation with no other income is $30 per month. This SSI payment is sometimes referred to as a "personal needs allowance." An exception is made for persons who enter a medical institution for a brief stay of 90 days or less. They can continue to receive regular SSI payments if they show that the benefits are needed to maintain the residence to which they plan to return.

Work Incentives for Blind and Disabled SSI Recipients

SSI benefits based on disability, like Social Security disability insurance benefits, are paid only to applicants who meet the definition of disability in the law. Beneficiaries who are found to have medically recovered from their disabilities are no longer eligible for benefits. When SSI recipients medically recover, Medicaid coverage also generally ends, unless the person is eligible for Medicaid based on criteria other than as an SSI recipient.

Unlike Social Security DI, under the SSI means test, benefits also generally are suspended if the person has a change in financial status that causes countable income or resources to exceed program limits. In such cases, the person can return to the SSI rolls without filing a new application if, within 12 months, countable income and resources are again within program limits. When SSI benefits are suspended or terminated because of excess countable income or resources, SSA notifies the state in which the person lives. The states then determine whether Medicaid coverage ends or whether the person qualifies for Medicaid in some way other than as an SSI recipient.

A number of SSI "work incentive provisions" modify the income and resource requirements in order to encourage SSI recipients to work. Although the foregoing description alludes to a number of these provisions, it may be useful to consider them as a whole.

The basic **earned income disregard** for blind and disabled recipients excludes from countable income the first $65 per month of earned income, plus one half of the remainder.

Under the **section 1619 work incentive provisions**, SSI eligibility and Medicaid coverage can continue after benefits are wholly offset because of earnings. Specifically:

- When a disabled beneficiary has earnings that indicate that he or she is able to engage in substantial gainful activity (now generally $500 a month) — that is the person no longer meets the regular definition of disability — SSI eligibility continues under a special section of the law, section 1619(a), as long as he or she has not recovered medically and continues to meet the other SSI eligibility requirements.

- When a blind or disabled beneficiary has earnings (or earnings plus other income) that are so high that he or she is not eligible for any SSI payment, he or she may retain SSI status for Medicaid eligibility purposes under section 1619(b), so long as: the person is still blind or disabled; the person would be eligible for an SSI payment were it not for his or her earnings; the person needs Medicaid in order to work; and the person's earnings are not so high that they could replace the value of the SSI benefits, Medicaid benefits, and any publicly funded attendant care the person receives.

For persons under age 22 who are regularly attending school, there is an additional **student earned income disregard** of up to $400 per month, not to exceed $1,620 per year.

For disabled SSI recipients, earnings needed to pay for **impairment-related work expenses** can be disregarded both for determining initial eligibility and benefit amounts and for determining whether the person is able to engage in SGA, a basic part of the determination of whether a person meets the definition of disability. The local SSA office determines which expenses can be deducted as IRWE. The expenses must be both impairment-related and work-related and the individual must pay the expense in order for it to be deducted from countable earnings.

For blind recipients, there is a special exclusion from countable income of earnings needed to meet **blind work expenses** that enable the person to work, such as guide dogs, attendant care and transportation to and from work. The work expenses do not need to be related the individual's blindness and may include meals eaten at work, federal, state and local income taxes, Social Security taxes, union dues and professional fees.

For both blind and disabled recipients, income and resources may be set aside under an approved **plan for achieving self-support (PASS)**. A PASS generally involves plans for specific job-related education, training or for setting up a business. A PASS must be in writing and must have a specific work goal that the individual probably can attain. It must cover a finite period (generally not more than three-years) and must detail the arrangements for setting aside income to reach the goal. A PASS must be approved by SSA and SSA staff will help individuals prepare a PASS. Income set aside under a PASS is excluded from countable income after all other applicable exclusions are applied.

Property essential for self-support (PES), which is used in a trade or business — such as tools or equipment — is excluded from countable resources. In addition, up to $6,000 of the equity value of non-business income-producing property is excluded from countable resources, provided that the property yields an annual rate of return of at least 6 percent.

---

11. The main sources for this section unless otherwise cited are: W.J. Nelson, Jr., "Workers' Compensation: Coverage, Benefits and Costs, 1990-1991," *Social Security Bulletin,* Fall 1993; and Social Security Administration, *Annual Statistical Supplement to the Social Security Bulletin* (Washington, DC: U.S. Government Printing Office, 1993), pp. 96-7 and table 9.B1, p. 324.

COMPENSATION PROGRAMS

Veterans' compensation (VC) and workers' compensation (WC) are the two main public programs for disability compensation. They are based on the idea that individuals who are injured on the job should be compensated by the employer. Compensation programs pay for health care, rehabilitation, and cash benefits, which are all financed by the employer. In workers' compensation, the benefits often are provided through insurance purchased by the employer. In veterans' compensation, the federal government, as employer of military personnel, pays directly for the benefits and often provides the services directly.

Compensation programs differ from most other cash disability benefit programs in the United States in that the same programs pay for health care, rehabilitation and cash benefits. The cash benefits are paid for partial as well as total disability.

Workers' Compensation

Workers' compensation was the first form of social insurance in the United States.[11] It was designed to provide cash benefits and medical care when workers were injured in connection with their jobs. It also provides survivor benefits to the dependents of workers whose death results from a work-related injury or illness. The first program was enacted in 1908 to cover civilian employees of the federal government. Other laws were enacted by nine states in 1911. By 1920, all but seven states and the District of Columbia had workers' compensation laws.

Today, each of the 50 states and the District of Columbia has its own program. In addition, two federal programs cover federal government employees and longshore and harbor workers throughout the country. A federal program enacted in 1969, also protects coal miners suffering from pneumoconiosis, or "black lung" disease.

Before the enactment of workers' compensation laws in the United States, injured employees seeking compensation for a work-related injury had to file a tort suit against their employer and prove that the employer's negligence caused the injury. The employer could use three common-law defenses to avoid compensating the worker: *assumption of risk* (showing that the injury resulted from an ordinary hazard of employment); *the fellow-worker rule* (proving that the injury was due to a fellow worker's negligence); and *contributory negligence* (proving that, regardless of any fault of the employer, the worker's own negligence contributed to the accident).

Because of these common-law defenses, workers often did not recover damages. While employers often prevailed in court, they were at risk for substantial and unpredictable losses if the worker's suit was successful. Consequently, both employers and employees favored legislation to ensure that a worker who sustained an occupational injury would receive predictable compensation without delay, irrespective of who was at fault. As a *quid pro quo,* the employer's liability was limited. Under the *exclusive remedy* concept, the worker accepted compensation as payment in full, without recourse to further tort suit.

Financing. Workers' compensation programs are financed almost exclusively by employers. Because employers pay for workers' compensation, it is argued that they have a financial incentive to invest in work place safety to prevent injuries and occupational disease.

Coverage and Administration. In 1991, state and federal workers' compensation laws covered about 93.6 million employees, or 87 percent of the nation's wage and salary workers. Many states exempt from coverage employees of nonprofit, charitable or religious institutions and some limit coverage provided to workers in hazardous occupations. Among the most common exemptions are domestic service, agricultural employment, casual labor, and state and local employees. In addition, not all workers in small firms (less than five employees) are covered.

Coverage is compulsory for most private employment except in New Jersey, South Carolina and Texas. In these states, the programs are elective, that is, employers may reject coverage under the law; but they then lose the customary common law defenses against suits filed by their employees.

Generally, workers' compensation laws require employers to obtain insurance or prove financial ability to carry their own risk. Insurance is usually purchased from commercial insurers (in all but six states) or from publicly-operated state funds (twenty-four states). Self-insurance is used primarily by larger employers or, depending on state law, by groups of employers in the same industry through what is called group self-insurance. Six states operate exclusive state funds (where commercial insurance is not permitted) and two states do not allow self-insurance.

Types of Benefits. Workers' compensation benefits include periodic cash payments and medical services to the worker during a period of disability and death and funeral benefits to the worker's survivors. Lump-sum settlements are permitted under most programs. Cash benefits are paid for temporary or permanent total disability and for permanent partial disability.

Temporary and permanent total disability. Aside from medical-only, the most common compensation cases involve temporary total disability; that is, the employee is unable to work at all while he or she is recovering from the injury, but the worker is expected to recover fully. When it has been determined that the worker is permanently and totally disabled for any type of gainful employment, permanent total disability benefits are payable.

Monthly payments for temporary and permanent total disability, as well as survivor benefits, are usually calculated as a percentage of the worker's average weekly total earnings at the time of accident — most commonly 66 and two-thirds percent. Some states are shifting to benefit formulas based on "spendable earnings" or take-home pay and provide benefits equal to 80 percent of these earnings.[12] In some states, the percentage replacement varies with the worker's marital status and the number of dependent children, particularly in survivor cases. All states place maximum dollar limits on weekly benefits. Other provisions limit the number of weeks for which compensation may be paid or the aggregate amount that may be paid in a given case.

If the total disability appears to be permanent, 44 programs provide for the payment of weekly benefits for life or the entire period of disability. Some states reduce the weekly benefits amount after a specified period, or they provide discretionary payments after a specified time.

Permanent partial disability. If the permanent disability of a worker is only partial and may or may not lessen work ability, permanent partial disability benefits are payable. Compensation for permanent partial disability is one of the more complicated aspects of workers' compensation. Broadly speaking, three different bases for determining compensation amounts are used:[13]

- Impairment-based methods provide compensation based on physical or mental loss of use of bodily function. This method pays a specified amount for such factors as loss of motion, loss of strength, or loss of a part of the body.

- Wage loss methods base the benefit on the actual partial loss of earnings experienced as a result of the permanent partial impairment. The amount of the benefit is calculated and paid as the loss is actually experienced.

- Earnings-capacity loss methods take into account the impact of the worker's age, education and work experience in combination with the permanent partial impairment to estimate the consequences of the injury for the worker's future stream of earnings.

A recent blue ribbon panel concluded that each of these methods has certain advantages as well as significant flaws. *Impairment-based* valuations of loss can be measured with relative ease, but the benefit is not related to the economic consequences of the loss for the particular worker. *Wage loss* systems come the closest to the traditional propose of workers' compensation, but they provide disincentives for workers to return to full employment if the amount of the benefit is related to the demonstrated partial wage loss. In addition, it is difficult to determine whether the wage loss experienced long after the injury is due to the injury or to other factors, such as economic conditions. Finally, assessment of *earnings-capacity loss* takes account of both the impairment and its future economic consequences, but the assessment is highly subjective and often involves dispute and litigation about the valuation of future earnings lost due to the injury.[14]

Medical benefits. All state workers' compensation laws require that medical aid be furnished to injured workers without delay, whether or not the injury entails work interruption. This care includes first-aid treatment, physician services, surgical and hospital services, nursing, medical drugs and supplies, appliances and prosthetic devices.

Benefits and Costs. In 1991, total workers' compensation benefits were $42.2 billion, or about $450 for every worker covered by workers' compensation laws. The benefits include $16.8 billion in medical and hospitalization payments, $23.4 billion in cash disability payments and $2.0 billion in survivor benefits. The total cost of workers' compensation, including the cost of administering the programs, was $55.2 billion or about $590 per covered employee.

---

12. If "spendable earnings" are less than 83 percent of total earnings, the formula based on 80 percent of spendable earnings is less than 66.6 percent of total earnings.
13. Blue Ribbon Panel on Workers Compensation, *Policy Statement on Permanent Partial Disability* (Denver, CO: National Conference of State Legislatures, 1992).
14. Ibid.

Integration with Social Security. The 1956 Social Security Amendments provided for offsetting Social Security disability insurance benefits due to WC receipt. The provision was eliminated in 1958 on the rationale that DI was the basic program, and state WC plans would do any offsetting. Legislation in 1965 reintroduced the Social Security offset. Under the law, Social Security benefits are reduced dollar for dollar for the amount of the workers' compensation benefit in order to limit the combined payment to 80 percent of the worker's pre-disability earnings, but not less than the Social Security benefit alone, before the reduction. In 1992, about 103,000 out of approximately 3.2 million Social Security disabled worker beneficiaries had their Social Security payments offset by their state WC payments. The average monthly offset amount was about $300.[15] A provision of the 1965 law allowed states to enact "reverse offset" laws, whereby states could reduce or offset the WC payment because of Social Security payments. Consequently, the savings from limiting combined benefits accrue to the WC program rather than to Social Security. The Omnibus Budget Reconciliation Act of 1981 eliminated the option for additional states to adopt reverse offset provisions. The provisions remain effective in 13 states.[16]

Coordination with Rehabilitation. In WC, the rehabilitation strategy is to return the worker to suitable employment. In some cases, the plans stipulate return to work priorities along the following lines: same employer same job; same employer different job; different employer same job; different employer different job; and lastly, training for a new occupation.[17] While vocational rehabilitation is included under workers' compensation, state plans vary considerably in terms of the discretion accorded to the employer, insurer or employee as to services that are provided and financed by the workers' compensation system.

States have experimented since the mid-1970s with policies that require employers to offer vocational rehabilitation, including education and training, to injured workers if the worker chooses to receiving these services. In more recent years, states have moved away from mandating these services and have placed limits on employer responsibility for financing education and training and placed renewed emphasis on placement in suitable jobs.[18]

Veterans' Compensation

Benefits available to veterans of military service include: disability payments; survivor and dependents' benefits; educational assistance; hospital and medical care; vocational rehabilitation; special loan programs and hiring preference for certain jobs. Most of the veterans programs are administered by the U.S. Department of Veterans' Affairs (DVA).[19]

Two types of cash disability benefits are available for veterans. Veterans' compensation pays benefits to veterans with service-connected disabilities and, on the veteran's death, benefits are paid to the eligible spouse and children. These benefits are not means-tested; they are paid regardless of other income or resources. Second, veterans' pensions are paid to needy veterans who have had wartime service and who have non-service-connected disabilities or are age 65 or older. These benefits are means-tested. This section considers only veterans' compensation. Veterans' pensions are described later.

Veterans' compensation pays monthly benefits to veterans whose disabilities resulted from injury or disease incurred or aggravated by active military duty, whether in wartime or peacetime. Individuals discharged or separated from military service under dishonorable conditions are not eligible for compensation payments.

---

15. U.S. Department of Health and Human Services, Office of the Inspector General, *State Reverse Offset Laws for Disability Beneficiaries*, December 1992.
16. No new reverse offset provisions could be put in after February 18, 1981 for workers injured March 1, 1981 or later with a month of entitlement of September 1981 or later.
17. Briefing by Viola Lopez, Lopez-Kramberg Associates, Houston, TX, October, 1993.
18. M. Berkowitz, "Should Rehabilitation be Mandatory in Workers' Compensation Programs?" *Journal of Disability Policy Studies*, Spring 1990.
19. Social Security Administration, *Annual Statistical Supplement to the Social Security Bulletin* (Washington, DC: U.S. Government Printing Office, 1993), pp. 101-2.

Benefit Amounts. The amount of monthly compensation depends on the degree of disability, rated as the percentage of normal function that is lost. Payments range from $85 a month, for a 10 percent disability, to $1,730 a month for total disability in 1993. In addition, special rates of up to $4,943 a month are paid when eligible veterans suffer specific severe disabilities. Veterans who have at least a 30 percent service-connected disability are entitled to an additional dependent's allowance. The amount is based on the number of dependents and degree of disability.

Recipients and Degree of Disability. In March of 1993, about 2.2 million veterans received compensation payments. Many had only partial impairments: 40 percent were compensated for a 10% disability; a total of 70 percent of the recipients were compensated for 30% or a lesser degree of disability (table 2-3). Fewer than 1 in 10 veterans were compensated for a 100% disability - they include 6 percent whose impairment was judged at 100% disability, and 3 percent whose impairment was assessed between 60-90%, but are compensated at the 100% disability rate because they were judged unable to secure or follow a substantially gainful occupation as a result of a service-connected disability. Less than 1 percent of those receiving veterans' compensation received additional payments for aid and attendance or a housebound allowance.

The number of persons who receive veterans' compensation has been remarkably stable over the last 40 years - fluctuating between 2.0 million and 2.2 million veterans since 1950. The number who are age 65 or older has increased and accounts for .9 million of the 2.2 million persons receiving veterans' compensation in September of 1992.[20]

Veterans' Medical Benefits. The Department of Veterans' Affairs provides a nationwide system of hospitals and other medical care for veterans. Care is furnished to eligible veterans at these facilities according to two categories: "mandatory" and "discretionary." Priority is granted to veterans with service-connected disabilities.

Nursing home care. Eligibility for admission to a DVA nursing home is the same as that for hospitalization in a DVA facility. Admission is based on a priority system with the highest priority given to veterans requiring nursing home care for a service-connected condition. DVA also contracts with community nursing homes to provide care at DVA expense to certain veterans.

Outpatient medical treatment. Extensive outpatient medical treatment is available to veterans: rehabilitation; consultation; training and mental health services in connection with the treatment of physical and mental disabilities. Outpatient care is furnished according to priority groups within the resources available to the facility.

Other medical benefits. Other DVA programs and medical benefits are available to certain eligible veterans: domiciliary care for veterans with limited income who have permanent disabilities, but who are ambulatory and able to care for themselves; alcohol and drug dependence treatment; prosthetic appliances; modifications in the veteran's home required by his or her physical condition, subject to prescribed cost limitations; and, for Vietnam-era veterans, readjustment counseling services. Under limited circumstances, the DVA may authorize hospital care or other medical services in the community at DVA expense.

The nature of the relationship between the veteran and the federal government differs from other employer/employee or government/citizen relationships. The government has the authority to recruit people into military service and subject them to extremely hazardous duty. This authority is considered necessary to meet the uncertain demands of national defense. As part of this arrangement, it is

---

20. Social Security Administration, *Annual Statistical Supplement to the Social Security Bulletin* (Washington, DC: U.S. Government Printing Office, 1993), p. 329.

generally accepted that those who serve honorably are owed more by the government than the typical employer owes its employees or than government owes the average citizen.

The special obligation of the federal government to veterans are reflected in the fact that the government provides veterans many other benefits beyond disability compensation — such as housing and education benefits. The full package of veterans' benefits can be used to improve the veteran's skills and earning capacity. The goal of the total package of veterans benefits is not limited to restoring the veteran to his former level of ability.

PRIVATE SHORT-TERM DISABILITY BENEFITS

Short-term disability benefits provide continuity in income for workers who miss work because of temporary illness or injury. While benefits provide income security to workers, they also promote health and safety in the work place by enabling workers to stay at home to accommodate a temporary health problem. Short-term disability benefits may also be used for paid maternity leave. In addition, they support workers through the early stages of what may turn out to be longer periods of disability. Social Security has a five-month waiting period after the onset of disability before cash benefits begin. Private long-term disability benefits also usually have a waiting period of several months during which short-term disability benefits are paid. Short-term benefits are a combination of union negotiated, employer-provided benefits and mandatory social insurance programs in five states.

---

21. U.S. Department of Labor, *Employee Benefits in Medium and Large Private Establishments, 1991* Bulletin 2422 (Washington, DC: U.S. Government Printing Office, May 1993); and U.S. Department of Labor, *Employee Benefits in Small Private Establishments, 1990* Bulletin 2388 (Washington, DC: U.S. Government Printing Office, September 1991).
22. Social Security Administration, *Annual Statistical Supplement to the Social Security Bulletin* (Washington, DC: U.S. Government Printing Office, 1993), pp. 99-100 and table 9.C1, p. 325.

Sick Leave

Sick leave is the most common type of short-term disability protection. It is available to about 50 percent of the private sector work force and is more commonly available to professional, technical and managerial workers (77 percent), than to clerical and sales workers (59 percent), or blue-collar workers (33 percent). Sick leave usually is payable from the first day of sickness, it usually replaces 100 percent of the worker's normal pay and typically lasts for several weeks. Sick leave, alone, rarely lasts long enough to cover the full five months after disability onset before Social Security disability benefits begin.[21] Consequently, short-term disability insurance is also important to cover the early periods of a long-term disability.

Mandatory Temporary Disability Insurance

Temporary disability insurance (TDI) programs are mandatory in five states — California, Hawaii, New Jersey, New York and Rhode Island.[22]

History and Financing. In all of the state programs, employees are required to contribute to the TDI systems. In all but California and Rhode Island, employers also are required to contribute. Employee financing was an integral part of TDI since the beginning of these programs. The TDI plans originated in the 1940s as amendments to the state unemployment insurance system, which were, and remain, financed largely by employers. The Federal Unemployment Insurance Tax Act was amended in 1946 to permit states, where employees made contributions to the unemployment insurance system, to use part or all of the employee contributions for temporary disability insurance. Four of the five state TDI programs began in the 1940s. Hawaii began its TDI program in 1969.

Administration. The method of administering these programs varies. In California and New Jersey, most of the coverage is provided through a state operated fund, although employers are allowed to "contract out" by purchasing group insurance from commercial insurance companies, by self-insuring, or by negotiating an agreement with a union or

Table 2-3: Veterans Compensation (Service Connected), March 1993
Persons Receiving Compensation by Degree and Type of Disability

Total recipients	Total	Persian Gulf	Vietnam	Korea	WW II	WW I[b]	Peacetime
Total number	2,188,061	54,167	676,678	200,258	786,866	1,639	468,453
Total percent	100	100	100	100	100	100	100
Men	98	100	99	99	99	97	94
Women	2	—[a]	1	1	1	3	6

Degree of disability[c]							
0% compensable	1	0	—[a]	3	1	1	1
10%	40	52	37	35	39	21	46
20%	16	22	16	15	15	26	19
30%	14	12	14	14	15	15	12
40%	8	6	9	9	9	9	6
50%	5	3	5	5	5	7	3
60% (total)	5	2	5	6	6	7	4
schedule	4	2	4	4	4	2	3
unemployable	1	0	1	2	1	5	1
70% (total)	3	1	3	3	3	3	2
schedule	2	1	3	2	2	1	2
unemployable	1	0	1	1	1	2	—[a]
80% (total)	2	—[a]	2	2	2	2	1
schedule	1	—[a]	1	1	1	0	1
unemployable	1	0	1	1	1	2	—[a]
90% (total)	1	—[a]	1	1	1	1	—[a]
schedule	—[a]	—[a]	—[a]	—[a]	—[a]	0	—[a]
unemployable	—[a]	0	1	—[a]	—[a]	1	—[a]
100%	6	2	8	8	5	8	6
Total paid 100% rate	9	2	10	12	8	18	8

Type of disability							
Psychological and neurological disorders	19	10	20	18	23	18	16
Other medical	81	90	80	82	77	82	84

Additional awards[d]							
Aid & Attendance							
Veterans	.5	.2	.5	.7	.3	.7	.6
Spouse	.1	0	—[a]	.1	.2	.7	—[a]
Housebound veterans	.3	.1	.4	.4	.3	.8	.3

a. Less than 1/2 of 1 percent.
b. World War I includes the Spanish-American War and Mexican Border Service.
c. Compensation is paid according to the combined degree of disability determined from the Schedule for Rating Disabilities. Veterans who have schedular ratings from 60 percent through 90 percent and are judged unable to secure or follow a substantially gainful occupation as a result of service-connected disabilities are classified as individually unemployed and compensated at the 100 percent disability compensation level.
d. Aid and Attendance and Housebound awards for Disability Compensation are granted under 38 U.S.C. 314 and 315.
Source: U.S. Department of Veterans Affairs, Analysis and Statistic Service, Demographics Division.

employees' association. The "contracted" plan must meet all requirements of the state plan. In Hawaii and New York, private insurance plans are the typical method of providing the required TDI. In Rhode Island, coverage is exclusively through a state operated fund.

Definition of Disability. The five state plans generally describe disability as the inability to perform regular or customary work because of a physical or mental condition. Some states also pay disability benefits during periods of unemployment, and these have a stricter test of disability. All five states pay TDI benefits for disability due to pregnancy.

Benefits. Benefits are typically 50 percent of prior pay and are subject to dollar minimums and maximums. The maximum duration of benefits ranges from 26 weeks in Hawaii, New York and New Jersey, to 30 weeks in Rhode Island, and 52 weeks in California. Generally, a seven-day waiting period applies before the TDI benefits begin.

Integration with Other Disability Benefits. All five states restrict payment of TDI if employees are also receiving workers' compensation (unless the WC payments are for a previous or partial disability). The state programs are integrated with sick leave in varied ways. Rhode Island pays TDI in full, regardless of sick leave. New York deducts from TDI other benefits paid by the employer, unless they are part of a collectively bargained agreement. California and New Jersey limit total TDI plus other benefits to not exceed 100 percent of the worker's prior pay.

Other Short-Term Disability Insurance

Outside of the five states where TDI is mandatory, workers may have short-term disability insurance (STDI) that is provided and financed, at least in part, by their employers.[23] Employers may purchase sickness and accident insurance from commercial insurers or they may self-insure the benefits. The insurance often has a waiting period of a few days before benefits are payable. Benefits usually last for up to 26 weeks and typically replace about 50 percent of the worker's prior earnings, although some plans replace as much as 70 percent.

Workers with the most comprehensive short-term disability protection are those with both sick leave — which pays benefits immediately, typically at 100 percent of pay, but often for only a few weeks — and temporary disability insurance — which typically pays 50 percent of prior earnings, but continues benefits for up to 26 weeks.

Coverage Under Sick Leave, STDI or TDI

The Department of Labor (DoL) provides estimates from its employee benefit surveys of the prevalence of either sick leave or sickness and accident insurance that is financed, at least in part, by employers. Those data show that about 30 percent of private sector employees have short-term sickness and accident insurance — and that 64 percent have either this insurance or sick leave.

The DoL data, however, do not include TDI coverage in California and Rhode Island, where benefits are wholly financed by employees. California and Rhode Island have about 11 million workers covered by TDI. When these mandatory state programs are included, then roughly 44 percent of private employees are estimated to have some short-term disability insurance. Overall, those with either STDI, TDI or sick leave would be about 70 percent of private employees. That is, of all private employees, about:[24]

---

23. U.S. Department of Labor, op. cit., footnote 21. Individually purchased insurance is not covered in this discussion.
24. Jack Schmulowitz, Social Security Administration, Office of Research.

- 30 percent have no sick leave or short-term disability insurance;
- 26 percent have sick leave only;
- 20 percent have short-term disability insurance only; and
- 24 percent have both.

Differences by occupation. When disaggregated by occupation, blue-collar workers are much more likely than upper status white collar workers to lack short-term disability protection. According to the DoL data, which leave out mandatory TDI in California and Rhode Island, the proportions of private sector workers without short-term disability protection are 17 percent for upper status white collar workers, 33 percent for clerical and sales workers, and 44 percent for blue-collar workers.

PRIVATE LONG-TERM DISABILITY BENEFITS AND PENSIONS

Social Security disability insurance is the primary source of earnings replacement income in the event of long-term disability for almost all workers in the United States. It is sometimes supplemented by private long-term disability insurance (LTDI) or disability pensions in private pension plans. Workers must meet a very strict definition of disability in order to qualify for Social Security. Private insurance or pension plans that use a less strict test of disability might pay benefits in situations where Social Security does not.

Private Long-Term Disability Insurance

Private LTDI is a union negotiated and employer-provided benefit. In all, about 25 percent of private sector employees have some type of private LTDI that is financed, at least in part by employers.[25] That LTDI protection is much more common among upper status white collar workers (47 percent), than among clerical and sales workers (28 percent) or blue-collar workers (13 percent) in private employment. As with almost all other private employee benefits, LTDI coverage is more common in medium and large establishments than in small ones (table 2-4).[26]

Benefits. Private long-term disability benefits usually are paid after a waiting period — typically three to six months after the onset of disability, or after temporary disability benefits are exhausted. The benefits are usually designed to replace a specified fraction of pre-disability earnings. The most common replacement rate is 60 percent, although replacement rates of 50 or 66 percent also are common.

Coordination with Social Security. Almost all private LTDI is coordinated with Social Security, such that private benefits are offset dollar for dollar by Social Security benefits. For example, as illustrated in table 2-5, if Social Security DI paid a benefit that replaced 40 percent of a worker's prior earnings, and the LTDI plan offers 60 percent replacement, the insurer would pay the remaining 20 percent to have the combined income from Social Security plus the private insurance replace 60 percent of the worker's prior earnings.

The rationale for offsetting the benefits against Social Security is to ensure that the target replacement rate is achieved and to preserve incentives for return to work by paying only partial replacement of earnings.

As noted earlier, Social Security benefits are designed to pay a higher percentage replacement of earnings for low earners than for higher earnings. Consequently, the integration of private LTDI with Social Security means that private benefits fill a relatively larger role for higher earners. Premiums and reserves for these plans generally are based on the assumption that the LTDI benefits will be offset $1 for $1 by Social Security. Consequently, it is common for private plans to require claimants to apply for Social Security disability benefits and to

---

25. U.S. Department of Labor, op. cit., footnote 21.
26. An establishment is defined as an economic unit that produces goods or services (such as a factory or a store) at a single location. An establishment is not necessarily a firm: it may be a branch plant, for example, or a warehouse.

assist employees in filing their Social Security claims and appeals, if necessary.

Definition of Disability. The definition of disability used in private LTDI plans varies, but one of the most common practices is to require, initially, that the worker be unable to perform his usual occupation. After a period, often two years, the test becomes more strict — "inability to perform the duties for any occupation for which one is qualified by training, education, or experience."[27] In these plans, the employee's LTDI benefits will end after two years if the disability does not meet the stricter test.

Coordination with Rehabilitation. Private insurers or employers may invest in individualized rehabilitation and return to work initiatives with an employee who is receiving LTDI. One study of the practices of large employers and private insurers concluded that private plans are very selective in terms of who is offered rehabilitation and return to work services. The criteria for selection are based largely on cost-benefit considerations. Individuals with the best prospects for successful return to work, and whose LTDI benefits represent the larger future benefit obligations are the most likely to be offered rehabilitation services that are financed by the employer or LTDI plan. The study reported the following criteria were used by employers or insurers in deciding whether to offer rehabilitation services:[28]

- medical stability — a physician's assessment of appropriateness of rehabilitation;

- age — workers under age 55 are more likely to be considered candidates for rehabilitation;

- severity and nature of impairment — traumatic, musculoskeletal injuries of recent onset and short duration (as opposed to chronic or progressive illness) are positive indicators for rehabilitation;

- occupation or type of job — white collar workers appear more likely to be offered rehabilitation, perhaps because they have transferrable skills and greater flexibility to shift among positions;

- cost recovery potential — which tends to favor younger workers and those with higher pre-disability earnings; and

- motivation — the employee's willingness to participate in rehabilitation was essential. Attempts to require rehabilitation were not considered cost effective.

Disability Pensions

While private pensions are designed mainly for retirement income, they may also provide income before normal retirement age to workers who are forced to retire early because of a career ending disability. Pensions may be paid before retirement age under either early retirement provisions or disability retirement provisions.[29]

Private pensions are of two types: defined benefit (DB) plans, which determine the benefit amount at retirement, or disability retirement, based on a formula specified in the plan. Usually the pension is based on the worker's earnings and years of service in the plan. In the case of disability, additional years of service may be granted for the period between the disability and normal retirement age. In this way, these plans have a disability insurance, or pooled risk, component. Defined contribution (DC) plans, in contrast, do not have a disability insurance component. They are more like an individual savings account. They specify the employer's, and sometimes the employee's, contribution to the plan and the benefit is the accumulated value of those contributions at the time of withdrawal. DC plans permit early withdrawal in the case of disability, but the value of the DC account would be very small if the worker became disabled after a relatively short service in the plan.

---

27. M.W. Kita, "Morbidity and Disability," *Journal of Insurance Medicine,* Winter 1992, p. 272.
28. D.E. Galvin, D. Dean, and K. Kirschner, *Applying State-of-the-Art Disability Management to Social Security Beneficiaries,* Washington Business Group on Health, Final Report to the Social Security Administration, September 1991.
29. U.S. Department of Labor, op. cit., footnote 21.

Table 2-4: Private Long-Term Disability Insurance, 1990-1991
Percent of Private Employees Covered, by Occupation, Amount of Employment and Establishment Size

Amount of employment and occupation	Total	Medium and large 1991	Small (under 100 employees) 1990
	Percent of employees with private LTDI		
All private employees	25	35	15
Professional, technical, executive	47	58	32
Clerical and sales	28	40	19
Production and service	13	21	7
Part-time — total	1	3	—[a]
Professional, technical, executive	8	16	2
Clerical and sales	1	2	1
Production and service	—[a]	1	—[a]
Full-time — total	29	40	19
Professional, technical, executive	51	61	36
Clerical and sales	35	49	25
Production and service	16	24	9

a. Less than 1/2 of 1 percent.
Abbreviation: LTDI = long-term disability insurance.
Sources: U.S. Department of Labor, *Employee Benefits in Small Private Establishments, 1990* Bulletin 2388 (Washington, DC: U.S. Government Printing Office, September 1991); U.S. Department of Labor, Bureau of Labor Statistics, *NEWS*, December 9, 1992; and U.S. Department of Labor, *Employee Benefits in Medium and Large Private Establishments, 1991* Bulletin 2422 (Washington, DC: U.S. Government Printing Office, May 1993).

Table 2-5: Integration of Private LTDI and Social Security, 1993
Illustrative Benefits and Replacement Rates under Private LTDI Plan that Provides 60% Replacement, by Earnings Level

Earnings level		Replacement rate (percent)		LTDI monthly amount	
Annual	Monthly	Social Security	LTDI	If no Social Security	With Social Security
$6,000	$500	78	0	$300	$0
12,000	1,000	55	5	600	50
18,000	1,500	49	12	900	188
24,000	2,000	44	16	1,200	328
36,000	3,000	36	24	1,800	707
48,000[a]	4,000	31	30	2,400	1,200
72,000[a]	6,000	20	40	3,600	2,400
120,000[a]	10,000	12	48	6,000	4,800

Abbreviation: LTDI = long-term disability insurance.
a. Monthly Social Security benefits for earnings of $48,000 or higher are estimated to be about $1,200.

Table 2-6: All Retirement Plans and Defined Benefit Plans, 1990-1991
Percent of Private Employees Covered, by Occupation, Amount of Employment and Establishment Size

Type of worker and retirement plan	Total	Medium and large	Small
Percent with retirement plans			
All employees:			
Any retirement plan	53	69	35
DB plan	35	52	17
Type of worker			
Part-time employees:			
Any retirement plan	21	40	10
DB plan	13	28	4
Full-time employees:			
Any retirement plan	60	78	42
DB plan	39	59	20
Type of occupation			
Professional and technical:			
Any retirement plan	66	81	44
DB plan	42	58	18
Clerical and sales:			
Any retirement plan	52	71	39
DB plan	32	51	19
Production and service:			
Any retirement plan	49	70	31
DB plan	33	54	15

Abbreviation: DB = defined benefit.
Sources: U.S. Department of Labor, *Employee Benefits in Small Private Establishments, 1990* Bulletin 2388 (Washington, DC: U.S. Government Printing Office, September 1991), tables 1 and 86; U.S. Department of Labor, *Employee Benefits in Medium and Large Private Establishments, 1991* Bulletin 2422 (Washington, DC: U.S. Government Printing Office, May 1993), tables 1 and 122.

Prevalence of DB Pension Plans. In 1990-91, DB pension plans covered about 35 percent of all private sector employees. The DB plan coverage rate was much higher for full-time employees in medium and large establishments (59 percent) than for full-time employees in small ones (20 percent) or for part-time employees (13 percent) (table 2-6).

Early and Normal Retirement Provisions. Information on retirement and disability provisions of DB plans is available only for full-time employees in medium and large establishments. In these plans, the most common normal retirement age at which unreduced pensions are payable is 65. Some workers, however, are in plans that allow retirement with full pensions before age 65 if the worker has long service with the plan. For example, 10 percent of the covered workers were in plans that allowed normal retirement after 30 years of service regardless of age. About a third of the workers were in plans that allow full benefits at age 60 or 62 if certain length of service requirements were met.

Almost all covered workers were in plans that would permit retirement on a reduced pension before normal retirement age. The most common minimum age for retirement was 55. Two-thirds of covered workers were in plans that would allow early retirement pensions at that age. While early retirement options allow workers choices about when to retire, they also may be used by those who have health problems. In addition, disability provisions of pension plans are specifically designed for workers who have career ending disabilities.

Disability Retirement Provisions. Disability provisions of private pension plans may substitute for long-term disability insurance (LTDI) in some cases. In other cases, pensions are integrated with LTDI. When employers provide LTDI, the pension plan might defer disability pensions until LTDI benefits have ceased at the plan's normal or early retirement age. These deferred disability pensions are more common among white collar workers than among blue collar workers (table 2-7). Under deferred plans, employees who qualify for LTDI benefits usually continue to earn credits for service in their pension plans until the normal retirement age is reached. At that time, the disability payments cease and pension payments begin.

In contrast with *deferred* disability pensions, *immediate* disability pensions are more common among blue collar workers and are likely to be the only form of disability protection other than Social Security. These plans commonly pay benefits under the normal retirement benefit formula, as if the retirement had occurred at the plan's normal retirement age.

Trends Over Time. The DoL data on employee benefits provide trends over time only for full-time workers in medium and large establishments — the private sector employee group most likely to have comprehensive employment-based benefits. These data indicate some decline in the prevalence of coverage under DB pension plans and an accompanying decline in the prevalence of immediate disability pensions protection under these plans (table 2-8).

Because of changes in the employee benefit surveys over the years, these data somewhat overstate the decline in DB plan coverage.[30] Nonetheless, some decline in coverage under plans that provide immediate disability pensions is evident during the 1980s — particularly for blue collar workers. During the same period, coverage under LTDI was fairly stable. Consequently, blue collar workers who, in the past relied on DB pensions, in lieu of LTDI, as a source of disability income protection are less likely now to have private long-term disability protection.

OTHER NEEDS-BASED DISABILITY CASH BENEFITS

Supplemental Security Income is the main source of means-tested benefits for low-income persons with disabilities. Veterans' pensions are akin to SSI for low-income elderly or disabled veterans who have had wartime service.

Veterans' Pensions

Wartime veterans who become totally and permanently disabled after their military service (with disabilities unrelated to active duty) are eligible for means-tested monthly pensions.[31] Those age 65 or

---

30. The 1980 survey did not distinguish between DB and DC plan coverage, because DC plans as the primary source of coverage was uncommon among full-time employees in medium and large establishments. The 1980 coverage rate includes all retirement plan coverage. In 1988, the scope of the survey was expanded to include more smaller establishments (with between 100 and 250 employees). The 1988a estimates are consistent with the surveys in prior years, while the 1988b estimates are consistent with later years.

31. Social Security Administration, *Annual Statistical Supplement to the Social Security Bulletin* (Washington, DC: U.S. Government Printing Office, 1993), pp. 101-2 and table 9.F1, p. 329.

Table 2-7: Disability Provisions of Defined Benefit Pension Plans, 1991
Percent of Full-time Employees in Medium and Large Private Establishments with Specific Plan Provisions

Plan provision	Total	White collar	Blue collar
Percent covered by			
Defined benefit pension plan	59	58	59
With disability retirement	47	43	50
Percent with age and service requirements for disability pension			
No age or service requirement	9	5	12
Service only	25	20	30
5 years	4	4	4
10 years	14	10	19
15 years	7	6	7
Age 40-49 [a]	1	2	—[f]
Age 50 or older [a]	2	3	2
Prior receipt of LTDI benefits	8	11	6
Percent with specific type of disability benefit provisions			
Immediate disability retirement [b]	29	23	36
Unreduced normal formula [c]	21	17	26
Reduced normal formula [d]	6	5	6
Other than normal formula [e]	2	1	4
Deferred disability retirement with benefits based on:	17	20	13
Service when disabled	4	3	4
Service and credit to retirement	13	16	9

a. Includes those with service as well as age requirements.
b. Immediate disability pensions may be supplemented by additional allowances until an employee reaches a specified age or becomes eligible for Social Security.
c. The disabled worker's pension is computed under the plan's normal benefit formula and is paid as if retirement had occurred on the plan's normal retirement date, either based on years of service actually completed or projected to a later date.
d. The disabled worker's pension is computed under the plan's normal benefit formula, based on years of service actually completed, and then reduced for early receipt.
e. The disabled worker's benefit is not computed by the plan's normal benefit formula. The methods used include flat amount benefits, dollar amount formulas, percent of unreduced normal benefits less Social Security, and percent of earnings formulas both with and without Social Security offsets.
f. Less than 1/2 of 1 percent.
Abbreviation: LTDI = long-term disability insurance.
Source: U.S. Department of Labor, *Employee Benefits in Medium and Large Private Establishments, 1991* Bulletin 2422 (Washington, DC: U.S. Government Printing Office, May 1993), tables 1 and 95.

Table 2-8: Disability Coverage under Defined Benefit Pension Plans and Long-Term Disability Insurance, 1980-1991

Percent of Full-time Employees in Medium and Large Establishments Covered, by Plans and Occupation

	1980	1986	1988[a]	1988[b]	1989	1991
All full-time employees						
With defined benefit pension plan	84[c]	76	70	63	63	59
Disability retirement provisions	73	68	—[d]	58	51	46
Immediate disability pension	51	37	—[d]	30	29	29
Deferred disability pension	22	31	—[d]	28	22	17
With LTDI coverage	40	48	47	42	45	40
White colar						
With defined benefit pension plan	86	78	69	64	63	58
Disability retirement provisions	71	69	—[d]	58	50	43
Immediate disability pension	36	26	—[d]	23	24	23
Deferred disability pension	35	43	—[d]	35	26	20
With LTDI coverage	55	64	62	58	61	55
Blue collar						
With defined benefit pension plan	81	74	71	61	63	59
Disability retirement provisions	74	67	—[d]	57	52	50
Immediate disability pension	62	50	—[d]	38	35	35
Deferred disability pension	12	17	—[d]	19	17	15
With LTDI coverage	27	30	29	24	27	24

a. Estimate consistent with scope of survey in previous years.
b. Estimate consistent with scope of survey in later years.
c. Includes all retirement plan coverage.
d. Not available.
Abbreviation: LTDI = long-term disability insurance.
Source: U.S. Department of Labor, *Employee Benefits in Medium and Large Private Establishments*, selected years.

Table 2-9: Veterans' Disability Pension (non-service connected), March 1993
Persons Receiving Pension by War Era, Gender and Type of Disability and Average Amounts

	Total	Persian Gulf	Vietnam	Korea	WW II	WW I[b]
Total recipients	474,801	15	42,018	97,604	329,099	6,065
Total percent	100	100	100	100	100	100
Male	98	100	98	99	98	98
Female	2	0	2	1	2	2
Average monthly payment	$373	$702	$565	$475	$316	$494
Type of disability						
Psychological and neurological	26	47	48	31	21	15
No disability	21	0	—[a]	1	29	18
Other	54	53	52	67	50	68
Additional payments[c] (percent receiving)						
Aid and Attendance	19	40	15	14	20	56
Housebond	3	7	3	4	3	3

a. Less tha 1/2 of 1 percent.
b. World War I includes the Spanish-American War and Mexican Border Service.
c. Aid and Attendance and Housebound awards for Disability Pension are granted under 38 U.S.C. 511, 512 and 521.
Source: U.S. Department of Veterans Affairs, Analysis and Statistics Service, Demographics Division.

older are presumed to be totally and permanently disabled, if they otherwise qualify based on need and prior wartime service. To qualify for these pensions, a veteran must have served in one or more of the following designated war periods: the Mexican Border Period, World War I, World War II, the Korean conflict, the Vietnam era, or the Persian Gulf War. The period of service must have lasted at least 90 days and the discharge or separation cannot have been dishonorable.

In 1994, maximum benefit amounts for non-service-connected disabilities range from $651.50 per month for a veteran without a dependent spouse or child, to $1,212 per month for a veteran who is in need of regular aid and attendance and who has one dependent. For each additional dependent child, the pension is raised by $108 per month. Benefits to veterans without dependents are reduced to not more than $90 per month if they are receiving long-term domiciliary or medical care from the Department of Veterans' Affairs.

In March 1993, 475,000 veterans received these means-tested pensions. The large majority were World War II veterans, (table 2-9). The number receiving these benefits has been declining since the mid-1960's. The large majority of recipients are men age 65 or older who served during World War II or the Korean conflict. Younger recipients of veterans' pensions, who served in the Vietnam era, are more likely to have psychological and neurological disorders than are the older recipients with earlier wartime service.

Chapter 3: The Population with Disabilitites

This chapter provides information about the population of persons with disabilities, including estimates of the prevalence of disability in the total population, the attributes of disability insurance (DI) and Supplemental Security Income (SSI) beneficiaries, and what is known about outcomes for persons who have been denied DI benefits in the past.

PREVALENCE OF DISABILITY

Estimates of the number of persons with disabilities vary greatly depending on how disability is defined and measured. For example, the preamble of the Americans with Disabilities Act (ADA) of 1990 estimates that 43 million persons in the United States have disabilities that are covered by that Act. Other estimates of the number of Americans with some type of chronic condition or impairment may be as high as half the total U.S. population. In contrast, the Social Security and SSI programs, together, paid benefits in December 1993, to about 6.7 million working age adults who were found unable to work because of disability. This section explores the different concepts of disability and how they affect counts of the number of persons with disabilities.

Persons Covered by the Americans with Disabilities Act of 1990

The ADA uses an inclusive definition of disability to encompass persons covered by the anti-discrimination and public accommodation protections of the Act. It defines a person with a disability as one who: has a physical or mental impairment that substantially limits one or more major life activities; has a record of such an impairment; or is regarded as having such an impairment. The estimate of 43 million persons covered by this definition includes children and elderly persons, as well as working age people. The estimate has been questioned as a count of those covered by the ADA for two reasons:[1]

First, it undercounts those potentially covered because it counts only certain types of impairments. It includes musculoskeletal and neuromuscular abnormalities and impairments of vision, hearing, speech and intelligence; but it does not include impairments of internal organs and tissue due to disease, such as HIV, or emphysema. If the definition of impairment included all chronic conditions as identified in the 1990 National Health Interview Survey (NHIS), the number of persons with impairments could be as high as half the U.S. population.

On the other hand, the estimate overcounts those *limited* by a disability because it is based on reports of impairments; it is not restricted to those whose impairment causes a limitation in major life activities. Most people identified in the NHIS as having

---

1. M.P. LaPlante, "The Demographics of Disability," *The Americans with Disabilities Act: From Policy to Practice*, J. West (ed.) (New York, NY: Milbank Memorial Fund, 1991).

Table 3-1. Disability and Work Status of Persons Age 18-64, 1990
Number and Percent of the Noninstitutionalized Population by Type or Activity Limitation and Work Status

Disability and work status	Number (thousands)	Percent
All persons 18-64	151,667	100.0
Unable to work	6,711	4.4
Limited only in kind or amount of work	7,421	4.9
Working full-time	4,247	2.8
Working part-time	1,542	1.0
Not working	1,633	1.1
Limited only in non-work activities	5,271	3.4
Working full-time	3,076	2.0
Working part-time	554	0.3
Not working	1,641	1.1
Not limited in activities	132,264	87.2
Working full-time	89,522	59.0
Working part-time	14,782	9.7
Not working	27,960	18.4

Source: M.P. LaPlante, unpublished tabulations from the 1990 National Health Interview Survey.

impairments or chronic conditions report they are not limited by their conditions.

If the count of people with disabilities who are covered by the ADA definition considered all types of impairments and chronic conditions, but counted only persons who are limited in major life activities — such as attending school, working or activities of daily living — by those impairments, then about 36 million persons would be counted in 1990. They include about 34 million people with disabilities who were living in households and about 2 million persons who were in institutions, such as nursing homes, mental hospitals, and facilities for persons with mental retardation.[2]

---

2. M.P. LaPlante, "How Many Americans Have a Disability?" *Disability Statistics Abstracts Number 5*, National Institute for Disability and Rehabilitation Research, December 1992.

Functional Limitations Among the Working-Age Population

Among working-age persons, chronic health conditions can limit activities in a variety of ways. Among those age 18-64 in 1990, about 19.4 million persons (12.8 percent) reported they were limited in some way because of a chronic condition (table 3-1). They include: 6.7 million (4.4 percent) who reported they were unable to work; 7.4 million (4.9 percent) who reported they were limited only in the kind or amount of work they could do; and 5.3 million (3.5 percent) who were limited only in non-work activities. The large majority of those who were limited only in the kind or amount of work they could do, or only in non-work activities were, in fact, working.

The large majority of persons who report some type of work limitation also report that they are able, without assistance of another person, to perform activities of daily living (ADLs) — such as bathing, dressing, eating, or getting around the home — and instrumental activities of daily living (IADLs) — such as doing household chores, doing necessary business, shopping or getting around for other purposes (table 3-2).

Those who do report a need for assistance include about 1.4 percent of the working-age population who need assistance with IADLs only, and 0.6 percent who need help with ADLs. Some of those who need assistance, nonetheless, are able to work.

PERSONS RECEIVING SOCIAL SECURITY OR SUPPLEMENTAL SECURITY INCOME

At the end of 1993, a total of 6.7 million persons age 18-64 were receiving Social Security or SSI benefits based on their own disability. To receive these benefits, individuals must meet the strict definition of work disability in the law — "inability to engage in any substantial gainful activity because of a medically determinable physical or mental impairment that is expected to last at least 12 months or result in death."[3] In addition, to receive Social Security DI benefits, a person must have worked in employment covered by Social Security. To receive SSI, a person must have limited income and assets. Also, at the end of 1993, 723,000 children under 18 were receiving SSI benefits based on disability.

Types of OASDI Benefits

Social Security benefits based on disability are paid to disabled workers who are insured based on their own covered work under Social Security, and the amount of their benefit is based on their own past earnings. In December 1993, benefits were paid to 3.7 million disabled workers. About 1 in 6 of these disabled workers received federally administered SSI benefits as supplements, because they had limited resources and their countable income, including their Social Security disability benefits, was less that the SSI income guarantee in their state (table 3-3).

---
3. For a more complete discussion of the program definition of disability, see the section on Social Security disability insurance in chapter 2.

Another 604,000 persons age 18-64 received Social Security benefits as adults disabled since childhood who are the child of a retired, disabled or deceased worker. Their benefits are based on the insured status and earnings of the parent, and amount to 50 percent of the parent's full benefit of the parent is alive (retired or disabled) and 75 percent if the parent is deceased. About 4 in 10 of these adults disabled since childhood receive SSI as supplements to the OASDI benefits. Because the benefit rate is smaller if the parent is alive and also receiving benefits, it is more likely to be supplemented by SSI than if the parent is deceased.

Finally, 147,000 persons received OASDI benefits as the disabled widow(er) aged 50-64 of a deceased worker. The benefit is based on the deceased worker's insured status and earnings and amounts to 71.5 percent of the full benefit based on that earnings record. About 2 in 10 of these disabled widow(er)s received SSI as a supplement to their OASDI benefits.

Type of SSI Benefits

Persons age 18-64 who received federally administered SSI benefits based on disability numbered 3.1 million at the end of 1993. They include 47,800 persons age 18-21 who are attending school and technically, are classified as children. SSI recipients age 18-21 who are not attending school are classified as adults. The SSI program statistics also include among blind and disabled recipients persons age 65 or older who first entered the SSI rolls as blind or disabled adults before age 65. At the end of 1993, there were 638,400 such persons age 65 or older receiving SSI on the basis of blindness or disability.

Age and Primary Diagnosis, DI and SSI Adult Beneficiaries

There is great diversity among DI and SSI beneficiaries in terms of their ages and the types of impairments that limit their ability to work. Disabled worker beneficiaries tend to be older. Over half (57 percent) were ages 50-64 at the end of 1992. Nearly 1 in 4 were age 60-64 (table 3-5).

Table 3-2. Need for Assistance and Work Limitations of Perssons Age 18-64, 1990
Number and Percent of the Noninstitutionalized Population by Need for Assistance and Degree of Work Limitation

Type of disability	Number	Percent
Total persons age 18-64	151,667	100.0
Type of activity limitation		
No limitation in any activity	132,264	87.2
Some activity limitation — total	19,403	12.8
Limited in non-work activity only	5,271	3.5
Limited in ability to work	14,132	9.3
Limited only in kind or amount of work	7,421	4.9
Unable to work	6,711	4.4
Need for assistance		
Does not need assistance	148,580	98.0
Needs assistance —	3,087	2.0
With IADLs only	2,190	1.4
With ADLs	897	0.6
Work limitation and need for assistance		
No work limitation, but needs assistance	275	0.2
Limited in kind or amount of work only and:		
Does not need assistance	6,778	4.5
Needs assistance	643	0.4
Unable to work and:		
Does not need assistance	4,542	3.0
Needs assistance		
With IADLs only	1,440	0.9
With ADLs	729	0.5

Abbreviations: IADL = instrumental activity of daily living, ADL = activity of daily living.
Source: M.P. LaPlante, unpublished tabulations from the 1990 National Health Interview Survey.

For many disabled workers, their disabling conditions are associated with aging, and include diseases of the musculoskeletal system, such as arthritis or back problems (20 percent), the circulatory or respiratory system (19 percent), or the nervous system or sense organs (10 percent). However, growing proportion of disabled workers, particularly younger workers, have mental illness as their primary diagnosis (24 percent). Detailed information about the primary diagnosis and age of disabled worker beneficiaries is in table 3-6. Similar information about those who receive only disabled worker benefits and about those whose disabled worker benefits are supplemented by SSI are in tables 3-7 and 3-8, respectively.

Disabled workers whose benefits are supplemented by SSI account for only 1 in 6 disabled worker beneficiaries and they differ from other disabled worker beneficiaries in several other respects. First, their benefits and other countable income are low enough to meet SSI eligibility criteria in the states in

Table 3-3. Persons Receiving OASDI Benefits Based on Disability by Type of Benefit and SSI Receipt, December 1993

Type of OASDI benefit	Total number (thousands)	Receiving SSI Number (thousands)	Percent
Disabled workers, 18-64	3,726.0	626.3	16.8
Disabled widow(er)s, 50-64	147.0	33.0	22.5
Disabled adult children, total	655.5	277.2	42.3
Age 18-64	603.6	258.6	42.8
Age 65 and older	51.8	18.6	35.9
Parent retired or disabled	230.7	129.8	56.3
Parent deceased	424.8	147.5	34.7

Abbreviations: OASDI = Old-Age, Survivors, and Disability Insurance, SSI = Supplemental Security Income.
Source: Social Security Administration, *Annual Statistical Supplement to the Social Security Bulletin* (Washington, DC: U.S. Government Printing Office, 1994), table 3.C6.

Table 3-4. Persons Receiving SSI Based on Disability or Blindness, by Age, December 1993
(Number in thousands)

Beneficiaries	Total	Under age 18	18-64	65 and older
Total	4,509.5	722.7	3,148.4	638.4
Adults	3,739.0	—	3,100.6	638.4
Blind	76.2	—	54.7	21.6
Disabled	3,662.7	—	3,045.9	616.8
Children	770.5	722.7	47.8	—
Blind	9.2	8.1	1.1	—
Disabled	761.3	714.6	46.7	—

Abbreviation: SSI = Supplemental Security Income.
Source: Social Security Administration, Office of Research and Statistics.

which the live. Second, they tend to be younger: 6 in 10 were under age 50, compared to 4 in 10 who received DI only. Third, they are more likely to have mental impairments as their primary diagnosis. Nearly half of the disabled worker beneficiaries who receive SSI supplements had mental impairments. For 14 percent, the primary diagnosis was mental retardation, and for 35 percent, it was mental illness. In contrast, among those receiving only disabled worker benefits, 4 percent had mental retardation, and 22 percent had mental illness as their primary diagnosis.

In contrast with disabled workers, blind and disabled SSI recipients under age 65 tend to be much younger. Many SSI recipients have developmental disabilities and enter the SSI rolls as children (if they live in low-income families) or as young adults, when their countable income and resources are considered independent of the financial status of their parents. Others, however, enter the SSI rolls at older ages and, like disabled worker beneficiaries, have impairments associated with aging, such as musculoskeletal, circulatory or respiratory system

Table 3-5. Disability Beneficiaries by Age, December 1992
DI Disabled-Worker Beneficiaries and SSI Blind and Disabled Recipients Under Age 65

Age	Total	DI - disabled workers Receiving DI only	DI - disabled workers Receiving DI and SSI	SSI, under age 65
Total number (thousands)	3,454.7	2,888.4	566.3	3,415.2
Total percent	100	100	100	100
Under 18	—	—	—	16
18-29	5	3	13	18
30-39	15	13	27	19
40-49	23	23	22	17
50-59	32	34	23	19
60-64	25	27	15	11
Under 18	—	—	—	16
18-49	43	40	61	54
50-64	57	60	39	30

Abbreviations: DI = Social Security disability insurance, SSI = Supplemental Security Income.
Source: Social Security Administration, Office of Research and Statistics.

Table 3-6. Total DI Disabled-Worker Beneficiaries by Age and Diagnostic Group, December 1992

Diagnostic group	Total	Under 18	18-29	30-39	40-49	50-59	60-64
	OASDI disabled-worker beneficiaries						
Total number (thousands)	3,454.7	—	158.5	536.0	798.1	1,103.9	858.2
Number with diagnosis	3,346.2	—	157.6	523.1	766.6	1,063.8	835.1
Total percent	100.0	—	100.0	100.0	100.0	100.0	100.0
Infectious and parasitic diseases	2.0	—	3.4	5.0	2.6	1.1	0.6
Neoplasms	3.3	—	2.9	2.0	2.8	3.9	3.8
Endocrine, nutritional and metabolic diseases	3.7	—	2.2	2.6	3.8	4.5	3.7
Diseases of the blood and blood forming organs	0.3	—	0.9	0.5	0.3	0.2	0.1
Mental disorders (other than mental retardation)	24.5	—	36.1	38.9	32.4	18.9	13.1
Mental retardation	5.3	—	16.1	10.8	6.3	3.1	1.8
Diseases of—							
Nervous system and sense organs	10.4	—	11.3	11.4	12.4	9.5	8.7
Circulatory system	14.9	—	2.2	3.2	7.6	18.8	26.5
Respiratory system	4.1	—	0.8	0.8	1.7	5.3	7.3
Digestive system	1.5	—	1.1	1.1	1.6	1.5	1.5
Genitourinary system	1.5	—	3.9	1.8	2.0	1.3	0.9
Skin and subcutaneous tissue	0.3	—	0.3	0.3	0.3	0.2	0.3
Musculoskeletal system	20.0	—	5.6	10.9	16.8	24.8	25.4
Cogenital anomalies	0.6	—	0.6	0.5	0.6	0.5	0.6
Injuries	6.5	—	11.8	8.9	7.5	5.4	4.6
Other	1.1	—	0.8	1.2	1.1	1.0	1.1

Abbreviations: DI = Social Security disability insurance, OASDI = Old-Age, Survivors, and Disability Insurance.
Source: Social Security Administration, Office of Research and Statistics, one percent sample, December 1992.

Table 3-7. Total DI Disabled-Worker Beneficiaries Not Receiving SSI, by Age and Diagnostic Group, December 1992

Diagnostic group	Total	Under 18	18-29	30-39	40-49	50-59	60-64
	\multicolumn{7}{c}{OASDI disabled-worker beneficiaries}						
Total number (thousands)	2,888.4	—	86.1	385.2	673.4	972.0	771.7
Number with diagnosis	2,798.0	—	85.7	376.0	647.9	937.0	751.4
Total percent	100.0	—	100.0	100.0	100.0	100.0	100.0
Infectious and parasitic diseases	2.0	—	4.1	5.4	2.5	1.1	0.6
Neoplasms	3.6	—	3.7	2.4	3.0	4.1	3.9
Endocrine, nutritional and metabolic diseases	3.6	—	2.0	2.5	3.7	4.3	3.5
Diseases of the blood and blood forming organs	0.2	—	1.0	0.4	0.3	0.1	0.1
Mental disorders (other than mental retardation)	22.4	—	32.4	36.6	31.2	17.8	12.3
Mental retardation	3.7	—	11.6	8.4	4.9	2.1	1.3
Diseases of—							
Nervous system and sense organs	10.8	—	12.8	12.3	13.1	9.8	9.0
Circulatory system	16.2	—	2.5	3.4	7.8	19.5	27.3
Respiratory system	4.2	—	0.6	0.8	1.6	5.2	7.4
Digestive system	1.5	—	1.2	1.3	1.8	1.5	1.5
Genitourinary system	1.6	—	4.4	2.0	2.1	1.4	0.9
Skin and subcutaneous tissue	0.3	—	0.2	0.3	0.3	0.2	0.3
Musculoskeletal system	21.5	—	7.2	12.2	17.9	25.7	25.8
Cogenital anomalies	0.6	—	1.1	0.6	0.7	0.5	0.5
Injuries	6.7	—	14.2	10.1	7.9	5.5	4.7
Other	1.1	—	0.9	1.3	1.2	1.0	1.1

Abbreviations: DI = Social Security disability insurance, OASDI = Old-Age, Survivors, and Disability Insurance, SSI = Supplemental Security Income.
Source: Social Security Administration, Office of Research and Statistics, one percent sample, December 1992.

disorders. Among SSI recipients at the end of 1992, for about 1 in 4, the primary diagnosis was mental retardation. For another 1 in 4, the primary diagnosis was mental illness. Impairments of the nervous system or sense organs (such as vision or hearing impairments) accounted for another 1 in 10 (table 3-9).

Figure 3-1 illustrates the relative number of persons receiving OASDI or SSI based on blindness or disability by age and primary diagnosis. For both groups of beneficiaries, mental illness is the most common diagnosis for those in their 30s and 40s. Very few people under 30 receive disabled worker benefits. For SSI recipients under age 30, mental retardation is the most common primary diagnosis. Among persons over age 50, musculoskeletal, circulatory and respiratory disorders together are the most common causes of disability for both OASDI and SSI recipients. The first panel of figure 3-1 includes all 6.2 million beneficiaries with disabilities including those receiving OASDI benefits as disabled widow(er)s or adults disabled since childhood. The other four panels include DI disabled workers and/or SSI recipients.

Children Receiving SSI

The number of children receiving SSI has grown rapidly, following implementation of the U.S. Supreme Court's 1990 decision in *Sullivan v. Zebley*. At issue was whether SSA policy satisfied the requirement in the Social Security law that a child under 18 be found disabled for the purpose of SSI eligibility "if he suffers from any medically determin-

Table 3-8. DI Disabled-Worker Beneficiaries Receiving SSI, by Age and Diagnostic Group, December 1992

Diagnostic group	Total	Under 18	18-29	30-39	40-49	50-59	60-64
	\multicolumn{7}{c}{OASDI disabled-worker beneficiaries}						
Total number (thousands)	566.3	—	72.4	150.8	124.7	131.9	86.5
Number with diagnosis	548.2	—	71.9	147.1	118.7	126.8	83.7
Total percent	100.0	—	100.0	100.0	100.0	100.0	100.0
Infectious and parasitic diseases	2.4	—	2.6	4.0	2.9	0.8	1.0
Neoplasms	1.9	—	1.8	1.0	1.5	2.6	3.0
Endocrine, nutritional and metabolic diseases	4.3	—	2.4	2.9	4.2	6.1	5.6
Diseases of the blood and blood forming organs	0.5	—	0.7	0.9	0.3	0.2	0.0
Mental disorders (other than mental retardation)	35.1	—	40.5	44.8	39.2	27.0	20.2
Mental retardation	13.8	—	21.4	17.0	14.2	10.3	6.0
Diseases of--							
Nervous system and sense organs	8.4	—	9.4	9.2	9.1	7.4	6.3
Circulatory system	8.4	—	1.9	2.4	6.6	13.6	19.0
Respiratory system	3.3	—	1.0	0.7	2.2	6.2	7.0
Digestive system	1.2	—	1.0	0.7	1.1	1.4	2.3
Genitourinary system	1.4	—	3.3	1.3	1.6	0.6	0.8
Skin and subcutaneous tissue	0.3	—	0.4	0.2	0.1	0.3	0.4
Musculoskeletal system	12.6	—	3.8	7.8	11.0	18.1	22.2
Cogenital anomalies	0.5	—	0.1	0.3	0.4	0.6	1.0
Injuries	5.4	—	8.9	5.7	5.1	4.2	3.8
Other	0.8	—	0.7	1.0	0.4	0.6	1.4

Abbreviations: DI = Social Security disability insurance, OASDI = Old-Age, Survivors, and Disability Insurance, SSI = Supplemental Security Income.
Source: Social Security Administration, Office of Research and Statistics, one percent sample, December 1992.

able physical or mental impairment of comparable severity" to that which would make an adult disabled for SSI or DI benefit eligibility. The Court found that the criteria in use did not meet the statutory requirement of "comparable severity" because there was no individualized functional assessment for children comparable to the assessment of residual functional capacity for adults.

Regulations implementing the *Zebley* decision were issued in February 1991. In addition, independent of the *Zebley* ruling, revised childhood mental impairment medical listings were issued in regulations in December 1990. The revised childhood mental listings, like those for adults issued earlier, included functional as well as medical criteria and, for the first time, included specific listings for attention deficit hyperactivity disorder for children,

developmental and emotional disorders for children under 1 year of age, and certain other mental disorders for children. After both sets of new regulations were in place, the number of SSI childhood disability claims and allowances rose significantly. At the end of 1989, fewer than 300,000 blind or disabled children received SSI. At the end of 1993, 770,000 children received these benefits. Among children on the rolls at the end of 1992, mental retardation was the primary diagnosis for about 40 percent. Other mental disorders — including autism, Downs syndrome, organic mental disorders, schizophrenia, mood disorder, attention deficit disorder, personality disorders, and developmental and emotional disorders for infants and other mental illness — together accounted for 16 percent. Another 16 percent of children on the SSI rolls had impairments of the nervous system or sensory

Table 3-9. SSI Blind and Disabled Recipients Unver Age 65 (not transferred from prior state program) by Age and Diagnostic Group, December 1992

Diagnostic group	Total	Under 18	18-29	30-39	40-49	50-59	60-64
	SSI blind and disabled recipients						
Total number (thousands)	3,415.2	542.1	615.6	653.9	583.8	637.1	382.7
Number with diagnosis	2,580.7	491.0	503.6	492.5	388.9	438.3	266.4
Total percent	100.0	100.0	100.0	100.0	100.0	100.0	100.0
Infectious and parasitic diseases	2.0	0.4	1.5	4.1	3.4	1.2	1.1
Neoplasms	1.7	2.1	0.8	0.8	1.7	2.5	2.8
Endocrine, nutritional and metabolic diseases	4.1	1.2	1.3	2.5	6.5	8.2	7.6
Diseases of the blood and blood forming organs	0.7	1.8	0.9	0.7	0.2	0.2	0.2
Mental disorders (other than mental retardation)	28.2	16.4	23.0	39.5	42.5	28.8	17.4
Mental retardation	27.2	40.0	47.4	29.2	16.1	9.6	6.6
Diseases of--							
Nervous system and sense organs	10.4	16.1	13.8	9.3	7.1	6.9	6.4
Circulatory system	6.0	0.9	0.9	1.9	5.8	13.8	20.2
Respiratory system	2.8	2.3	0.6	0.8	2.2	5.4	7.5
Digestive system	0.8	0.4	0.2	0.4	1.4	1.6	1.7
Genitourinary system	1.1	0.5	1.2	1.3	1.4	1.0	0.9
Skin and subcutaneous tissue	0.2	0.1	0.1	0.2	0.2	0.3	0.2
Musculoskeletal system	7.1	1.5	1.8	3.9	5.9	15.2	21.7
Cogenital anomalies	2.0	6.6	2.0	0.9	0.6	0.3	0.5
Injuries	2.9	0.7	3.7	3.4	3.7	3.4	2.9
Other	2.8	9.0	1.0	1.1	1.3	1.6	2.3

Abbreviation: SSI = Supplemental Security Income.
Source: Social Security Administration, Office of Research and Statistics, one percent sample, December 1992.

system, such as vision or hearing impairments, as their primary diagnosis.

Representative Payees

Under the Social Security Act and regulations, representative payees may be assigned to Social Security or SSI beneficiaries to receive and manage payments for the use and benefit of these beneficiaries, when the Secretary determines that the interests of the individual would be served by having a representative payee.[4] For beneficiaries under 18, parents or legal guardians usually serve as representative payees. For beneficiaries age 18 or older, payment is generally made directly to the beneficiary, unless he or she is: judged legally incompetent; is mentally incapable of managing the benefit payment; is physically incapable of managing or directing the management of the benefits; or is receiving SSI based on disability and is identified as having drug addiction or alcoholism as the primary diagnosis. The large majority of adults receiving disability are capable of managing their own benefits.

The extent to which disabled Social Security or SSI beneficiaries are assigned representative payees is another indication of the diversity among the beneficiary population. Among adults receiving Social Security based on disability, nearly one million had representative payees at the end of 1992 (table 3-10). They include about 500,000 persons

---

4. In addition, the law requires that SSI recipients who have drug addiction or alcoholism as their primary diagnosis have representative payees. They are also required to accept available treatment for their addictions.

Figure 3-1. Number of Persons Receiving OASDI or SSI Benefits, December 1992 Based on Disability, by Age and Primary Diagnosis

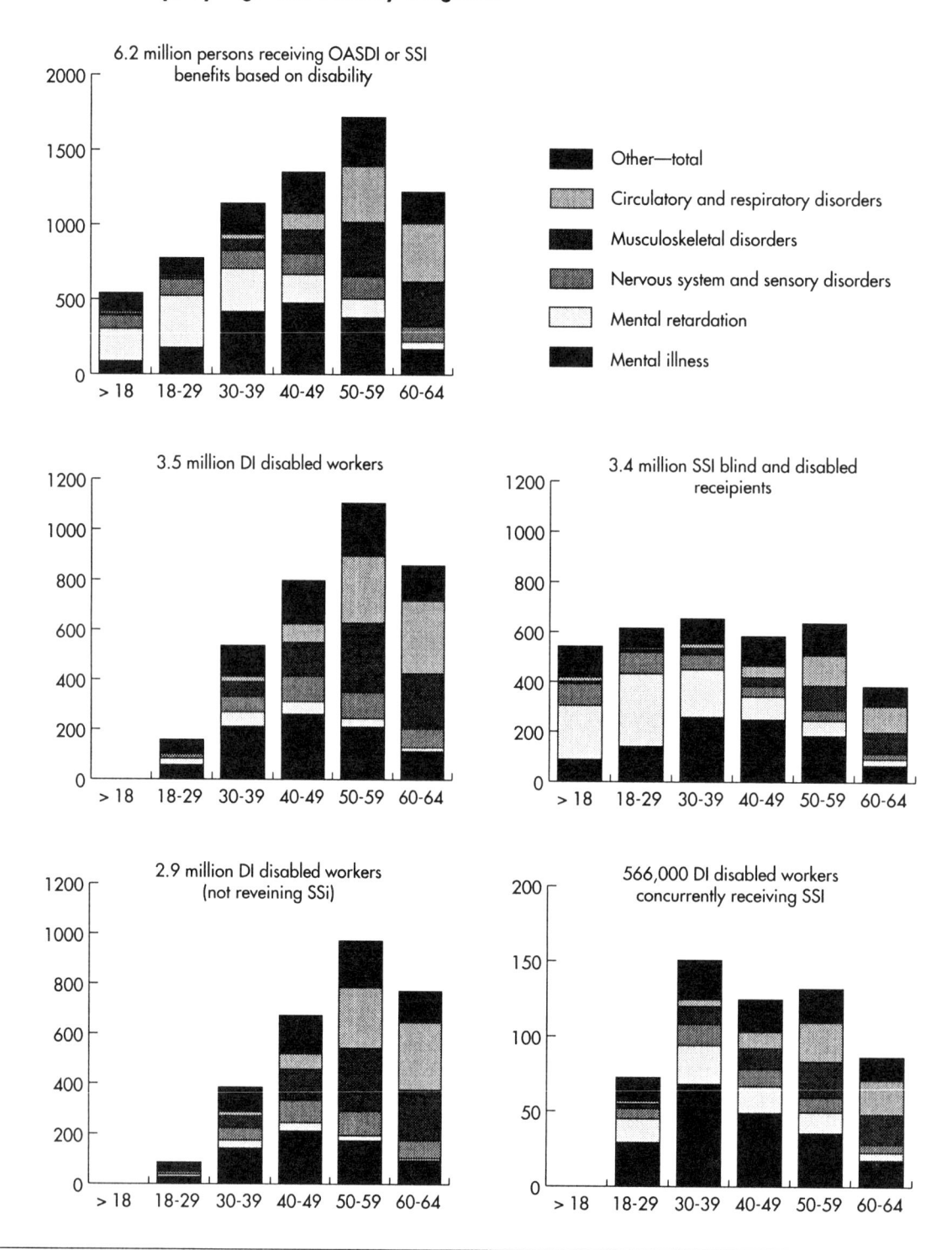

Abbreviations: DI = Social Security disability insurance, OASDI = Old-Age, Survivors, and Disability Insurance, SSI = Supplemental Security Income.
Source: Social Security Administration, Office of Research and Statistics, one percent sample, December 1992.

54 The Environment of Disability Income Policy

who account for 1 in 8 disabled worker beneficiaries and about 500,000 persons who account for 8 in 10 adults disabled since childhood. Among SSI recipients, those with representative payees account for about 3 in 10 adults receiving benefits on the basis or blindness or disability, including some who are elderly.

OUTCOMES FOR PERSONS DENIED BENEFITS

This section provides an overview of the results of five major studies and surveys of denied and allowed DI applicants that were done between 1964 and 1987. The primary focus is on the subsequent employment, economic, and health status of individuals who applied for and were denied DI benefits because they were found not to be disabled under the Social Security definition. In general, the studies interviewed denied applicants three to five years after their DI claims had been denied.

Data on employment from these studies and surveys are often reported in several different ways. In an effort to maintain as much consistency as possible among the employment data from the various studies, estimates of the percentage of applicants who are working (or not working) at a particular time were developed using a denominator that *excludes* applicants who died or retired prior to that time.

The data on denied applicants from five studies in the 1960s, 1970s, and 1980s show certain similarities.

- Between 1964 and 1987, the various studies found the work status of denied applicants of working age to fall within a fairly narrow range: from a high of 47 percent working in 1972 to a low of 40 percent in 1977. In those years with the lowest percentages of denied applicants working, 1977 and 1987, the nationwide unemployment rates were higher, and were higher still in the years just preceding 1977 and 1987.

- Denied applicants tend to be younger than allowed applicants and, on average, those denied applicants who work are likely to be the younger and better educated members of the denied group.

- The economic status of the non-working denied applicants is, on average, poor—in both senses of the word. Their primary sources of income appear to be the earnings of other family members and government income maintenance programs.

- The self-reported health status of the non-working denied applicants appears not to be appreciably better than the health status of those receiving disability benefits.

General Accounting Office Study

The most recent study of denied applicants for DI was issued in 1989 by the U.S. General Accounting Office (GAO),[5] which studied the status of DI applicants and beneficiaries who had applied for disability benefits in 1984 and who, at the time of a national survey conducted in 1987, were between ages 18 and 64.

The GAO surveyed 1,081 persons who were initially allowed DI benefits in 1984 and were receiving benefits in June 1987, and 1,109 persons who were initially denied benefits in 1984 and were not receiving benefits in June 1987. (Both samples excluded individuals who had applied for benefits in 1984 but had died or retired by 1987.) The potential sampling errors for estimates from the survey ranged from plus or minus 3 to 5 percent at a 95 percent level of confidence.

Demographic Characteristics. The demographic characteristics of the study populations in 1987 can be summarized as follows.

- Denied applicants were generally younger than allowed applicants. The median age of the

---

5. U.S. General Accounting Office, *Denied Applicants' Health and Financial Status Compared with Beneficiaries*, HRD-90-2, November 1989.

Table 3-10. OASDI and SSI Beneficiaries with Representative Payees, December 1992

OASDI	Total number of beneficiaries (thousands)	With representative payees Number (thousands)	Percent
OASDI beneficiaries			
Total number	41,497	4,179	10.1
Benefits based on disability			
Total	4,245	998	23.5
Disabled workers	3,473	468	13.5
Disabled widow(er)s	132	14	10.5
Disabled adult children	640	516	80.7
Not based on disability			
Adults	34,583	517	1.5
Children under 18	2,669	2,663	99.8
SSI			
Total	5,566	1,696	30.5
Benefits based on blindness or disability			
Adults[a]	3,471	1,048	30.2
Children	624	594	95.3
Not based on blindness or disability			
Aged adults	1,471	54	3.6

a. Includes some adults age 65 or older.
Abbreviations: OASDI = Old-Age, Survivors, and Disability Insurance, SSI = Supplemental Security Income.
Source: Social Security Administration, *Annual Supplement to the Social Security Bulletin* (Washington, DC: U.S. Government Printing Office, 1993), tables 5.L1 and 7.E4.

allowed population was 54, while that of the denied population was 45.

- Both allowed and denied populations were roughly two-thirds men and one-third women.

- More denied applicants (33 percent) than allowed applicants (25 percent) were non-white.

- About half of both the allowed and the denied applicants were married.

- Although a slightly larger proportion of the allowed applicants had not completed high school (44 percent, versus 38 percent of the denied), GAO concluded that the overall difference in educational levels between the allowed and denied populations was insignificant when age was held constant. Only 17 percent of each population had any post-secondary education.

Employment Status. Of those individuals receiving DI benefits in 1987, 91 percent were not working and not looking for work, 1 percent were looking for work, and 8 percent were working. Nearly all of those who were working had annual earnings below the substantial gainful activity (SGA) level (at that time $300).

Among denied applicants, 58 percent were not working in 1987. They include 51 percent who were neither working nor looking for work and 7 percent who were unemployed (actively looking for work). Over two-thirds of those not working said they had been out of work since 1984 or before, and over three-quarters said they were unable to work because of poor health.

Those who were working accounted for 42 percent of the denied applicants. The younger and the better educated denied applicants were more likely than others to be working.

- **Age.** Those working account for 50 percent of the denied applicants age 18 to 44, compared with 39 percent of those 45 to 54 and 29 percent of those 55 to 64 years of age.

- **Education.** Of the denied applicants with at least some college education, 58 percent were working, compared to 44 percent for high school graduates and 33 percent of those who had not completed high school.

Of the denied applicants who were working, 71 percent said they were limited in the kind or amount of work they could do, and about a third who reported being limited said they could work only part-time. Two-fifths of those working said they were not doing the type of job they had done most of their lives because of health reasons. After adjusting for inflation, 62 percent of those denied applicants who were working in 1986 (the full year prior to the survey) earned a lower annual amount than they did in 1980.

Economic Status. In 1986, the median family income for denied applicants was about the same as that of the allowed: $8,400 for the denied and $8,700 for the allowed. However, median family income of the working denied applicants was $11,800, while that of the non-working denied applicants was only $6,500. (Median income for all U.S. households in 1986 was around $24,900). A significant portion of both the allowed and the denied populations had family incomes below the poverty level. About 61 percent of the non-working denied applicants reported income below the poverty level in 1986, as did 43 percent of the allowed applicants and 36 percent of the working denied applicants.

The sources of income of denied disability applicants has long been a subject of particular interest. There are some inconsistencies in the income data developed by GAO because the GAO study used 1986 as the base year for determining income, but used 1987 for determining whether or not an individual was working and/or receiving DI benefits. Hence, a person may have reported earnings or receipt of Social Security benefits in 1986 but neither in 1987. The GAO found that in 1986, the denied proportion of and allowed DI applicants in the study who reported receiving 50 percent or more of their 1986 family income from various sources are shown in table 3-12.

Health and Medical Insurance. The GAO survey collected self-reported assessments of the health of the allowed and denied applicants. About 29 percent of the allowed and 4 percent of the denied had died by the time of the survey, so the comparison of health status is representative only of survivors and therefore may not be representative of the comparative status of allowed and denied applicants at the time they applied for DI benefits in 1984.

A fairly consistent pattern of self-identified health status emerges when the applicants are divided into three groups: those allowed, those denied and not working, and those denied and working. In terms of perceived overall health status, ability to perform activities of daily living, dependency on others for personal care, and severity of functional limitations, the allowed applicants and the non-working denied applicants looked very much alike. The working denied applicants reported a much more favorable status in all of these categories. For example, 76 percent of the allowed and 71 percent of the non-working denied applicants reported "severe" functional limitations, while only 41 percent of the working denied applicants reported "severe" limitations.

Although self-assessments of health and functional limitation appeared similar for the non-working denied and the allowed populations, impairments reported as most limiting were different for the two populations. The allowed population most fre-

Table 3-11. Percent of Denied Applicants for DI Benefits who were Working Several Years Later:
Summary of Five Studies by Year of Study

	1964-66	1971	1972	1977	1987
Percent working	46	45	47	40	42
Civilian unemplyment rate	5.5	5.9	5.6	7.1	6.2

Abbreviation: DI = Social Security disability insurance.

quently reported mental and heart problems, while both groups of the denied (working and non-working) most frequently reported back problems as limiting them the most.

A significant proportion of denied applicants did not have health insurance coverage. Twenty-nine percent of the working denied applicants and 25 percent of the non-working denied applicants were without medical insurance coverage when surveyed by the GAO in 1987. Those who had private insurance through their own or their spouses' current or former employment account for about 58 percent of the working denied applicants and 37 percent of the non-working denied applicants. A little under 20 percent of the non-working denied applicants were covered by Medicaid; roughly 20 percent of each category of denied applicants were eligible for veterans' or military health care coverage.

Three Studies from the 1970s

Several surveys and studies of denied disability applicants were done by the Social Security Administration in the 1970s. The *1972 Survey of Disabled and Non-Disabled Adults and the 1978 Survey of Disability and Work* asked DI beneficiaries and denied applicants a variety of questions about their employment, income, and health. SSA researchers also used administrative records to study the status in 1972 of applicants who had initially been denied benefits in 1967.

The 1972 and 1978 surveys of the disabled found a somewhat older disabled population than GAO found in the next decade. According to John Bound, who analyzed the data from the 1970s,[6] more than 80 percent of DI beneficiaries were age 45 or older. Bound therefore restricted his analysis of the 1972 and 1978 survey data to denied applicants over the age of 45. Their average age in 1972 was 57.9; it declined to 55.6 in the 1978 survey.

The average educational attainment of denied applicants was 8.1 years in the 1972 survey and 9.2 years in 1978. In contrast to the GAO survey, which found only half were married, approximately three-quarters of the denied applicants in Bound's analysis were married.

Key findings from the 1972 and 1978 surveys, as reported by Bound, were:

- Less than half of the denied applicants worked at any time in 1971 and 1977: 45 percent worked in 1971 and 40 percent worked in 1977. Those who worked full time account for twenty-one percent and sixteen percent, respectively. To the extent that younger denied applicants are more likely to work than older ones, Bound's decision to limit analysis to denied applicants over age 45 may tend to understate the number.

- Roughly two-thirds of the working denied applicants experienced a decline in real annual earnings in comparison to their earnings levels prior to application for disability benefits.

---

6. J. Bound, "The Health and Earnings of Rejected Disability Insurance Applicants," *American Economic Review*, June 1989, pp. 482-503.

- In 1971, the mean family income of non-working denied applicants was $4,100. This compares with $5,100 for beneficiaries, $9,800 for working denied applicants, and $13,400 for the general population of working age. Comparable data for 1977 are $8,300 for the non-working denied, $10,700 for beneficiaries, $13,500 for the working denied, and $17,800 for the general population.

Bound also reports that the SSA study of administrative records found that, of those disability applicants who had been denied in 1967, and who were alive and below retirement age in 1972, 47 percent worked at some time in 1972.

A 1960s Study

The Social Security Administration contracted with the Johns Hopkins University to perform a study examining a group of applicants for DI who had been denied, and to contrast their experience with applicants who had been allowed benefits. The study population all lived in Baltimore, Maryland. The study was conducted between March 1964 and September 1966.[7]

The study found that 12 percent of those who were allowed benefits and 46 percent of those who were denied benefits returned to work. Disability applicants who returned to work were likely to have been younger (average age 49) at the time of the onset of their impairments than those who did not (average age 54), and to have as their disability a disease of the circulatory or musculoskeletal system. The less skilled the occupations of workers prior to disability application, the greater the proportion of workers who did not return to work.

---

7. R.T. Smith and A.M. Lilienfield, *The Social Security Disability Program: An Evaluation Study*, Research Report No. 39, Social Security Administration, Office of Research and Statistics, June 1971.

Table 3-12. Percentage of 1984 DI Applicants Receiving 50 Percent or More of 1986 Family Income from Specified Sources

Source	Denied applicants Working	Denied applicants Not working	Allowed applicants
Social Security	3[a]	8[a]	63
Earnings	80	32	17
Own	(63)[b]	(15)[b]	(2)
Spouse	(14)	(16)	(15)
Pension/insurance	1	10	5
Asset income	1	—	—
Other government:	10	35	8
Entitlement	(4)	(11)	(2)
Welfare	(6)	(23)	(6)
Other private	3	5	1

a. Although the denied applicants in the sample were not receiving Social Security benefits in 1987, these cases reported receiving benefits in 1986. It was not possible to determine whether these benefits were for the sample person, the spouse or dependent children.
b. The working and nonworking classifications are based on the employment status of the respondents at the time of the interview in 1987. The earnings data, however, are based on the amount respondents reported to have received during 1986. Thus, some respondents who were classified as not working (in 1987) reported receiving earnings in 1986, and some of those who were classified as working reported no earnings in 1986.
Abbreviation: DI = Social Security disability insurance.
Source: U.S. General Accounting Office, *Denied Applicants' Health and Financial Status Compared with Beneficiaries*, HRD-90-2, November 1989.

Table 3-13. Percent of Non-Working Denied DI Applicants Receiving Specified Sources of Income 1971 and 1977

Source	Percent receiving income 1971	Percent receiving income 1977
Spousal/family earnings	37	47
Public income maintenance (excluding Social Security)	51	44
Private pensions	16	28
Asset income	20	28

Abbreviation: DI = Social Security disability insurance.
Source: J. Bound, "The Health Earnings of Rejected Disability Insurance Applicants," *American Economic Review*, 1989.

Chapter 4 Fluctuations in Disability Benefit Awards

This chapter examines cyclical changes in the economy and trends in the receipt of Social Security disability insurance (DI) and Supplemental Security Income (SSI) disability benefits over the last two decades. In general, it shows that the number of people entering the disability benefit rolls has fluctuated greatly over the last two decades. The number of people who leave the disabled-worker benefit rolls has also varied, although to a lesser extent. The trends reflect significant changes in the Social Security Act, in administrative policy and in the economy as well as other factors that are discussed in chapters 5 and 6 of this report.

CYCLICAL CHANGES IN THE ECONOMY

It is generally recognized that cyclical changes in the unemployment rate affect the likelihood that workers will apply for disability benefits and that benefits will be awarded. In times of economic expansion and low unemployment, workers with significant disabilities have far better prospects for finding jobs and those who become disabled have better prospects for remaining on their jobs. When unemployment is low, employers are more inclined to accommodate employees' health problems, rather than to seek and train new workers to replace them. Figure 4-1 summarizes cyclical fluctuations in the economy over the past three decades.

Since the beginning of the DI program, the strict definition of disability in the law has been designed to limit access to disability benefits among unemployed workers with only marginal disabilities. At the same time, it is recognized that some workers with significant disabilities are in the work force and would qualify for DI if they lost their jobs. Unfortunately, basic data are lacking to estimate the number of such workers. Yet, such data are critical for conducting research to better understand and anticipate the dynamics of how cyclical changes in the economy affect claims for disability benefits. One small study conducted disability determinations using longitudinal medical records of persons in one community and found that about 1 in 8 men had an impairment that met or equalled Social Security's medical listings at some time before age 65. Most of those men were alive four years after the disabling condition was determined and most of those survivors were in the labor force despite the disabling condition.[1] While that study was small and localized, it suggests that much could be learned about the dynamics of the disability program if more were known about people who have conditions that meet the medical criteria for disability benefits, but are nonetheless working. Investment in nationwide research in this area would be very productive.

---

1. H.P. Brehm, and T.V. Rush, "Disability Analysis of Longitudinal Health Data: Policy Implications for Social Security Disability Insurance," *Journal of Aging Studies*, vol. 2, no. 4, 1988, pp. 379-399.

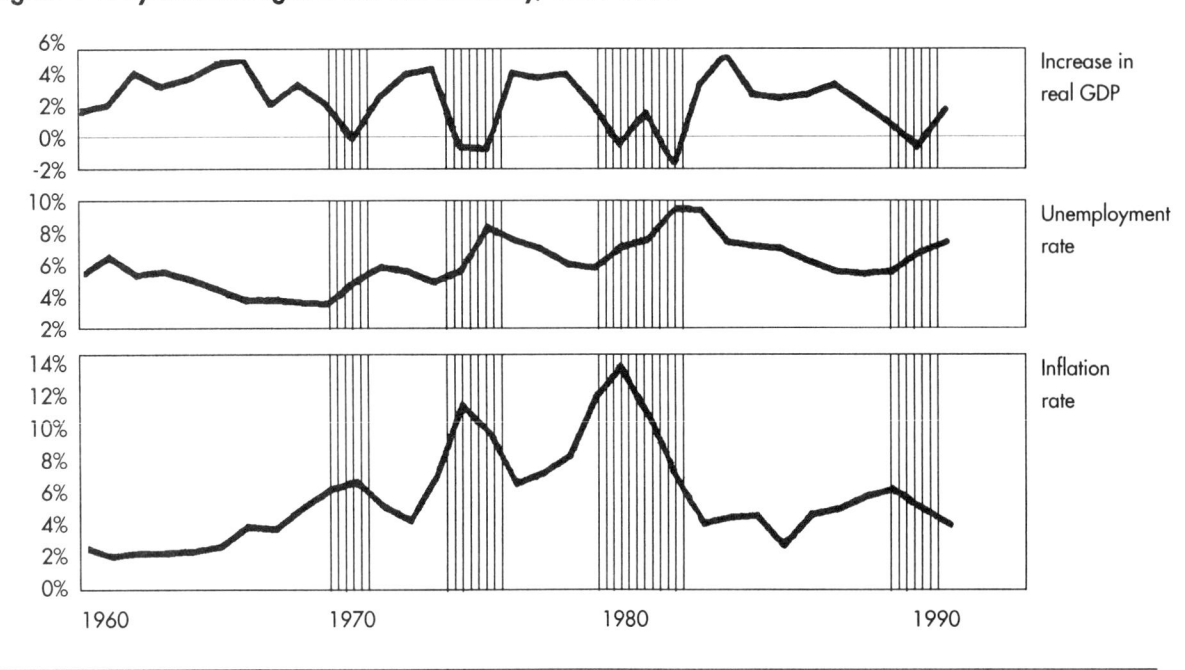

Figure 4-1. Cyclical Changes in the U.S. Economy, 1960-1993

Abbreviation: GDP = gross domestic product.
Source: Social Security Administration, Office of the Actuary.

THE BENEFICIARY ROLLS

Trends in the disability benefit rolls are shown in terms of the number of people entering the rolls (benefit awards), incidence rates based on awards, and termination rates based on the proportion of beneficiaries who leave the rolls.

Number of Benefits Awarded

The number of people awarded disability benefits has fluctuated considerably over the last two decades (figure 4-2). Those awarded DI benefits as disabled workers rose sharply in the first half of the 1970s. That growth coincided with the implementation of the Supplemental Security Income program, which brought a large influx of new claims, and with economic recessions in 1969-1970 and in 1974-1975. It also coincided with growth in the real level of benefits in the late 1960s and early 1970s. After the mid-1970s, the number of new disabled-worker benefit awards declined gradually to a low in 1982, then rebounded and leveled off later in the 1980s.

Between 1989 and 1992, the number of disabled-worker benefit awards again rose sharply. Even though the 652,000 people who entered the disabled worker benefit rolls in 1993 represents the highest number to date, the rate of growth was less than that experienced in the prior three years, from 1989 to 1992.

Data on SSI benefit awards begin in May of 1974. The first full year of SSI award data in 1975 reflects the enrollment of the initial caseload from state assistance rolls. After the initial influx, the number of people entering the SSI disability rolls followed a pattern somewhat similar to that for disabled workers although the 1982 drop in awards was sharper and the "leveling-off" in the late 1980s was brief. Since 1988, the growth in the SSI rolls has been more rapid than the DI disabled-worker rolls, and, since 1990 the number of new SSI disability awards has exceeded the number of DI awards. Children with disabilities account for part of the recent growth in the SSI disability rolls. In 1992,

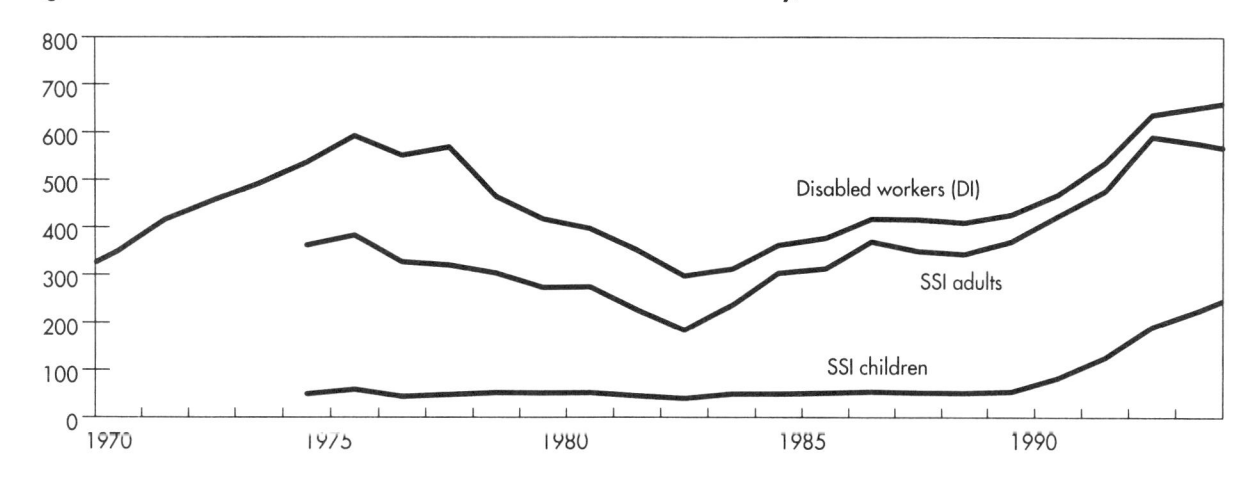

Figure 4-2. Number of Persons Awarded Benefits Based on Disability, 1970-1993

[Figure: Line graph showing three lines — Disabled workers (DI), SSI adults, and SSI children — from 1970 to 1993, with values ranging from 0 to 800.]

Abbreviations: DI = Social Security disability insurance, SSI = Supplemental Security Income.
Source: Social Security Administration, Office of Research Statistics.

after regulations implementing the 1990 U.S. Supreme Court decision in *Sullivan v. Zebley*, and after new mental impairment listings for children were in place, the number of children awarded SSI benefits grew rapidly to 191,000 children in 1992 and to 225,600 children in 1993. Before 1990, about 40,000 to 50,000 children entered the SSI rolls each year. When SSI children are excluded, the number of adults entering the SSI disability rolls in 1992 was still at an all time high (590,000), a 60 percent increase over the number of such awards three years earlier in 1989. In 1993, the number of SSI awards to blind and disabled adults was slightly smaller (576,000) than in 1992.

Disabled-Worker Benefit Incidence Rates

Part of the growth in the number of people entering the benefit rolls reflects an increase in the size of the population who could potentially receive benefits. Disability incidence rates show the proportion of the eligible population who enter the benefit rolls in a given year.

The Office of the Actuary of the Social Security Administration (SSA) calculates the disability incidence rate as the number of persons who are awarded DI disabled-worker benefits in a year per 1,000 persons who are insured for DI benefits but are not receiving them. To be insured, that is "eligible," a person must have sufficient work experience in employment that is covered by Social Security.[2]

The gross incidence rates in figure 4-3 follow a pattern similar to that of the number of awards. However, the incidence rate has not returned to the peak level reached in 1975.

Incidence rates factor out the growth in the number of awards that can be attributed to the growth in the eligible population, which in turn is due to growth in the number of people age 18-64 and an increase in the proportion of them, particularly women, who have enough covered work experience to be insured. The 1992 incidence rate of 5.36 was the highest since the late 1970s, but still below the peak rate of 7.2 in 1975. The 1993 incidence rate was no higher than that in 1992.

---

2. The eligible population is defined as those who have enough covered employment to be insured for benefits. There are no data with which to estimate the number of people who might meet the medical or vocational criteria for eligibility.

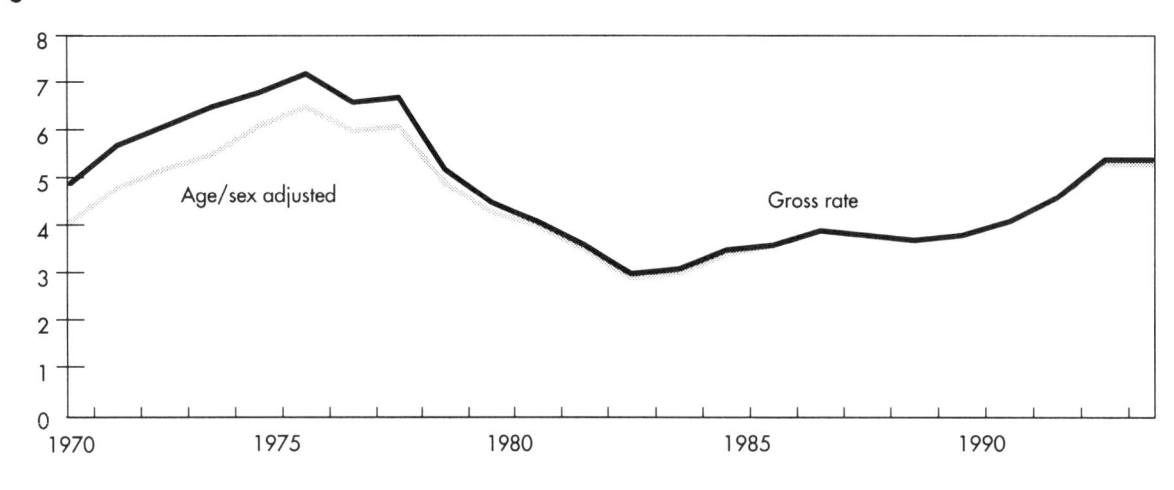

Figure 4-3. DI Disabled Worder Incidence Rate,ᵃ 1970-1993

a. The number of disability awards per 1,000 insured workers not already receiving benefits.
Abbreviation: DI = Social Security disability insurance.
Source: Social Security Administration, Office of the Actuary.

The "age-sex adjusted" incidence rate nets out changes in the composition of the eligible population as well as its size. It, in effect, shows what the incidence rates would have been in prior years if the eligible population had the same age and sex distribution as was the case in 1992. During the 1970s, particularly the early 1970s, more of the eligible population was concentrated at older ages, where disability is more common. If the eligible population in 1975 had the same age/sex composition as experienced in 1992, then the 1975 disability incidence rate would have been 6.5 per 1,000, compared to 5.3 per 1,000 in 1992 or 1993.

Disabled-Worker Benefit Terminations

People generally leave the disabled-worker benefit rolls for one of three reasons: they reach age 65, at which time their benefits are automatically converted to retired-worker benefits; they die; or they recover. SSA's Office of the Actuary defines the disabled-worker benefit termination rate as the number of people who leave the benefit rolls in any given year as a percent of the average number of beneficiaries on the rolls in that year. As illustrated in figure 4-4, the termination rate for disabled-worker benefits declined during the early 1970s from 15.9 in 1970 to 13.3 in 1975, then stabilized through the rest of the 1970s. It peaked in the early 1980s, then declined and stabilized in the rest of the 1980s. In the 1990s, the termination rate declined steadily. In 1993, the rate of 10.0 is the lowest in the history of the disability benefit program.

The largest single reason people leave the disabled-worker benefit rolls is that they reach age 65 and enter the retirement rolls. The second most common reason is that they die. The termination rate reflecting conversions to the retirement rolls has declined since the mid-1980s. This has occurred because disabled-worker beneficiaries, on average, are somewhat younger than in the past. The median age of those receiving disabled-worker benefits declined from about 56 in 1980 to 55 in 1986 and to 52 in 1992.[3]

---

3. Social Security Administration, *Annual Statistical Supplement to the Social Security Bulletin* (Washington, DC: U.S. Government Printing Office, 1981), table 66, p. 124; Social Security Administration, *Annual Statistical Supplement to the Social Security Bulletin* (Washington, DC: U.S. Government Printing Office, 1988), table 5.A1, p. 143; and Social Security Administration, *Annual Statistical Supplement to the Social Security Bulletin* (Washington, DC: U.S. Government Printing Office, 1993), table 5.A1, p. 177.

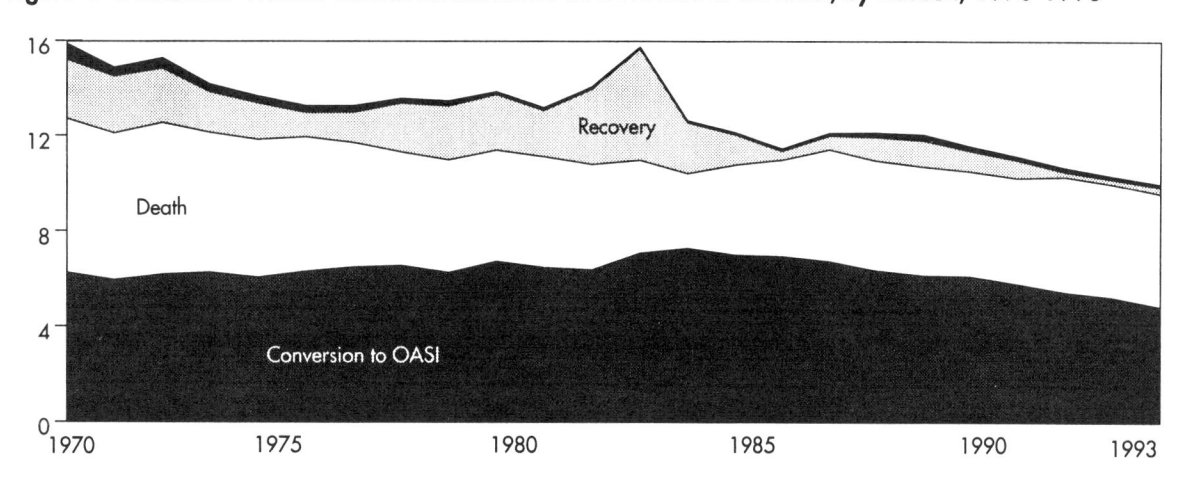

Figure 4-4. Disabled-Worker Benefit Terminations as a Percent of the Rolls, by Reason, 1970-1993

Abbreviation: OASI = Old-Age and Survivors Insurance.
Source: Social Security Administration, Office of the Actuary.

Individuals whose benefits are terminated because of "recovery" may leave the rolls under one of three types of circumstances: by their own assessment that they have "medically recovered," returned to work and report their change in status to SSA so that benefits will stop; they have not medically recovered, but return to work despite their impairments under various work incentive provisions, and ultimately leave the benefit rolls because of their continued employment; and SSA reexamines their disability under its continuing disability review (CDR) process, determines they have "medically recovered" and terminates their benefits. Those whose benefits are terminated in this way have the right to appeal that decision and have the option to continue to receive benefits until their case is decided by an administrative law judge on appeal. Data are not available to distinguish the prevalence of the three types of "recovery," although variations over the last two decades in the recovery rate are due, largely to the way in which CDRs are conducted. This is an area where more research and database development are needed in order to evaluate the disability programs. The proportion of beneficiaries who leave the disabled-worker benefit rolls because of recovery has never been large. During the 1970s, it generally ranged between 1.5 and 2.5 percent of the benefit rolls. Terminations due to recovery peaked in the early 1980s, when SSA pursued an aggressive policy of reviewing the rolls and terminating benefits.

In the 1990s, terminations for recovery are at an all time low, in 1991-93 they were below 0.5 percent. The trends in terminations for recovery during the 1980s are influenced by changes in both law and in administrative policy with regard to conducting CDRs. These changes are discussed in the following chapter.

Chapter 5 History of Disability Income Policy

Much of the fluctuation in the number of people awarded Social Security disability insurance (DI) or Supplemental Security Income (SSI) disability benefits, and in disabled-worker benefit incidence rates and in benefit termination rates shown in the prior chapter reflect legislative and administrative changes in the programs in conjunction with cyclical changes in the economy.

THE EARLY 1970S: GROWTH IN THE DISABILITY ROLLS

The early 1970s were characterized by rapid growth in the number of people awarded DI disabled-worker benefits as well as a large influx of disabled public assistance recipients before and after the development of the new federal SSI program that was enacted in 1972 and implemented in 1974. Economic recession and high unemployment in 1969-70 and in 1974-75 and legislative expansions in DI before and during this period contributed to the growth in the disability rolls. Under pressure to process new claims in an era of government-wide restrictions on personnel, staff resources were diverted from reviewing the accuracy of disability decisions by the states and conducting continuing disability reviews to processing new claims.

Disability Insurance Legislation

Modifications in the Social Security Act during the 1960s and early 1970s both increased the numbers of persons who could qualify for DI benefits and increased the real value of the benefits.

Larger Eligible Population. The potentially eligible population was expanded by such changes as: in 1965, liberalizing the definition of disability from "long-continued and indefinite duration" to "expected to last at least one year, or to result in death," and a more generous, occupational definition of disability for blind workers age 55 or older; change, in 1967, to a less strict insured status requirement for disabled workers under age 31; and in 1972, reducing the waiting period for DI benefits from 6 months to 5 and increasing from 18 to 22 the age before which a disability must have begun in order for a person to qualify as an adult disabled in childhood.

Increased Benefit Levels Legislation that increased the value of DI benefits included: ad hoc benefit increases enacted in 1967, 1969, 1971 and 1972 that exceeded growth in the consumer price index and, consequently, raised the real value of the benefits; increases in the level of workers' earnings that are counted for tax and benefit purposes, which further increased the level of benefits; and automatic cost of living adjustments which assured that benefits in force would not lose purchasing power. The combined effects of these changes brought an increase in the replacement rate (benefits as a percent of recent earnings) in the early 1970s for newly entitled disabled workers, particularly for young workers, as illustrated in figure 5-1.

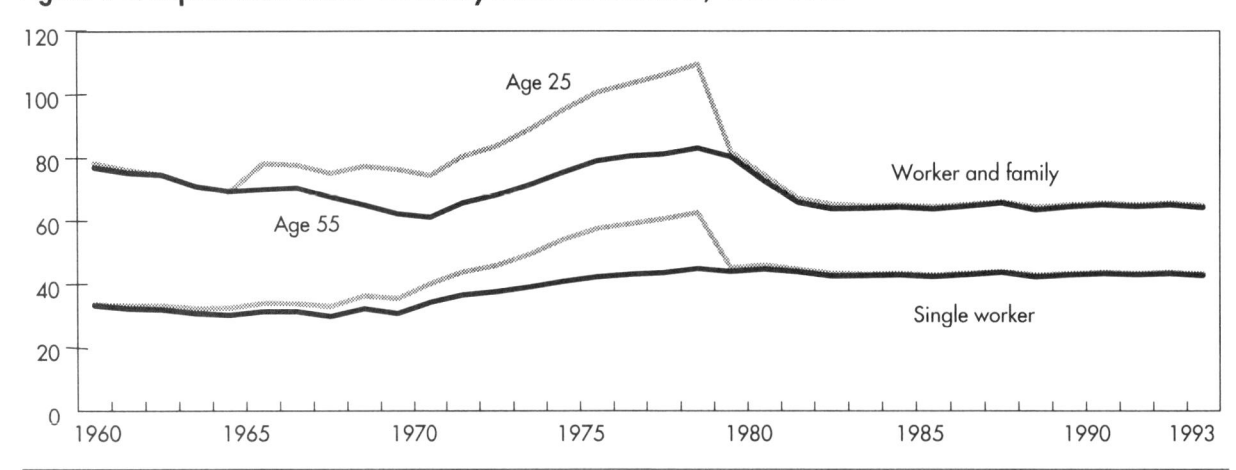

Figure 5-1. Replacement Rates[a] for Newly Disabled Workers[b], 1960-1993

a. The replacement rate is the ratio of benefits to pre-disability earnings.
b. Examples shown are for workers who had steady earnings at the average level for all workers.
Source: Social Security Administration, Office of the Actuary.

The examples illustrated in figure 5-1 reflect replacement rates for a worker whose pre-disability earnings had always been equal to the average earnings of all workers. For such a worker, who became disabled at age 55, the replacement rate rose from 31 percent for those first entitled in 1969 to 45 percent for those first entitled in 1978. For a young worker with comparable earnings, benefits were considerably higher, with replacement rates rising from 36 to 63 percent for those entitled in 1969 and 1978, respectively. (As discussed later in this chapter, 1977 legislation that took effect in 1979 caused replacement rates for young disabled workers to drop to the level experienced by older disabled workers.)

Medicare Coverage In 1972, Medicare coverage was extended for the first time to persons who had been receiving cash disability benefits for 24 months. The availability of Medicare coverage, even with a 24-month waiting period, increased the value of entitlement to disability benefits. Because Medicare coverage ended when cash benefits ended, the change may also have made it more difficult for a beneficiary to risk leaving the rolls because of return to work.

Enrolling SSI Eligibles. The federal SSI program was enacted in 1972 and implemented in 1974, to replace the prior federal/state matching programs of Aid to the Permanently and Totally Disabled (APTD) and Aid to the Blind (AB) as well as Old-Age Assistance. There were widespread publicity and outreach efforts to enroll eligible persons in the new SSI program. These activities undoubtedly brought new claims for Social Security disability benefits. SSI, as an income guarantee of last resort, requires that applicants first claim all Social Security benefits to which they are entitled before they qualify for SSI. While this was also a requirement of the prior APTD program, new applications for SSI may have brought additional DI applications.

Supplemental Security Income

When the SSI program began, there were a number of reasons to expect that SSI recipients would outnumber those who had been on the prior state APTD rolls.

Prior Growth in APTD Rolls. The APTD rolls had been growing rapidly well before enactment of SSI. Beginning in 1968 — when the APTD rolls stood at

68   The Environment of Disability Income Policy

702,000 — the number of recipients grew by over 100,000 a year and reached nearly 1.3 million persons when the SSI program took over the APTD rolls in 1974. The AB program caseload, on the other hand, had peaked at 110,000 in 1958 and declined gradually thereafter, except for a sharp drop of 10,000 in 1965. When SSI took effect, only about 78,000 persons received AB.[1] The decline in AB probably reflects the more liberal eligibility provisions for blind workers under DI after 1965.

While there is anecdotal evidence that some states tried to increase the numbers of persons receiving APTD in anticipation of the federal takeover of that caseload in 1974, the trends suggest that the APTD rolls had been growing well before the SSI legislation was enacted. That growth may have been related to an economic recession in 1969-70 as well as "deinstitutionalization" of persons in mental hospitals that began in the mid-1950s and accelerated after 1965 when Medicaid and Medicare were enacted.[2]

"Grandfather" Provision. Special provision was made to ensure that persons already receiving APTD could qualify for SSI, even if they had entered the APTD rolls under a less strict test of disability than that used in the new federal SSI program, which adopted the strict test of disability used for DI. To protect APTD recipients who would have difficulty meeting this test, the 1972 law included a "grandfather" provision that would convert persons on the state rolls as of December 1973, to the SSI rolls without having to meet the SSI test of disability. In 1973, before the SSI program took effect, the grandfather provision was amended to apply only to persons who had been on the state assistance rolls in or before July 1973, as well as in December 1973, in order to temper possible state incentives to "load up" the APTD rolls just prior to the federal takeover.

SSI Payment Levels. More people were expected to qualify for SSI than the prior state benefits because the SSI payment level, or "federal benefit rate," was higher than assistance payment levels in some states. Furthermore, states that had been paying benefits higher than the new federal rate were required, under the law, to provide supplements to the federal SSI benefit. Consequently, the new federal income guarantee meant that more people would qualify.

Income and Resource Criteria. The income and resource (or asset) criteria for SSI eligibility were somewhat more generous than those in some state APTD programs. An important feature of the new SSI program was that individual adults had their income and resources considered independent of the income and resources of relatives other than a spouse. This meant that low-income elderly individuals could qualify for SSI without regard to the financial status of their adult children, even if they lived with their children. It also meant that young adults with disabilities could qualify without regard to the income and resources of their parents. To take account of shared living arrangements, however, the law provides that if an SSI recipient is living in another person's household and is receiving support and maintenance in-kind from such person, the federal SSI benefit for the individual is reduced by one-third.

Childhood Disability. The SSI program provided benefits for disabled children, a group not covered by APTD, although children could have been covered under AB. According to the Committee on Ways and Means report on the original SSI legislation, disabled children in low-income households were included in the SSI program because they were "certainly among the most disadvantaged of all Americans" and deserved "special assistance in order to help them become self-supporting members of our society."[3]

---

1. Social Security Administration, *Annual Statistical Supplement to the Social Security Bulletin* (Washington, DC: U.S. Government Printing Office, 1975), p. 186.
2. The deinstitutionalization trend is discussed further in the section on "Changes in Treatment for Severe Mental Illness" in chapter 6 of this report.
3. U.S. House of Representatives, Committee on Ways and Means, *Social Security Amendments of 1971: Report to Accompany H.R.1*, H. Rpt. 92-231 (Washington, DC: U.S. Government Printing Office, 1971), pp. 147-148.

Administrative Developments in the Early 1970s

Just a few years prior to acquiring new responsibility for implementing the SSI program, the Social Security Administration (SSA) became responsible for implementing the Black Lung program (Part B of the Federal Coal Mine Health and Safety Act of 1969), which first took effect in 1970. Shortly thereafter, as part of a government-wide effort to reduce the number and average grade level of federal employees, SSA reduced staff for certain disability-related activities. In November 1971, the Commissioner of Social Security announced the U.S. Department of Health, Education, and Welfare's plans to comply with the new directives to reduce staffing and spending. The administrative changes included reducing SSA's review of state disability determination service (DDS) allowances of initial DI claims from close to 100 percent to a 5 percent sample. This and other measures were "designed to free up personnel and put us in the best position possible, under the circumstances, to get ready to implement new legislation and to cope with current heavy workloads such as black lung reconsiderations and hearings."[4] Also in this period, annual reviews of the continuing disability of persons on the rolls were reduced from about 10 percent to less than 4 percent.[5]

1975-1980: CONTROLLING EXPANSION

The period after 1974 was characterized by growing concern about the rapid rise in the number of people receiving DI benefits, the resulting escalation of the cost of benefits and projected insolvency of the DI trust fund. Reasons generally offered for the rapid growth included: high unemployment during the recession of 1974-1975; "excessive replacement rates" for some disabled workers, particularly higher earning young workers, that were seen as making disability benefits too attractive relative to work; lack of work incentives to encourage disabled workers to leave the benefit rolls; lack of rigor in administering the program; and increased rates of benefit allowances on appeals to administrative law judges. In this period, legislation reduced future benefits and administrative initiatives tightened administration of the program.

1977 Amendments — Reducing Benefit Replacement Rates

The 1972 amendments, which had provided for indexing Social Security benefits to keep pace with the cost of living, when combined with unanticipated high rates of inflation after 1972, resulted in unintended increases in benefits and replacement rates for newly entitled beneficiaries. The amendments of 1977 revised the method of calculating initial benefits to stabilize replacement rates for future new beneficiaries. The main reasons for the change were the clearly unintended increases in future replacement rates and the resulting projected insolvency of the Social Security trust funds. The remedy enacted in 1977 was implemented gradually for new retirees, beginning in 1979 and phased in over the next several years. For disabled workers, however, the remedy was effective immediately in 1979 and brought an abrupt reduction in replacement rates for new young disabled-worker beneficiaries that is illustrated in figure 5-1. As discussed later, the replacement rate level for disabled workers receiving family benefits was further reduced in 1980.

Modest SSI Legislation

A number of relatively minor changes in the SSI program were enacted after 1974. Many involved relationships with the states or clarifying and expanding certain income disregards, and clarifying the relationship between SSI and other means-tested benefits. Some changes reflected administrative difficulties in SSI implementation. For example,

---

4. Social Security Administration, *Commissioner's Bulletin*, November 5, 1971.
5. U.S. Department of Health and Human Services, *The Social Security Disability Insurance Program, An Analysis*, requested by the Board of Trustees for the Federal Old-Age and Survivors Insurance and Disability Insurance Trust Funds (Washington, DC: U.S. Department of Health and Human Services, December 1992), p. 5 and p. 8.

amendments provided for reimbursing states directly for interim assistance the state furnished to SSI applicants while an SSI claim was pending. Other amendments provided for continuing payments to disabled persons who did not meet the conditions for the "grandfather" provision and for whom a new disability determination would be needed.

Administrative Tightening in the Late 1970s

After 1975, SSA instituted measures to tighten administration of disability adjudication in the states agencies for both DI and SSI disability claims. SSA issued more definitive procedural instructions, policy guidance, and training for DDS adjudicators. SSA also stepped up quality assurance reviews of initial decisions, and increased the number of reviews of the continuing disability of persons on the disability benefit rolls. These initiatives followed closely a critical report by the U.S. General Accounting Office (GAO) in 1976, *The Social Security Administration Should Provide More Management and Leadership in Determining Who is Eligible for Disability Benefits*. Among the administrative changes were a new emphasis on "objective" criteria and a change in criteria for terminating disability benefits.

Emphasis on "Objective" Criteria.
One theme evident in congressional committee reports as well as in SSA efforts during the late 1970s was a desire to achieve greater uniformity in disability determinations (and possibly to tighten adjudicative standards) by increasing reliance on "objective" as opposed to "subjective" criteria in making disability determinations. In this context, "objective" evidence was that which required no discretion or judgment on the part of the adjudicator. For example, a match between medical evidence in the file (such as the applicant's score on a laboratory test) and criteria in the medical listings would show that the individual met the medical listings (step three in the sequential determination process)[6] and benefits could be allowed. "Subjective" criteria, in contrast, involved assessing the individual's residual functional capacity and its relationship to the person's ability to work, taking account of age, education and prior work experience (steps four and five in the process).[7] These assessments were more labor intensive on the part of DDS staff, and required judgment on the part of the adjudicator. Consequently, there was greater risk that different decision-makers might reach different conclusions on the same case. In the quest for greater uniformity and control over DDS determinations, medical allowances were considered "objective" and allowances based on functional assessments were suspect.

In contrast with this philosophy was the view of administrative law judges (ALJs) who constitute the recourse for appeal of claims denied by state DDSs. Typically, the ALJ hearing is the first face-to-face meeting between the decision-maker and the claimant. While the judges are expected to be "objective," in the sense of being unbiased, they are expected to exercise judgment in deciding each case on its merits. The ALJs' decisions are governed by the definition of disability in the law and the sequential decision-making process in regulations. But ALJs are not governed by SSA's subregulatory policy that is issued in instructions to the DDSs.

In 1979, after more than a decade of work, SSA published in regulations the so-called vocational grid, which was designed to introduce more objectivity in the assessment of applicants' residual functional capacity (RFC) and vocational factors (age, education and work experience) in considering their ability to work. The grid did promote greater uniformity in that it required a finding of "disabled" or "not disabled" based on specified combinations of RFC and age, education and work experience. It, however, was based largely on physical requirements

---

6. The sequential process for making disability determinations is illustrated in figure 2-1 of this report.
7. This distinction between objective and subjective evidence of disability reflects a fundamental dilemma in implementing the statutory definition of disability: "inability to engage in substantial gainful activity (SGA) because of a medically determinable ... impairment." If claimants are not working and their conditions meet the medical listings, they are *presumed* to be unable to engage in SGA. The objective evidence supports a *presumption*. In contrast, evidence that the claimant is functionally unable to engage in SGA because of a severe impairment is considered "subjective" and therefore suspect, although, arguably, closer to the literal definition in statute.

of jobs — such as strength and endurance. It was not well suited to assessing RFC and vocational criteria for claimants with mental impairments. In the quest for "objectivity," assessing disability for claimants with mental impairments remained problematic.

Terminations Without Medical Improvement.
After 1975, SSA also modified its criteria for conducting continuing disability reviews. Since 1969, SSA had followed a policy of terminating benefits only in cases where the beneficiary did not meet current disability criteria and there was indication of medical improvement. In 1976, the policy was changed to no longer require that medical improvement be shown before state agencies could terminate benefits. The change in policy was cited as one reason for a significant increase in the rate of cessation decisions on continuing reviews by state agencies, from about 16 percent in 1975 to 50 percent in 1978. According to a survey by staff on the Social Security Subcommittee of the Committee on Ways and Means, state DDS administrators attributed the increase in cessations to a new policy of *de novo* review of continuation cases, as well as elimination of the requirement to show medical improvement. State agency staff also pointed out that many of the cases in which benefits were terminated had, in fact, been allowed by ALJs after having been previously denied by state agencies.[8]

Results. Between 1975 and 1980, the number of people entering the DI and SSI disability rolls declined steadily. The disabled-worker benefit incidence rate declined from an all-time high of 7.2 in 1975 to 4.1 in 1980, a level lower than any that had been observed in the prior 15 years of the DI program.

The drop in the disabled-worker incidence rate came about in part, because of a decline in the application rate from 17 per 1,000 insured workers in 1974 to 13 per 1,000 in 1978-1980 (table 5-1). More importantly, the incidence rate declined because fewer claims were allowed by state agencies. In the early 1970s, more than half of initial claims were allowed; by 1980, state agencies allowed just 32 percent of initial claims. The decline in initial allowances was offset, somewhat, by an increase in the proportion of appealed claims that were allowed by administrative law judges at the hearing level, from 41 percent in 1974 to 56 percent in 1980.

The decline in initial allowance rates by state agencies in the late 1970s was accompanied by a shift in the basis for allowance. In the early 1970s, DDS allowances based on "equalling the listings" or "vocational factors" were quite common. Virtually all of the decline in initial allowances was in allowances based on these criteria (table 5-2). Between 1975 and 1980, when the total initial allowance rate declined from 53 percent to 32 percent, the allowance rate based on meeting the listings rose from 16 to 19 percent, while allowance rates declined from 24 to 5 percent based on equalling the listings and declined from 14 to 8 percent based on vocational factors.

The 1980 and 1981 Amendments

The 1980 disability amendments were the culmination of several years' work in Congress, in collaboration with the Carter administration, to develop legislation to enhance disability work incentives by further limiting the level of disability benefits and easing the transition from benefits to work for DI beneficiaries. In 1980, Congress also legislated new requirements for strict administration of the disability programs.

Limiting DI Benefits. The 1980 amendments set new limits on the total family benefits that could be paid to disabled workers to generally not exceed the lesser of 85 percent of the worker's prior earnings or 150 percent of the worker's benefit. This limit on family benefits for workers becoming entitled after June 1980 is reflected in figure 5-1. The amendments further limited potential benefits for young

---

8. U.S. House of Representatives, Committee on Ways and Means, Subcommittee on Social Security, *Actuarial Condition of Disability Insurance — 1978*, WMCP-96-5, (Washington, DC: U.S. Government Printing Office, February 1, 1979).

Table 5-1. Trends in Disability Application and Allowance Rates, 1970-1993

Calendar year	Incidence rate[a]	Application rate[b]	Allowance rate[c] Initial	Reconsideration[d]	Hearing[d]
1970	4.9	12.2	54	35	42
1971	5.7	12.7	51	—[e]	—[e]
1972	6.1	12.7	55	—[e]	—[e]
1973	6.5	14.0	57	—[e]	46
1974	6.8	17.0	54	31	41
1975	7.3	15.9	53	33	42
1976	6.7	14.9	47	—[e]	43
1977	6.7	14.6	43	23	47
1978	5.4	13.7	40	19	50
1979	4.6	13.1	36	17	54
1980	4.2	13.3	32	15	56
1981	3.6	11.9[f]	27	13	55
1982	3.0	10.2[f]	27	11	53
1983	3.1	10.0	31	14	53
1984	3.6	10.1	33	16	52
1985	3.7	10.2	36	14	51
1986	4.0	10.5	36	17	48
1987	3.9	10.2	35	15	54
1988	3.8	9.2	34	14	56
1989	3.8	8.7	36	15	59
1990	4.1	9.2	37	17	63
1991	4.6	10.3	39	17	66
1992	5.4	11.2	39	17	69
1993	5.3	11.8	35	14	68

a. Number of disabled-worker benefit awards per 1,000 insured workers not already receiving benefits.
b. Number of applications for disabled-worker benefits per 1,000 insured workers not already receiving benefits.
c. Ratio of disability awards to total disability decisions at initial determination, reconsideration or hearing level of appeals.
d. Fiscal year rates. Reconsideration allowance rates are combined experience for DI and SSI. Hearing allowance rates include all hearings (including SSI and Medicare) the vast majority of which involve disability issues.
e. Not available.
f. The abrupt decline in applications in 1981 and 1982 is due, in part, to improvements in SSA's computer systems implemented in October 1981. With the new system, local district office staff were able to check immediately whether an applicant met the insured status requirements for disabled-worker benefits and, if that requirement was not met, a formal application was not filed. Before then, more applications were filed and then denied for lack of insured status.
Abbreviations: DI = Social Security disability insurance, SSI = Supplemental Security Income.
Sources: U.S. Department of Health and Human Services, *The Social Security Disability Insurance Program: An Analysis*, requested by the Board of Trustees of the Federal Old-Age and Survivors Insurance and Disability Insurance Trust Funds (Washington, DC: U.S. Department of Health and Human Services, December 1992), table 2; and Social Security Administration, Office of the Actuary.

disabled workers.[9] Legislation in 1981 further limited replacement rates from DI benefits in combination with other types of disability benefits, by extending the concept of a cap on combined benefits from DI and workers' compensation to apply to benefits from DI and other public programs that pay benefits not based on Social Security covered earnings.

Work Incentives in 1980. Positive "work incentives" provisions in the 1980 legislation included:

- deducting the amount of impairment-related work expenses (IRWE) from earnings in determining whether a DI or SSI applicant or beneficiary is engaging in substantial gainful activity;

- continuing benefits for DI or SSI beneficiaries who medically recover while in an approved vocational rehabilitation program;

- extending Medicare coverage for at least 36 months beyond the month DI cash benefits ended for beneficiaries who have returned to work but have not medically recovered;

- eliminating a second Medicare waiting period for people who have left the benefit rolls because they returned to work, but later become reentitled to DI benefits within five years;[10]

- for SSI, counting sheltered workshop income as earnings rather than as unearned income; and

- an SSI work incentives demonstration program — the first "1619 provision." On a time limited (three-year) basis persons could remain eligible for SSI benefits and Medicaid, despite their demonstrated ability to engage in SGA (then monthly earnings of $300). The "1619 provision" was later extended and, in 1986, made a permanent part of the SSI program.

Legislating Administrative Review. Finally, and perhaps most important in terms of later developments, the 1980 legislation set in law requirements that SSA tighten adjudication of the disability programs. Specifically:

- Before disability benefits are paid, SSA must review state agency allowances of disability benefits. The purpose of the review was to ensure that the applicants did, in fact, meet the disability criteria before benefits were paid. If SSA found that the cases did not meet eligibility criteria, it could reverse the allowance or refer it back to the state agency for further development. The 1980 law specified that SSA was to review 35 percent of allowances in the first year, 50 percent in the second year and 65 percent of all state agency allowances in subsequent years. While the statutory requirement applied only to DI, committee report language strongly suggests that SSA should conduct similar reviews of SSI cases.

- Beginning in 1982, SSA must conduct continuing disability reviews (CDRs) every three years of persons receiving either DI or SSI whose impairment(s) had not been found to be permanent. If a beneficiary's disability was found to be permanent, review of the beneficiary's condition was to be made at such times as the Secretary of the U.S. Department of Health and Human Services considers appropriate.

- SSA's Appeals Council was required to reinstate "own-motion review" of a percentage of decisions by administrative law judges, with the aim of improving consistency among ALJ decisions.

---

9. The Social Security benefit formula calculates workers' benefits based on their average earnings in Social Security covered employment. In general, the number of years' earnings that are included in the measure of "average earnings" is the number since age 21, minus the lowest five years. The 1980 amendments provided fewer dropout years for younger workers: for those under age 27, no dropout years; for those 27-31, one dropout year; for those 32-36, two dropout years, and so on, with five dropout years for those age 47 or older.

10. The elimination of a second Medicare waiting period applied to those who become reentitled to DI disabled-worker benefits within five years and to those reentitled as disabled adult children or disabled widow(er)s within seven years.

Table 5-2. Basis for Allowance of Initial DI Claims by State Agencies, FY 1970-1993

Year	Total Initial Allowances	Meets Listings	Equal Listings	Vocational Factors
	Percent distribution of allowances			
1970	100	39	43	18
1975	100	29	44	27
1976	100	29	45	26
1977	100	34	42	24
1978	100	46	32	22
1979	100	55	23	22
1980	100	58	16	26
1981	100	64	12	24
1982	100	73	9	19
1983	100	74	8	18
1984	100	67	9	25
1985	100	63	9	28
1986	100	68	9	23
1987	100	66	10	24
1988	100	64	11	25
1989	100	62	11	27
1990	100	59	12	29
1991	100	56	12	32
1992	100	51	15	34
1993	100	51	15	34
	Percent of initial decisions			
1970	54	21	23	10
1975	53	16	24	14
1976	47	14	21	12
1977	43	15	18	10
1978	40	18	13	9
1979	36	20	8	8
1980	32	19	5	8
1981	27	17	3	6
1982	27	20	2	5
1983	31	23	3	5
1984	33	22	3	8
1985	36	23	3	10
1986	36	25	3	8
1987	35	23	4	8
1988	34	22	4	8
1989	36	22	4	10
1990	37	22	4	11
1991	39	22	5	12
1992	39	20	6	13
1993	35	18	5	12

Abbreviation: DI = Social Security disability insurance, FY = fiscal year.
Sources: D. Koitz, et al., *Status of the Disability Programs of the Social Security Administration*, Congressional Research Service Report for Congress, 92-691 EPW, September 8, 1992, p. 101, table 36; U.S. Department of Health and Human Services, *The Social Security Disability Insurance Program, An Analysis*, requested by the Board of Trustees for the Federal Old-Age and Survivors Insurance and Disability Insurance Trust Funds (Washington, DC: U.S. Department of Health and Human Services, December 1992), table 2 for initial allowance rate; and Social Security Administration.

1981-1984: RETRENCHMENT AND REACTION

In the early 1980s, administrative initiatives to reduce the disability benefit rolls were implemented abruptly in the midst of a deep economic recession with record high unemployment. In response to widespread dismay at human suffering caused by the abrupt retrenchment, the courts, the states, the administration and Congress all acted to rectify the situation.

Administrative Retrenchment in 1981-1982

With the 1980 legislative mandate in place, the new Reagan administration, which had promised to reduce the size and cost of government, sought through administrative initiatives to significantly reduce the cost of disability benefits, applying a very restrictive interpretation of eligibility criteria.

Accelerated CDRs The administration pursued a policy of aggressively reviewing the rolls, beginning in March 1981, and terminated benefits to those who did not meet a restrictive interpretation of the eligibility requirements. This administrative retrenchment was reenforced by a GAO report issued in March 1981 (but available in draft form during 1980) which urged more rigorous review of continuing disability. The report, entitled *More Diligent Follow-up Needed to Weed Out Ineligible SSA Disability Beneficiaries*, cited an internal, unpublished SSA study to conclude that as many as 20 percent of DI beneficiaries might not meet current eligibility criteria.[11]

An indication of the shift in policy from that envisioned in the 1980 amendment is the significant increase in estimated benefit savings that would result from the new policy of aggressive review of the rolls. The 1980 conference report on those amendments estimated savings from the periodic reviews over fiscal years 1982-1985 of $218 million, with a net loss in the early years as increased investment in administrative resources would outweigh benefit savings in those years.[12] In contrast, the new administration, in documents submitted to Congress, estimated $2.4 billion in savings over fiscal years 1981-1985 without the investment in administrative resources envisioned in the 1980 legislation. The stepped up reviews were begun without adequate staffing or training in new procedures.

Many of those whose benefits were terminated were beneficiaries with mental impairments. There were widespread cases of severe hardship among those whose benefits were terminated and many whose benefits were terminated later won benefits on appeals through the courts. The change in the role of the U.S. district courts in allowing or continuing disability benefits was striking. In 1975, those courts had received just over 5,000 DI appeals. In 1984, the number was 28,000. The change in reversal rates was also dramatic. While in 1975, SSA's denial of benefits had been reversed or remanded by district courts in only 19 percent of the cases filed, in 1984, courts reversed or remanded benefit denials in 62 percent of the cases.[13] Not only did the number of court cases increase dramatically, the number of individuals represented in class action cases also grew sharply.

The policy of aggressively reviewing the disability rolls and terminating benefits to those who did not meet a restrictive interpretation of disability criteria ultimately met with resistance from the states. Many states resisted sharing responsibility for the individual hardship caused by benefit terminations and many recognized that former disability beneficiaries were likely to turn to state assistance rolls for support. In state after state, governors first protested the new policy and then, citing judicial opinion in

---

11. U.S. General Accounting Office, *More Diligent Follow-up Needed to Weed Out Ineligible SSA Disability Beneficiaries*, HRD-81-48, March 3, 1981, reprinted in U.S. Senate, Committee on Finance, *State Data and Materials Related to the Social Security Disability Insurance Program*, CP 97-16 (Washington, DC: U.S. Government Printing Office, August 1982).
12. P. Dilley, "Social Security Disability: Political Philosophy and History," *Psychiatric Disability: Clinical, Legal, and Administrative Dimensions*, A.T. Meyerson and T. Fine (eds.) (Washington, DC: American Psychiatric Press, Inc., 1987), pp. 393-394.
13. J.L. Mashaw, "Disability Insurance in an Age of Retrenchment: The Politics of Implementing Rights," *Social Security: Beyond the Rhetoric of Crisis*, T. Marmor and J.L. Mashaw (eds.) (Princeton, NJ: Princeton University Press, 1988), pp. 166-167.

support of their actions, announced they would no longer conduct the reviews.[14]

In April 1984, the Secretary announced a temporary nationwide moratorium on periodic reviews. By that time, nine states were operating under a court-ordered medical improvement standard for continuing reviews, and nine states had suspended reviews pending implementation of a court-ordered medical improvement standard, or pending action by the circuit court.[15]

The Case of Mental Impairments. The emphasis on "objective," or medical, criteria in the late 1970s appears to have evolved into a restrictive criteria for adjudicating claims based on mental impairments. That policy evolved in SSA instructions to the DDSs in 1979-1980, before the Reagan administration took office and accelerated continuing disability reviews. The policy came to light in *Mental Health Association of Minnesota v. Schweiker*,[16] a class action suit brought in 1982 on behalf of all severely mentally ill individuals in SSA's Chicago region (covering six states) whose benefits had been denied or terminated under the adjudicative policy at issue. The plaintiffs charged that DDS office in the Chicago region was not applying the five-step sequential decision-making process as called for in regulations. Instead, any severely mentally-impaired claimant or beneficiary whose condition did not meet the medical listings, was *presumed* to be able to perform at least unskilled work. The effect of this presumption was to bypass the assessment of the individual's residual functional capacity and steps four and five in the sequential decision-making process. Consequently, those whose impairments did not meet the medical listings were denied benefits. The allegations were substantiated to the satisfaction of the judge who ruled in favor of the plaintiffs, declaring SSA's policy to be "arbitrary, capricious, irrational, and an abuse of discretion." The Eighth Circuit Court of Appeals[17] upheld the district court's finding.

In February 1983, a similar class action was brought in New York, against the Secretary of Health and Human Services and the Commissioner of Social Security on behalf of all persons with a severe mental impairment residing in the state who had been denied benefits or whose benefits were terminated after April 1980. In *City of New York v. Heckler*, the District Court in 1984 held that SSA had followed the "covert" policy alleged by plaintiffs and that the policy was illegal.[18]

According to a GAO study reported to Congress in April 1983, the policy at issue had its origins in a policy issuance in April, 1979. The GAO further cited SSA correspondence to the regions clarifying the policy during 1980:

> SSA's chief psychiatrist elaborated on this issue in a May 1980 memo to SSA's New York regional office, when he said that a psychiatric impairment rating below meeting the listings signifies the ability to engage in SGA at a level of unskilled work or higher... He also said that making an RFC assessment would be 'redundant.'[19]

The GAO testimony identified serious deficiencies in SSA's handling of mental impairment claims that followed from the courts' findings and extended to other procedures in DDSs. All of the deficiencies cited by GAO were in the direction of applying overly strict criteria to deny claims. They included: overly restrictive interpretation of medical criteria, without appropriate evaluation of functional criteria in the medical listings for mental impairments; inadequate consideration of the claimants' residual functional capacity and vocational factors; inadequate use of existing medical evidence and over-reliance on consultative exams (medical exams

---

14. Ibid., p. 168.
15. U.S. Senate, Committee on Finance, *Report on Social Security Disability Amendments of 1984*, S. Rpt. 98-466 (Washington, DC: U.S. Government Printing Office, May 1984), p. 8.
16. 554 Fed. Supp. 157 (D. Minn. 1982).
17. 720 F. 2d 965 (C.A. 8, 1983).
18. *City of New York v. Heckler*, 742 F 2d 729 (CA2; 1984); and on appeal: *Bowen v. City of New York*, 746 U.S. 467 (1986).
19. U.S. Senate, Special Committee on Aging, *Social Security Reviews of the Mentally Disabled*, Hearing 98-170, 1983, p. 7.

purchased by SSA) in lieu of evidence from treating sources; and inadequate use of psychiatrists or psychologists in the DDSs.

In June 1983, the Secretary issued a moratorium on denial or termination of disability claims based on mental impairments until SSA had developed new guidelines. For that purpose, SSA, in collaboration with the American Psychiatric Association, set up a work group that included psychiatrists, psychologists and other professionals from both government and the private sector who were concerned with assessment of mental impairments.[20] Their meetings began in July 1983, and culminated with publication of new mental impairment listings in August 1985.

The new mental impairment criteria emphasized what research has shown, and what most psychiatrists believe, to be of key relevance to a disability determination: the person's functional skills which do not necessarily correlate with severity of medical signs and symptoms.[21] The work group recognized that the emphasis on evaluation of functional skills meant that the disability determination would be more labor intensive, but they were convinced that the investment in adjudicative resources was needed in order to have a valid assessment of disability for people with mental impairments.[22]

Legislation in 1982 and 1984 — Undoing Retrenchment

In 1982, Congress enacted legislation authorizing the Secretary to slow down the rate of continuing disability reviews that were mandated in the 1980 law. It also provided, on a temporary basis, that persons who were appealing decisions that terminated their benefits could elect to have their benefits and Medicare coverage continued pending review by an ALJ. (This provision was extended several times and was made permanent in 1990.)

By 1984, Congress responded to continued widespread dismay with administrative retrenchment in DI and SSI policy by enacting into law a number of administrative reforms, including those recommended by GAO and under development in SSA. The amendments required:

- **New mental impairment standards.** Mental impairment standards were to be implemented in regulations that would focus on evaluating the individual's ability to perform substantial gainful work in a competitive work place environment. The provisions were consistent with a moratorium announced by the Secretary in June 1983, to defer CDRs of DI or SSI beneficiaries with mental impairments until new regulations were in place.

- **Medical improvement standard** A medical improvement standard was to be implemented in regulations which would require proof of medical improvement in a beneficiary's condition before benefits could be terminated.

- **Frequency of CDRs** The Secretary was required to issue regulations establishing standards to be used in determining the frequency of CDRs. Following a build-up of CDR-related backlogs in 1982 and 1983, the Secretary had announced in April 1984, a complete moratorium on CDRs. This provision of the amendments was intended to facilitate scheduling of CDRs where an individual was recently found eligible after a lengthy appeal, where recovery was expected in less than three years.

- **Combined effects.** The combined effects of all of a claimant's impairments must be considered in determining whether an claimant can engage in substantial gainful activity.

- **Notice of CDRs.** Advance notice must be given to beneficiaries who are selected for CDRs, including information on the nature of the

---

20. H.H. Goldman and A.A. Gattozzi, "Balance of Powers: Social Security and the Mentally Disabled, 1980-1985," *The Milbank Quarterly*, vol. 66, no. 3, 1988.
21. Ibid., p. 539.
22. H.H. Goldman, member of the work group on mental impairments.

review, the potential for benefit termination, and the individual's right to provide medical information for use in the review.

- **Use of psychiatrists/psychologists.** The Secretary must make reasonable efforts to involve psychiatrists or psychologists in DI and SSI determinations involving mental impairments.

- **Consultative exams and 12-month medical histories.** The Secretary must publish regulations covering standards for deciding when a consultative examination (CE) — an exam by a physician employed by SSA — should be obtained, standards for CE referrals, and monitoring procedures. The law also required the Secretary to seek medical evidence from the treating physician before evaluating evidence from a CE and required that a complete medical history covering at least 12 months be developed prior to a decision to terminate benefits.

1985-1989: ECONOMIC EXPANSION, AGENCY DOWNSIZING

As SSA implemented the administrative reforms called for in the 1984 amendments, the nation enjoyed a sustained period of economic growth and unemployment rates fell from rates over 9 percent in 1982-83 to 5.5 percent in 1988 and 5.3 percent in 1989. The DI application rate stabilized at levels lower than had been observed at any time during the 1970s.

After new regulations were in place in 1985, continuing disability reviews were resumed on a gradual basis. Also, when new mental impairment regulations were issued in August 1985, SSA resumed processing claims based on mental impairments. It was generally agreed that deciding claims using the functional criteria in the new mental impairment regulations would be more labor intensive than the approach that was invalidated by the courts.

---
23. These are described in chapter 6.

A major administrative initiative during this period was a decision to significantly reduce the number of SSA staff — from about 80,000 employees in FY 1985 to about 63,000 in 1989. The agency had begun a systems modernization initiative earlier in the decade that was part of the rationale for the staff reductions.

Along with the agency downsizing plan, SSA leadership sought ways to streamline operations with a vision of service based on that of a financial institution rather than a social agency. Instituting an 800 number to conduct routine business and scheduling appointments rather than handling walk-in service were examples of the new service plan. In the process, with fewer field office personnel, fewer resources were available to provide individualized attention to vulnerable populations — such as SSI recipients, who may have difficulty understanding their benefit rights, or severely disabled beneficiaries who need representative payees that SSA is supposed to assign and monitor. Congressional concerns with Social Security during this period focussed on problems in individualized service to the public. In this period, Congress called for improvements in telephone service, representative payee services and SSI outreach to enroll eligible persons. Also during this period, a number of incremental changes were made in SSI and Medicaid to enhance access to these benefits for people with serious mental illness.[23]

THE EARLY 1990S: GROWTH OF THE DISABILITY ROLLS

The early 1990s, like the early 1970s, were characterized by rapid growth in the disability rolls, in this case with particularly rapid growth in SSI claims. The growth coincided with an economic recession in 1990-1991. It also followed various legislative, administrative and judicial actions that were designed to enhance access to SSI for vulnerable populations through SSI outreach and new standards for determining childhood disability. While allowance rates on initial claims rose somewhat in the 1990s, the number of denied applicants who appealed also grew, and the administrative law judge (ALJ) allowance rate on those appeals rose to unprecedented levels. In the wake of agency downsizing during the 1980s, and increased workloads in the 1990s, SSA has not allocated agency resources to conducting CDRs in order to process the large influx of new claims and appeals.

SSI Outreach

The Bush administration entered office in 1989 with a promise of a "kinder and gentler" approach to domestic policy than its predecessor and that theme is reflected in SSA's response to congressional interest in outreach efforts to enroll eligible persons in SSI.

Beginning in 1989, Congress earmarked appropriations over five successive years for SSI outreach activities, with $3 million in FY 1989 and $6 million in each of the next four fiscal years, for a total of $27 million. With the earmarked funding, SSI outreach became an SSA priority in 1989. Outreach activities included field offices, agreements with other federal agencies, and demonstration projects involving community groups and advocacy organizations.

In **field offices**, managers were encouraged to work with community-based providers to serve the homeless, ethnic or linguistic minorities or other underserved populations. In some areas, local social service agencies, soup kitchens, shelters and churches would screen homeless people for possible SSI eligibility, refer them to the local Social Security district office and help them through the application process. In other areas, field office staff would visit shelters and other sites to explain SSI and help people apply.[24] The field office outreach activities varied greatly in capacity due to SSA staff reductions in the 1980s that have significantly affected urban offices that serve low income populations.

SSA has entered into **interagency agreements** with other federal agencies, such as the U.S. Department of Veterans' Affairs (DVA) Homeless and Chronically Mentally Ill Program. At project sites in New York City, Dallas and Los Angeles, SSA has joined with the DVA to serve chronically mentally ill veterans, many of whom are also substance abusers. SSA's role is to provide cash benefits. The DVA provides shelter, detoxification, and rehabilitation services.

As of September 1993, with funds earmarked by Congress, SSA had used $21 million to fund 82 **SSI outreach demonstrations** with various organizations across the country including national advocacy organizations such as the American Association of Retired Persons, the Judge David L. Bazelon Center for Mental Health Law in Washington, D.C. (for national outreach for children with disabilities), the National Urban League and state and local providers of services. The availability of grants has been published in the *Federal Register*. The most recent announcement, which closed in August 1993, specifies models of outreach and service integration that grantees must provide. For example, the "one-stop-shopping model" requires a grant applicant to do intensive case management for a specified population, such as: take SSI applications; assist in collecting medical evidence; provide medical exams, if needed; obtain representative payees' services, if needed; and provide linkage with other needed services — such as housing, food stamps and supported employment. The new emphasis is on funding projects that will serve vulnerable populations in a comprehensive way.

New Childhood Disability Standards

The U.S. Supreme Court decision in *Sullivan v. Zebley* in February 1990, expanded eligibility criteria for SSI among children with disabilities in low-income families. The SSI provision for disability benefits for children in 1972, indicated children would will be considered disabled for purposes of SSI if they suffered from "any medically determinable physical or mental impairment of comparable severity" to that which would make an adult dis-

---

24. U.S. House of Representatives, Committee on Ways and Means, *Overview of Entitlement Programs, (1993 Green Book)*, WMCP 103-18 (Washington, DC: U.S. Government Printing Office, 1993), p. 861.

abled.[25] Prior to the *Zebley* ruling, childhood disability had been determined using only medical listings. A special set of medical listings had been developed for children, and children were found disabled if their condition met or equalled conditions found in either the medical listings used for adults, or the special childhood disability listings. There was no equivalent to the "residual functional capacity" assessment used for adults to determine whether they could do their past work or other work. In *Zebley*, the Court found that this did not meet the statutory requirement for determining "comparable severity."

SSA convened a work group of experts to help develop functional criteria to assess disability for children whose conditions did not meet the medical listings. Under these new rules, children who did not meet or equal the medical listings would undergo an "individualized functional assessment," as called for in the Supreme Court's decision, to determine whether their impairments severely limit their ability to function independently, appropriately, and effectively in an age appropriate manner. The *Zebley* regulations were published in February 1991.

At about the same time, in December 1990, SSA published new updated mental impairment listings for children. The childhood mental listings emphasized functional criteria (like the adult listings published in 1985), and for the first time, included attention deficit hyperactivity disorders for children, developmental and emotional disorders for infants under one year of age, and certain other mental disorders for children.

The change in standards required by the courts, the updated mental impairment listings for children, and publicity and outreach activities to enroll eligible children together have brought rapid increase in the number of children receiving SSI benefits based on disability — from less than 300,000 in December 1989 to 770,000 in December 1993.

Increased Initial Claims

The increase in initial claims over the period since 1989 is striking — with total disability claims rising from about 1.5 million in fiscal year 1989 to about 3.0 million estimated for fiscal year 1994. Childhood disability claims contribute to the growth, but the vast majority of cases remain adult claims, with SSI adult claims rising more rapidly than DI claims. Between 1988 and 1992, DI disabled-worker benefit claims rose by 39 percent while adult SSI disability claims rose by 48 percent.

The increased claims undoubtedly reflect the economic recession and higher unemployment of 1990 and 1991. They may also reflect increased awareness of the SSI program among vulnerable populations.

Increased Appeals to ALJs

The recent rapid growth in appeals before ALJs is illustrated in figure 5-2.[26] The ALJ level of appeal is the one most likely to reverse prior denial of benefits.

The number of appeals rose sharply in the early 1980s, when SSA was applying very strict criteria for deciding disability claims and was aggressively reviewing the continuing disability of those on the rolls. In the later 1980s, the number of appeals declined.

In the early 1990s, however, following shortly after the rapid increase in initial claims in 1989, the number of appeals rose sharply. In fiscal year 1993, the number of appeals received at the ALJ level reached an all time high of over 500,000 cases. The number of cases processed — 374,000 — also reached an all time high, but the number of cases left pending at the end of the year soared to a record 358,000, compared to 218,000 just 12 months earlier.

---

25. Section 1614(a)(3)(A) of the Social Security Act.
26. The number of cases includes appeals of all OASDI, SSI and Medicare claims. Of these, about 90 percent are DI or SSI claims.

CDRs Are Not Being Done

In the wake of agency downsizing in the 1980s and increased claims workloads in the 1990s, agency resources are not allocated to conducting continuing disability reviews in order to process new claims. While the proportion of beneficiaries who leave the DI rolls because of recovery has never been large, it is now at an all time low — with less than 0.5 percent of DI beneficiaries leaving the rolls for this reason in 1993.

Limitations on Staffing

In the wake of agency downsizing in the 1980s, staff resources were not adequate to handle the rapid increase in claims that followed the economic recession of 1990-91. In the face of government-wide initiatives to reduce the number of federal employees, the Social Security Administration is developing plans to "reengineer" its administrative procedures, with first emphasis on ways to expedite initial disability claims decisions.

SUMMARY

Several lessons emerge from the tumult of the past 20-25 years in the DI and SSI disability programs. First, stable administration of these programs is critical to the economic security of people with severe disabilities who rely on these benefits, as well as to the fiscal integrity of the programs.

Second, cutbacks in administrative resources during the 1980s were accompanied by growing concern that vulnerable populations were not being well-served. Problems were identified in such needed individualized services as: appropriate assignment and monitoring of representative payees, clear and accurate answers to individuals' questions about their benefits, post-entitlement benefit updates to avoid underpayment or overpayment problems and outreach to those eligible for, but not receiving, benefits. Individuals with disabilities must be able to count on receiving the individualized attention and accurate information they need in order to understand their rights and responsibilities with regard to cash benefits.

Third, adequate staff and other resources to administer the programs are essential. The investment of resources in making correct initial disability decisions, and documenting those decisions fully, should shorten delays in getting correct benefits to applicants, reduce appeals and avoid the cost of paying any incorrect allowances. If the required medical improvement standard for conducting continuing disability reviews is to be implemented effectively, allowances must be sufficiently documented to support an assessment of whether there has been a change in the beneficiary's condition between the allowance and the review. To be fair to the beneficiary, there must be adequate staff to assure that the record is fully developed at the time of the review. For program integrity and public confidence in the programs, resources must be adequate both to decide and document initial claims promptly and correctly, and to conduct appropriate quality reviews and continuing disability reviews.

Fourth, changes in regulations that were called for in legislation and court decisions in the 1980s require greater emphasis than in the past on assessing claimants' functional capacity in conjunction with medical evidence. These changes in adjudicative requirements were based on expert medical judgment about disability assessment. If properly conducted, these functional assessments are likely to be more time consuming than determinations based solely on medical evidence. This shift toward more labor intensive adjudicative requirements needs to be taken into account in resource allocations.

Fifth, it is reasonable to expect some volatility in disability claims with cyclical changes in the economy. Disability claims have risen during every economic recession since the late 1960s—with the one exception of the early 1980s, when harsh retrenchment policies offset those effects. Persons with disabilities have much better prospects for finding work, despite severe impairments, when jobs are plentiful. When they lose their jobs during recessions and exhaust other sources of support, it is reasonable to expect they will apply for disability benefits. Flexibility in administrative resources is

Figure 5-2. ALJ Hearings, Number of Appeals Received, Processsed, Pending and Percent of Decisions Allowed,[a] **1976-1993**

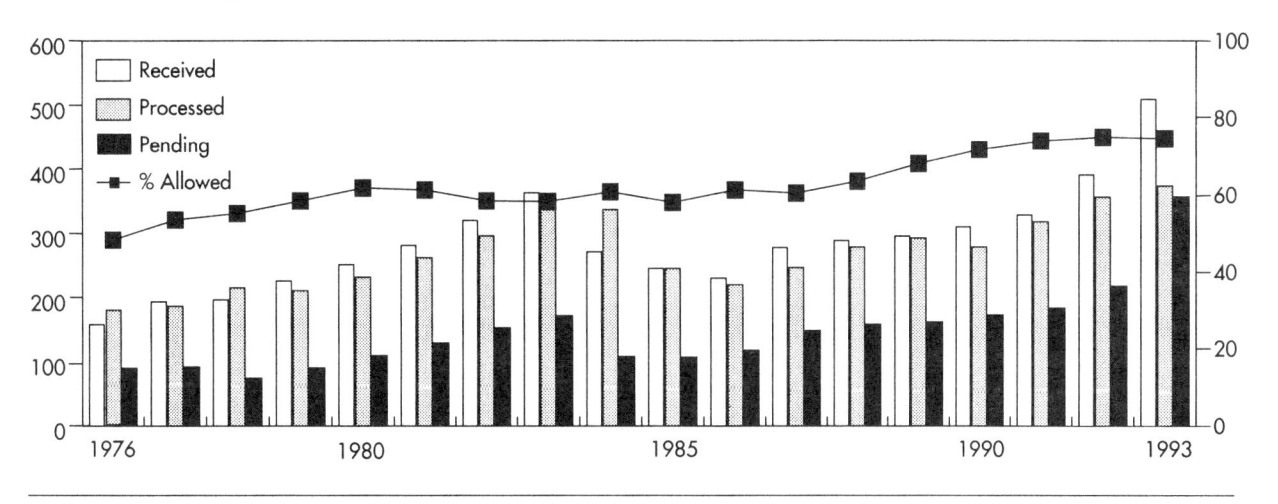

Abbreviations: ALJ = administrative law judge, DI = Social Security disability insurance, OASDI = Old-Age, Survivors, and Disability Insurance, SSI = Supplemental Security Income.
a. Percent allowed is of decisions made on the merits of the case. (Excludes cases that were dismissed without a decision to allow or deny.) Number of appeals include all OASDI, SSI and Medicare appeals. About 90 percent are DI or SSI disability cases.
Source: Social Security Administration, Office of Hearings and Appeals

needed to accommodate cyclical changes in disability claims.

Finally, research is needed to better understand the size and attributes of the underlying population of persons with disabilities who could meet the program definition of disability if they were not working. Such research is needed in order to anticipate the consequences of cyclical changes in the economy, of outreach efforts to enroll eligible persons, or other changes such as routine updates in the medical and other criteria for making disability determinations. Such research would also provide information about the circumstances that distinguish persons with disabilities who are successfully integrated into the work force from those who become unable to work because of their impairments. That information could help develop ways to expand opportunities for successful integration of beneficiaries into the world of work.

Chapter 6: The Broader Context of Disability Income Policy

The Disability Policy Panel believes that the prevalence of work disability in the population reflects the interaction between individuals — who may have physical or mental impairments — and the capacity of the economy and of the body politic to respond to their diverse abilities and needs. The prior chapter described how cyclical changes in the economy in conjunction with changes in the legislative, judicial and administrative policy environment have influenced access to the Social Security disability insurance (DI) and Supplemental Security Income (SSI) programs over the past 20-25 years.

This chapter explores some of the broader environmental changes beyond the specific programs that influence the context in which disability benefits are claimed and decisions are made to allow benefits. The purpose of this chapter is not to offer definitive explanations for cash benefit trends, nor to forecast their future. Rather it is to explore plausible connections between the demand for disability benefits and the broader environment. Those environmental factors include:

- structural changes in the economy that alter work opportunities for workers in general, and for persons with disabilities in particular;

- the relative role of other components of the social safety net (both public and private) beyond the DI and SSI programs;

- changes in the availability of health care coverage and its role in influencing choices about work and benefits;

- changes in the recognition and treatment of disabling conditions, particularly mental illness, that represent advances in the integration of people with disabilities into the community (in the past, more people with disabilities may have been institutionalized or otherwise wholly excluded from the community or the world of work); and

- growth in the number and sophistication of claimants' representatives and growing interest on the part of state and local governments, employers and insurers to ensure that SSI and DI serve as the first payor of disability benefits.

STRUCTURAL SHIFTS IN THE LABOR MARKET

Structural changes in the labor market have long-term effects on employment opportunities for particular subgroups of workers, including those with disabilities. Industrial shifts in the 1950s and 1960s brought a decline in extremely arduous jobs and that decline is projected to continue. The industrial shift from manufacturing to service industries is projected to continue into the next century, with the largest growth in occupations projected to be in those that generally require a college degree or other post-secondary school education. The continued growth in these jobs is likely to enhance opportunities for well-educated or highly skilled persons with physical disabilities. Growth is also projected in service occupations, many of which require less formal education.

Research on earnings levels of workers finds a decline in demand for workers with limited education and job skills, particularly in the 1980s. To the extent that such workers have disabilities, they are likely to be doubly disadvantaged in competing for available jobs. At the same time, workers with cognitive impairments or mental illness may have difficulty finding work.

Industrial and Occupational Shifts

One study of the physical demands of jobs found a significant decline in extremely arduous jobs in the 1950s and 1960s, but much slower decline since then. With arduous jobs defined as those requiring "heavy or very heavy strength," the study found that the proportion of U.S. workers in such jobs declined from 20.3 percent in 1950, to 9.9 percent in 1970 and to 9.1 percent in 1980, with further declines projected into the next century.[1] Requirements other than "heavy strength," however, are important in determining job opportunities for people with disabilities.

The Department of Labor studies of the industrial and occupational mix of U.S. jobs indicate that the long-term decline in the goods-producing sector and the long-term growth in service industries continued during the 1980s and is projected to continue into the next century (table 6-1). Within the service-producing sector, major growth industries are in health services, business services, other services and retail establishments, such as restaurants. At the same time, a shrinking share of U.S. jobs are in manufacturing of durable or nondurable goods.

The industrial shift brings an increased demand for workers in highly skilled occupations. The most rapid growth is among professional specialty workers, such as computer systems analysts, physicians, nurses, therapists, and teachers (table 6-2). Large growth is also projected in service occupations, such as nurses aides, orderlies, attendants, home health aides, food preparation workers, child care workers, and protective services. While these service occupations often require less formal education, they often require regular contact with the public and many require mobility, stamina and endurance. Clerical and administrative support positions, which tend to be more sedentary, declined as a share of the work force in the 1980s and that decline is projected to continue. The Labor Department concludes that the economy will continue to generate jobs at all educational levels, but the most rapid growth will be in highly skilled occupations. That growth is likely to generate job opportunities for highly skilled workers with physical disabilities as well as for those without disabilities. It is less clear how less skilled workers with physical disabilities or progressive impairments will fare in competing for jobs that require less formal education. To the extent that occupational shifts emphasize the cognitive aspects of jobs or require regular contact with the public, persons with cognitive limitations or mental illness may continue to have difficulty findings jobs.

Declining Demand for Workers with Limited Skills

Using earnings levels of workers as a measure of the demand for their services, research on trends since the 1960s, and particularly during the 1980s, finds a deterioration in labor market opportunities for low-skilled workers, which seems to affect an important subset of people with disabilities. One study finds, for example, that over the 15 year period ending in 1987, average annual earnings (after adjusting for inflation) rose slightly for workers who had some college education and rose somewhat more for those with a college degree, but declined for workers with only a high school education, and declined even more for high school dropouts. That study found

---

1. Social Security Administration, *Increasing the Social Security Retirement Age: Effect on Older Workers in Physically Demanding Occupations or Ill Health*, study pursuant to Section 201(d) of P.L. 98-21, appendix B. tables B-1 and B-3.

Table 6-1. Employment by Industry, 1979, 1992, and Projected to 2005 (moderate growth scenario)

Industry	1979	1992	2005	Annual growth rate 1979-1992	Annual growth rate 1992-2005
Total employment (thousands)	101,363	121,093	147,483	1.4	1.5
Total non-farm wage & salary (thousands)	89,491	107,888	132,960	1.4	1.6
Total percent	100.0	100.0	100.0	—	—
Goods-producing	29.6	21.4	17.8	-1.0	0.2
Mining	1.1	0.6	0.4	-3.2	-0.9
Construction	5.0	4.1	4.2	0.0	1.8
Manufacturing	23.5	16.7	13.2	-1.2	-0.2
Durable goods	14.2	9.5	7.3	-1.7	-0.4
Nondurable goods	9.3	7.2	5.9	-0.5	0.0
Service-producing	70.4	78.6	82.2	2.3	2.0
Transportation, communication and utilities	5.7	5.3	4.9	0.8	1.0
Wholesale trade	5.8	5.6	5.4	1.1	1.3
Retail trade	16.7	17.9	17.9	2.0	1.6
Eating and drinking places	5.0	6.1	6.6	2.1	2.2
Other	11.7	11.8	11.3	1.5	1.3
Finance, insurance, and real estate	5.6	6.1	6.0	2.2	1.5
Services	18.7	26.3	31.4	4.1	3.0
Business services	2.7	4.9	6.3	6.3	3.6
Health services	5.6	7.9	9.4	4.2	3.0
Other	10.4	13.5	15.7	2.4	2.0
Government	17.8	17.3	16.6	1.2	1.3
Federal	3.1	2.8	2.1	0.5	-0.4
State and local	14.7	14.5	14.4	1.1	1.3
Education	7.2	7.4	7.8	1.4	1.6
Other	7.5	7.1	6.6	3.4	1.2

Source: J.C. Franklin, "The American Work Force, 1992-2005: Industry Output and Employment," *Monthly Labor Review*, November 1993.

that the growing inequality in earnings was not simply the result of shifts from manufacturing to service jobs. It was evident within both goods-producing and service-producing industries.[2]

2. G. Burtless, *A Future of Lousy Jobs? The Changing Structure of U.S. Wages* (Washington, DC: The Brookings Institution, 1990), p. 74.
3. G. Burtless and L. Mishel, "Recent Wage Trends: The Implications for Low-Wage Workers," unpublished paper presented at a conference sponsored by the Social Science Research Council, Washington, DC, November 9-10, 1993.

The fall in weekly earnings among the less well educated is sharpest among younger workers.[3] The decline in labor market opportunities for less skilled workers is also reflected in higher rates of involuntary unemployment among both younger and older workers.

Among older workers, the decline in opportunities for the less skilled is also revealed by early withdrawal from the labor force. Employment rates for less well educated men aged 45-64 have fallen much

Table 6-2. Employment by Occupation, 1979, 1992, and Projected to 2005 (moderate growth scenario)

Occupation	1979	1992	2005	Average annual rate of growth 1979-1992	1992-2005
Total, all occupations (thousands)	101,363	121,099	147,482	1.4	1.5
Total percent	100.0	100.0	100.0	—	—
Executive, administrative, managerial	7.8	10.0	10.3	3.2	1.8
Professional specialty	11.4	13.7	15.5	2.8	2.5
Technicians and related support	2.7	3.5	3.8	3.6	2.2
Marketing and sales	9.7	10.7	10.6	2.1	1.4
Administrative support, including clerical	19.0	18.5	17.2	1.1	1.0
Service	15.2	16.0	17.5	1.7	2.2
Agriculture, forestry, fishing	3.6	2.9	2.5	-0.4	0.3
Precision production, craft, and repair	12.7	11.2	10.4	0.3	1.0
Operators, fabricators, and laborers	17.8	13.5	12.1	-0.8	0.7

Source: G.T. Silvestri, "The American Work Force, 1992-2005: Occupational Employment: Wide Variations in Growth," *Monthly Labor Review*, November 1993.

more sharply than they have for male college graduates of the same age. Early retirement pensions, or other early retirement incentives offered by downsizing firms, appear to be used to accommodate the declining demand for less skilled older workers.

Downsizing and employer restructuring brings tight competition for remaining available jobs. In such an environment, early retirement incentive windows are one way to achieve work force reductions. In addition, firms may find that it is more feasible to pay private disability benefits, or encourage workers to claim public disability benefits, rather than to invest in job site accommodations for employees with progressive disabilities.[4] In an environment of declining demand for workers with limited skills, workers with limited skills who also have disabilities are doubly disadvantaged.[5]

---

4. We have anecdotal evidence from private insurers that firms, on occasion, using private long-term disability insurance claims to accommodate corporate restructuring, downsizing or plant closings.
5. R.V. Burkhauser, R.H. Haveman, and B.L. Wolfe, "How People with Disabilities Fare When Public Policies Change," *Journal of Policy Analysis and Management*, vol. 12, no. 2, 1993.
6. See table 6-3 notes for measure of work disability used.

The strong connection between limited education, labor market disadvantage and work disability is evident in household survey data in 1992. When disability is defined in terms of limitations in ability to work, the prevalence of severe work disability is highest among persons with limited educations (table 6-3). In fact, among workers under age 55, those with less than a high school education are 10 times more likely than college graduates to be identified as having a severe work disability.[6] For both men and women in all age groups under age 55, severe work disability rates are low for college graduates (about 1 percent), while for those without a high school diploma, severe work disability rates range from 10 to 19 percent. Among older workers, work disability rates are much higher, but differences by educational attainment remain; those with severe work disabilities account for about 1 in 4 workers age 55-64 without a high school degree and about 4 - 5 percent of those who have college degrees.

CHANGES IN OTHER PUBLIC AND PRIVATE SUPPORT

All western European countries as well as the United States face the problem that a large number of people lose their connection with the labor force

Table 6-3. Number and Percent of the Population with a Severe Work Disability by Age, Education, and Gender, March 1992

	\multicolumn{4}{c}{With severe work disability}
	Number (thousands)		Percent	
Age and years of school completed	Men	Women	Men	Women
Ages 25-34				
Under 12 years	295	278	9.9	10.0
12 years	330	270	4.1	3.4
13 to 15 years	101	110	2.0	1.9
16 years or more	46	42	0.9	0.9
Ages 35-44				
Under 12 years	323	273	13.8	11.6
12 years	373	243	5.9	3.4
13 to 15 years	149	125	2.9	2.3
16 years or more	59	43	1.1	0.9
Ages 45-54				
Under 12 years	431	438	19.1	18.1
12 years	273	326	6.4	5.8
13 to 15 years	102	157	3.7	5.0
16 years or more	61	38	1.6	1.4
Ages 55-64				
Under 12 years	697	778	24.9	27.0
12 years	450	514	13.9	10.7
13 to 15 years	133	193	7.7	9.8
16 years or more	103	69	4.5	4.7

Source: U.S. Bureau of the Census, Current Population Survey, March 1992.
Notes: In these data, persons are classified as having a work disability if any of the following conditions are met: 1) they have a health problem or disability that prevents them from working or that limits the kind or amount of work they can do; 2) they have ever retired or left a job for health reasons; 3) they did not work in the survey week because of a long-term physical or mental illness or disability that prevents any kind of work; 4) they did not work at all in the previous year because of illness or disability; 5) they are under age 65 and covered by Medicare; 6) they are under 65 and receiving Supplemental Security Income; 7) they receive disability compensation from the Department of Veteran's Affairs. If one or more of criteria 3 through 6 are met, the person is classified as having a severe work disability.

before retirement age. It happens particularly during economic recessions, but occurs in normal times as well. One researcher has characterized the social welfare responses to this problem in four areas: *work-based interventions*, which provide rehabilitation or training or expand job opportunities; *unemployment benefits*, which provide income continuity to those actively seeking work; *disability benefits*, which provide income security to those severely limited in their ability to work; and *assistance*, which provides universal income guarantees or means-tested benefits for the poor.[7]

---

7. R.V. Burkhauser, *Employing People with Disabilities: What to Expect from the Americans with Disabilities Act*, CPR paper no. 9, Maxwell School, Syracuse University, 1994.

That comparative research suggests that the difference in the size of the disability rolls across countries depends much more on the relative strength of these four social welfare responses than on differences in the underlying health of the population. The United States, in contrast with many other western countries, has relatively weak support systems other than for disability. For example: job creation, rehabilitation and training programs serve small numbers of persons relative to the numbers receiving disability benefits; unemployment benefits are paid to only about half of those seeking work and are limited in duration; federal funding for assistance, other than that based on disability, is available only to certain low-income families with children and those benefits have declined in value over the past two decades. The same analysis suggests that policies that seek to reduce reliance on one or more of these sources of support are likely to increase reliance on others.

Work-Based Interventions

Vocational Rehabilitation. In the United States, the federal/state vocational rehabilitation (VR) program is designed to enhance work opportunities for persons with disabilities. The Rehabilitation Act authorizes federal grants to states to provide vocational rehabilitation and related services to enable individuals with disabilities to become employed and to live independently. The programs are designed and administered by states with 80 percent of funding from the federal government. Legislation in 1973 stipulated that states should give priority to serving persons with severe disabilities, defined in part as persons who need multiple services over an extended period of time. In fiscal year (FY) 1993, funding for programs under the Rehabilitation Act was $2.1 billion. Since 1975, funding for the VR programs has not kept pace with inflation.[8] In inflation adjusted dollars, FY 1990 funding was about 80 percent of the 1975 level, an increase since 1982 when funding was roughly 60 percent of the 1975 level. The number of people served has also declined — from 1,244,000 to 942,000 — and the number who were successfully rehabilitated (worked for at least 60 days) dropped — from 324,000 to 203,000 — between fiscal years 1975 and 1991.[9] While fewer persons were served and fewer were successfully returned to work, the number of persons with severe disabilities who were successfully rehabilitated increased from 123,000 to 140,000 between fiscal years 1976 and 1991.[10]

Targeted Jobs Tax Credit. The targeted jobs tax credit (TJTC), section 51 of the Internal Revenue Code, was enacted in 1978 to provide employers with an incentive to hire specific targeted groups of individuals that include: recipients of benefits under mean-tested programs; economically disadvantaged persons (as measured by family income); and persons with disabilities.

The TJTC is available as a subsidy to employers on an elective basis for hiring individuals from nine targeted groups, which include persons referred by VR agencies and SSI recipients, among others. Individuals must be certified as being in one of the targeted groups in order for the employer to receive the credit. The TJTC subsidy would amount to nearly 19 percent of the first-year wages of a full-time employee hired at the minimum wage ($4.25 a hour) by a corporate employer. In fiscal year 1990, about 445,000 employees qualified for the credit. Of the 452,000 who qualified in the prior year, 7,400 were SSI recipients and 40,650 were VR referrals.[11]

Job Training and Partnership Act. The Job Training and Partnership Act (JTPA) provides federal funds for employment and training of disadvantaged persons. The primary target is the

---

8. M.F. Smith and C. O'Shaughnessy, *Rehabilitation Act Reauthorization and Funding*, Congressional Research Service Issue Brief, November 30, 1993.
9. U.S. Department of Education, *Annual Report to the President and Congress, FY 1991: On Federal Activities Related to the Rehabilitation Act of 1973, as Amended* (Washington DC: U.S. Government Printing Office, 1991).
10. Ibid., table 10.
11. U.S. House of Representatives, Committee on Ways and Means, *Overview of Entitlement Programs (1993 Green Book)*, WMCP 103-18 (Washington, DC: U.S. Government Printing Office, 1993), pp. 1031-1034.

low-income population, not necessarily people with disabilities. Title II-A of the JTPA provides block grants to states to fund training and related services for economically disadvantaged youths and adults. The activities are administered by states and localities, which select participants and design projects within federal guidelines. The purpose of the program is to increase participants' future employment and earnings and reduce their reliance on cash assistance. Services authorized under the JTPA include institutional and on-the-job training, job search assistance, counseling, and other work-related assistance. At least 90 percent of the participants must be economically disadvantaged. Members of families receiving Aid to Families with Dependent Children, Supplemental Security Income or Food Stamps are defined as economically disadvantaged.[12]

In fiscal year 1992, budget authority under the title II-A of the JTPA was $1.6 billion. In inflation-adjusted dollars, 1992 funding is less than half of that available in 1975 for training activities under the Comprehensive Employment and Training Act (CETA). The CETA program was replaced by the JTPA activities in 1984. The number of people enrolled in such training programs also declined by roughly half from 1.1 million in 1975 to 0.6 million in 1992.[13]

Title II-B of the JTPA authorized a summer employment and training program for economically disadvantaged young people aged 16-21. Services include a full range of remedial education, classroom and on-the-job training, as well as work experience for which participants are paid the minimum wage. In the summer of 1993, $683 million was available to serve approximately 565,000 young people. The 1992 appropriation is less in absolute dollars than what was appropriated in 1984, the first year of the JTPA programs.

---

12. Ibid., p. 1690.
13. Ibid., p. 1692.
14. Ibid., p. 503.

Unemployment Benefits

Receipt of unemployment benefits in the United States is conditioned upon the individual being available for work and willing to accept suitable employment. Nonetheless, the generosity and duration of unemployment benefits may influence demand for disability benefits in several ways. First, many workers with severe disabilities do work. If they become unemployed, they may turn to disability benefits for support if those benefits are more attractive than unemployment benefits. Also, individuals in declining health who lose their jobs may turn to disability benefits if they exhaust unemployment benefits.

Unlike many European systems, unemployment benefits in the United States are time limited and paid only to those who were in employment covered by the unemployment insurance system before they became unemployed. Labor force entrants do not receive benefits, and those with long spells of unemployment may exhaust their benefits.

Although the unemployment insurance system covers 91 percent of all employees, only 52 percent of those officially counted as "unemployed" were receiving benefits in an average month in 1992. Those counted as unemployed are people without jobs who are actively seeking work. They do not include discouraged workers who have stopped looking. The 52 percent receipt rate compares with a peak of about 75 percent of the unemployed receiving benefits in 1975 and a low of 32 percent in 1987 and 1988. The insured unemployment rate rose after December 1991, due to the temporary Extended Unemployment Compensation program. Variations in the proportion of unemployed who receive benefits are influenced by the availability of extended benefits, which are activated during periods of unusually high unemployment, or temporary supplemental benefits that are enacted by Congress when regular and extended benefits are considered insufficient.[14] Variations in the proportion who receive benefits also reflect state or federal changes in eligibility and qualification requirements.

Other Sources of Disability Benefits

Unlike many European countries, the United States does not have a national network of temporary disability insurance or short-term sickness benefits. Federal legislation in 1946 was designed to permit and encourage states to add temporary disability insurance to their state unemployment insurance systems. Only five states did so — California, New York, New Jersey, Rhode Island and Hawaii. In other states, employment-based temporary disability insurance is available through union negotiation or at the discretion of the employer. In the absence of short-term disability insurance, individuals may seek federal DI or SSI benefits earlier than they might if temporary disability benefits were available.

Private long-term disability insurance generally is designed to supplement rather than substitute for Social Security disability benefits. Private, employment-based long-term disability insurance (LTDI) covers about 25 percent of the private sector work force. It is much more commonly available to upper status white collar workers than to blue collar workers.

Defined benefit (DB) pension plans have traditionally been a more common sources of disability protection for blue collar workers (particularly those in medium and large firms). About half the private sector workers covered by these plans are in plans that offer immediate pensions for disability retirement before the plan's early or normal retirement age. A decline in coverage under defined benefit pension plans has weakened this source of alternative disability protection for blue collar workers. In 1991, only about 35 percent of private sector workers were covered by defined benefit pension plans. About half of these, or 17 percent of private sector workers, were in plans that provided immediate disability retirement pensions.[15] The shift to defined contribution pension plans, which do not provide comparable disability protection, means that pensions are filling a smaller role in disability protection.

Assistance

Aid to Families with Dependent Children (AFDC) is the main assistance program other than SSI for low-income persons in the United States. AFDC provides cash benefits to low-income families for needy children who have been deprived of parental support because their father or mother is absent from the home or is incapacitated, deceased or unemployed. It also provides benefits to an adult in the household caring for the needy child. It is financed by federal grants to states and state matching funds. States determine the benefit levels and eligibility rules. Unlike Social Security and SSI benefits, AFDC benefits usually are not automatically adjusted for inflation.

The number of families receiving AFDC was fairly stable throughout the 1980s, ranging between 3.5 and 3.8 million families. In 1991, 4.4 million families received benefits in an average month — they included 8.7 million children. Disability of a parent in the home was the basis for AFDC eligibility for 10.2 percent of AFDC children in January 1973. This figure declined to 5.3 percent in March 1979 and to 3.2 percent for 1986 and was 3.8 percent for 1991.[16]

AFDC has filled a declining role in meeting the needs of low-income families with children over the past two decades. The proportion of poor children receiving benefits declined from 75 percent in 1974 to 60 percent in 1990.[17] Further, the adequacy of AFDC benefits for those who receive them has declined. The inflation-adjusted value of the maximum benefit for an AFDC family of three in the median state declined by 43 percent between 1970 and 1992.[18]

---

15. Tables 2-6, 2-7 and 2-8 of this report present data on DB plan coverage and disability provisions of pension plans.
16. U.S. House of Representatives, Committee on Ways and Means, op. cit., footnote 11, p. 696.
17. Ibid., p. 663.
18. Ibid., p. 645.

Figure 6-1. Percent of All Unemployed Workers[a] Who Received Unemployment Insurance Benefits, Annual Averages, 1970-1991

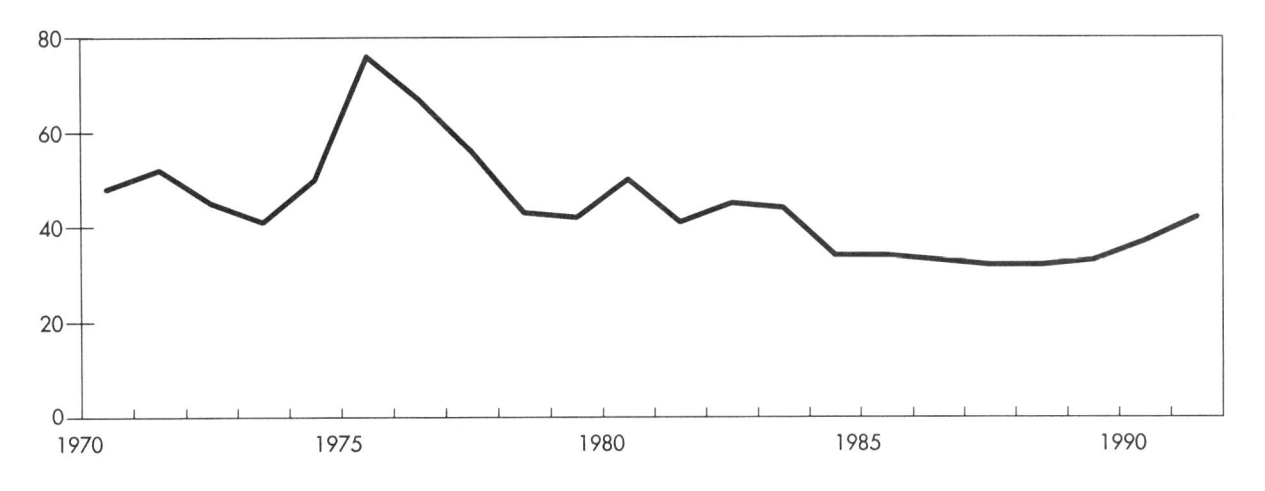

a. All unemployed workers are those without jobs who are actively seeking employment.
Source: U.S. House of Representatives, Committee on Ways and Means, *Overview of Entitlement Programs, (1993 Green Book)*, WMCP 103-18 (Washington, DC: U.S. Government Printing Office, 1993).

General Assistance is the only assistance program for non-disabled adults without children. Its availability, benefits and financing are determined exclusively by states and localities. About 1.3 million people received these benefits in 1991.[19] Some states have reduced or terminated their General Assistance programs under budget constraints and are actively encouraging former recipients of state assistance to apply for SSI.

AVAILABILITY OF HEALTH INSURANCE

Health care is critically important to persons with chronic health conditions or disabilities. Employment-based group insurance is a potential source of coverage for those who can work despite chronic conditions. This is the main alternative to Medicare or Medicaid for persons with chronic conditions.

Coverage under employer-sponsored health insurance has declined in recent years. Between 1988 and 1992, the proportion of the non-elderly population who were covered by employment based health insurance declined from 66.8 percent to 62.5 percent. The decline was also evident for those in families in which the head worked full time throughout the year. Their coverage rate from employer-sponsored insurance declined from 79.5 percent to 76.6 percent. Over that period, the proportion of the non-elderly population covered by Medicaid increased from 8.6 percent to 11.6 percent, while the number of people under age 65 without any health insurance coverage rose from 33.7 million to 38.5 million.[20] In the absence of universal health care protection, individuals with disabilities who lack the coverage they need may turn to DI and SSI to gain coverage under Medicare

---

19. Social Security Administration, *Annual Statistical Supplement to the Social Security Bulletin* (Washington, DC: U.S. Government Printing Office, 1993), p. 338 and p. 125.
20. Employee Benefit Research Institute, *Sources of Health Insurance and Characteristics of the Uninsured: Analysis of the March 1992 Current Population Survey*, EBRI Special Report and Issue Brief Number 133, January 1993; and Employee Benefit Research Institute, *EBRI Notes*, December 1993, vol. 14, no. 12, table 2.

or Medicaid, which accompanies entitlement to cash disability benefits.

CHANGES IN TREATMENT FOR SEVERE MENTAL ILLNESS

An important change in DI and SSI that occurred in the 1980s is an increase in the number of persons with severe mental illness who qualified for benefits. Contributing to this growth were changes in DI and SSI adjudicative policy in the early and mid-1980s, a longer term trend toward community-based care for people with severe mental illness, and incremental changes during the later 1980s, that were designed to increase access to SSI for persons with severe mental illness. It is likely that SSI outreach activities since 1989 also contributed to increased claims among persons with severe mental illness.

Today, disability beneficiaries whose primary diagnosis is mental illness account for about 1 in 4 disabled-worker beneficiaries in the DI program and about 1 in 4 adults under age 65 receiving SSI on the basis of blindness or disability. In the 1970s, mental illness was the primary diagnosis for about 1 in 8 disabled-worker beneficiaries.

Revised Mental Impairment Listings

As reported in chapter 5 of this report, Social Security adjudicative policy that was applied to claimants with mental illness went through a tumultuous period in the early 1980s. At that time, people with mental illness accounted for many applicants who were denied DI or SSI disability benefits, as well as many of those whose benefits were terminated. In class actions brought on behalf of mentally ill persons whose benefits were denied or terminated, federal district courts ruled in 1982 and again in 1984 that overly restrictive standards applied to claimants with mental illness violated the disability adjudication process called for in law and regulations.

Following the 1982 court decision, SSA began work on revising and updating the standards used to evaluate mental impairments. In June 1983, the Secretary of Health and Human Services (HHS) had issued a moratorium on benefit denials or terminations until the new regulations were in place. Legislation in 1984 lent congressional support to that activity by requiring SSA to update and revise the mental impairment criteria to "realistically evaluate a person's ability to do substantial gainful work in a competitive work place environment." In 1986, the first full year under the new rules, the backlog of pending claims were adjudicated. Since then, benefit awards based on mental illness have accounted for about 1 in 4 new awards of Social Security disabled-worker benefits and SSI benefits to blind or disabled adults.

Figure 6-2 shows the number of allowances based on mental illness for adults age 18-64 over the period since 1986. The number of allowances declined slightly in 1993 from 1992, largely because administrative initiatives in 1992 expedited allowances for claims that could be decided without further evidence.

Shift from Institutional to Community-Based Care

The preferred treatment site for people with severe mental illness has shifted from institutional to community-based care. This is a long-term trend that began in the 1950s out of concern that patients in state mental institutions were not receiving appropriate care. As evidence of the trend, the number of people residing in state mental hospitals declined from about 560,000 in 1955 to about 100,000 in 1988.[21] Today, a rate of institutionalization comparable to that of 1955 would involve nearly 1 million people.[22]

---

21. D. Mechanic and D.A. Rockefort, "Deinstitutionalization: An Appraisal of Reform," *Annual Review of Sociology*, 1990, 16:301-27; and U.S. Department of Health and Human Services, *Mental Health in the United States*, 1992, table 1.5.
22. Assuming the number institutionalized grew at the same rate as the U.S. population age 16 and older.

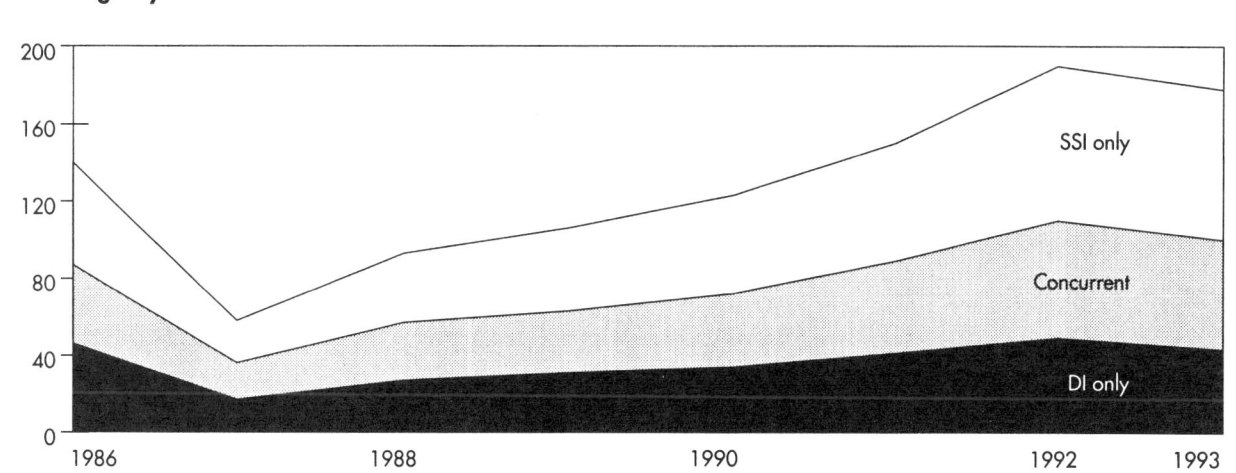

Figure 6-2. Number of DDI and SSI Allowances Based on Mental Illness, 1986-1993
State Agency Initial Decisions

Abbreviations: DI = Social Security disability insurance, SSI = Supplemental Security Income.
Source: Social Security Administration, Office of Disability.

The major decline in the resident population of state mental hospitals occurred after the mid-1960s, when Medicaid and Medicare were enacted and in the 1970s after the federal SSI program was enacted and Medicare was extended to Social Security disability beneficiaries.[23] In fact, these programs are credited with helping to make deinstitutionalization feasible, by affording care in the community to former residents of institutions. As noted in chapter 5 of this report, the rapid growth during the late 1960s and early 1970s in the APTD rolls may have reflected, in part, the deinstitutionalization trend.

It is plausible that the growth in claims and allowances based on mental impairments might have risen more in the mid- and late 1970s, had that period not coincided with initiatives to tighten adjudicative standards in the wake of the rapid growth in the disability rolls during the early 1970s. Between 1975 and 1980, DI allowances based on "meeting the listings" increased slightly, while allowances based on "equalling the listings" and on assessment of residual functional capacity and vocational factors decline precipitously.

In the past, state and local mental hospitals[24] were the primary locus of treatment for persons with severe mental illness. The custodial and medical care provided in state hospitals is financed by state and local governments. In general, neither Medicaid nor Medicare pays for care of working-age adults who reside in state mental hospitals and these residents are not eligible for SSI.

The move to "deinstitutionalize" mental health care reflects changes in philosophy. The prevailing view is that community-based care is far preferable treatment for all but the most severely disabled. Also contributing to the trend are advances in psychotropic medications that help to stabilize disabling conditions so that, with appropriate treatment and support, individuals with quite severe illnesses, nonetheless, can function in the commu-

---

23. D. Mechanic and D.A. Rockefort, op. cit., footnote 21.
24. In the following discussion, "state hospital" includes both state and local mental hospitals.

nity. In-patient care, when needed during acute episodes of illness, is now usually provided in psychiatric units of general hospitals. That care is covered by Medicare or Medicaid if the individual is otherwise eligible.

The decline in the institutional population reflects both the release of long-term residents from state facilities and a sharp reduction in new placements in those hospitals. Young persons with severe mental illness today are much more likely to remain in the community — with occasional episodes in acute care hospitals — than were their counterparts a generation ago.

Thus, a growing professional consensus about the preference for community-based care, where possible, and the availability of federal benefits and funding through SSI and Medicaid for mentally ill persons who live outside of institutions, have brought major changes in the treatment of mental illness. The changes also bring new challenges to meet the needs of persons with serious mental illness in the community. For example, in many cases there remains a need to replicate in the community — through community-based mental health centers or other means — the services that were previously the responsibility of state hospitals, such as continuity of care, case supervision, coordination of medical and psychiatric care, and assistance with other needed services such as housing, transportation, education and training.

Because of the importance of SSI and Medicaid for their clients, many mental health practitioners now consider it part of their job to help their clients qualify for these programs. In this sense, the growth in the number of people with mental illness receiving SSI, and therefore Medicaid, represents a significant improvement in the care they can receive in the community. At the same time, while SSI and Medicaid help pay for needed services, these programs are not designed to organize and deliver all the services needed. The need remains for community-based organizations to coordinate and provide those services needed by mentally ill individuals in the community.

It is plausible that the increase in the number of persons, with mental illnesses who qualify for work-based DI benefits reflects positive consequences of community integration as well as improvements in prescription drug therapy that help stabilize otherwise disabling conditions. People who, in the past, may have been wholly excluded from the world of work may now experience stable periods during which they are able to work and gain insured status for DI benefits as workers.

The shift from institutional to community-based care as the preferred method of treatment is not unique to the mental health field. A similar shift is occurring for the frail elderly in nursing homes and for people with developmental disabilities who reside in intermediate care facilities for the mentally retarded (ICF/MR). In fact, Medicaid policy has been modified expressly to encourage community-based care for these populations as a way to reduce the cost of institutional care paid by Medicaid. In 1992, the average Medicaid expenditure for nursing home care was $15,000. For care in ICF/MR, the average expenditure was $56,500.[25] Under the 1915(c) Medicaid waivers that were enacted in 1981, states with plans approved by the Secretary of HHS can provide social services in the community to people who, without these services, would require institutional care that would be covered by Medicaid. The services allowed under the waivers go beyond the medical services that Medicaid traditionally pays for and include: case management, homemaker/home health aide services, personal care, adult day care and habilitation services, which help people with developmental disabilities acquire the socialization and adaptive skills they need to live successfully in the community.[26]

---

25. Social Security Administration, *Annual Statistical Supplement to the Social Security Bulletin* (Washington, DC: U.S.. Government Printing Office, 1993), table 8.E.1, p. 301.

26. Congressional Research Service, *Medicaid Source Book: Background Data and Analysis (A 1993 Update)*, a report for the use of the Subcommittee on Health and the Environment of the Committee on Energy and Commerce, U.S. House of Representatives, Committee Print 103-A (Washington, DC: U.S. Government Printing Office, January 1993).

Institutional care in state mental hospitals also is costly. In 1988, expenditures for state and local mental hospitals per average daily census of patients was about $70,000.[27] Pursuing policies that foster community-based care can be less costly than institutional alternatives. But for persons with severe mental illness, it also represents a shift in source of financing, with DI and SSI and Medicaid and Medicare serving as critical sources of support. Several incremental legislative changes were enacted in the 1980s to improve access to SSI and Medicaid for individuals with severe mental illness.

Incremental Changes in SSI and Medicaid

The following incremental changes in Medicaid and SSI policy were enacted by Congress during the 1980s to improve access to these benefits for persons with severe mental illness, including homeless persons.[28]

Medicaid for Persons with Mental Illness in Group Homes.
In general, as noted, Medicaid is not available to working-age people in public mental institutions. Legislation in 1988 defined such mental institutions as facilities with more than 16 beds so that mentally ill residents of group homes with 16 or fewer beds would not be excluded from Medicaid.

SSI for Residents of Public Shelters.
In general, SSI is not available to residents of public institutions. Prior to 1984, public shelters were considered institutions, and SSI was not payable for any month a person lived in a public shelter. Legislation in 1984 and 1987 extended SSI eligibility to temporary residents of emergency shelters for up to six months in any nine-month period.

Pre-release Procedures for Residents of Mental Institutions.
Legislation in 1986 required federal agencies to collaborate in pre-release procedures for persons with chronic mental illness who are being discharged from a state institution so as to ensure that their SSI and Food Stamp benefits are available upon release. Residents of institutions who expect to be released can apply for these benefits well in advance of the release date and use their expected new living arrangement as the basis for eligibility.

Temporary Stays in Hospitals.
In general, when a person resides in a medical institution where Medicaid covers the care, for one month or more, the SSI benefit amount is reduced to the personal needs allowance — currently $30 a month — on the theory that the person's need for food, clothing and shelter for the month is being met by the institution. Legislation in 1987 changed the rule to permit payment of regular SSI benefits for up to three months of hospitalization, if the person is expected to be hospitalized no longer than three months and benefits are needed to maintain the living arrangement to which the person plans to return. The change in law applies to persons hospitalized for all types of conditions. It is particularly important for persons with episodic mental conditions.

CLAIMANT REPRESENTATION AND THIRD PARTY INTEREST

Over the past 15-20 years, there has been a significant increase in the number of Social Security disability claims that are appealed after initially being denied, as well as an increase in the likelihood that benefits will be allowed by administrative law judges (ALJs) on appeal. There has also been a significant increase in the size and sophistication of organizations of claimants' representatives and growing interest of third parties in helping individuals gain access to Social Security or SSI disability benefits.

---

27. U.S. Department of Health and Human Services, *Mental Health in the United States, 1992,* R.W. Manderscheid and M.A. Sonnenschein (eds.) (Washington, DC: U.S. Government Printing Office, 1992), tables 1.4, 1.10a and 1.10b. (The high expenditures per resident reflect, in part, the fact that those who remain in state institutions are likely to be the most seriously ill. Also, full-time equivalent staff at state mental hospitals has not declined as rapidly as the number of patients. For a discussion of challenges faced in diverting resources from institutional to community-based care, see G.K. Robinson, *Journey to Passage: Establishing a Community-Based State Mental Health System* (Washington, DC: Mental Health Policy Resource Center, 1991).)

28. C. Koyanagi and H. Goldman, *Inching Forward: A Report on Progress Made in Federal Mental Health Policy in the 1980s,* (Washington, DC: National Mental Health Association, 1991).

Social Security Policy on Paying Claimants Representatives

The Social Security Act does not provide for paying claimants' representatives — attorneys or otherwise — out of Social Security trust funds or other federal funds. It does, however, authorize the Secretary of HHS to set maximum fees that claimants' representatives are allowed to charge their clients (Social Security claimants) and, under some circumstances, provides for paying those approved fees directly out of past-due benefits the government owes the claimant when the claim is successful.[29]

Background. The 1939 amendments to the Social Security Act authorized the Social Security Board to prescribe maximum fees that attorneys could charge Social Security claimants for representing them. The Board, in regulations, set $10 as the maximum fee an attorney could charge unless the attorney filed a petition with the Board and a greater fee was authorized. In 1960, the Secretary raised that maximum amount to $50 for representation before a hearing examiner or the Appeals Council. For any higher fee, the representative had to file a petition and receive SSA approval.

In the mid-1960s, Congress revisited the issue of attorney fees and two concerns were paramount — ensuring claimants had access to effective legal representation and allowing fees that were fair compensation. In 1965, Congress provided for withholding up to 25 percent of past-due benefits toward payment of attorney fees in court cases (appeals beyond the Appeals Council). In 1967, Congress extended the concept of withholding past-due benefits to pay attorneys for representation at the administrative level (up through the Appeals Council) and gave the Secretary the responsibility for approving "reasonable" fees in all cases of claimant representation at the administration level.

The SSI program enacted in 1972 generally follows the same rules as the Old-Age, Survivors, and Disability Insurance (OASDI) program with regard to the Secretary's responsibility to set fees that representatives may charge claimants. However, SSI has never provided for paying attorneys directly out of past-due benefits, on the theory that the benefits are intended to meet basic subsistence needs for food, clothing and shelter, not for other purposes.

Under the policy in effect prior to the Omnibus Budget Reconciliation Act (OBRA) 1990, persons who represented either OASDI or SSI claimants at the administrative level could, after the case was completed, file a fee petition with the Social Security Administration. The petition had to provide information for SSA to determine whether the fee was "reasonable," by detailing services provided, time spent, and so on. SSA would ultimately approve a fee. If the representative was an attorney and the claim was for OASDI benefits, SSA could pay the approved fee directly to the attorney out of up to 25 percent of past-due benefits.

As the number of appeals rose in the 1980s, so did the number of representatives seeking SSA approval of fee petitions. Consequently, significant backlogs developed in SSA's attorney fee approval process during the 1980s. In OBRA 1987, Congress directed the Secretary to conduct a study of the attorney fee process and suggest ways to expedite the payment process.

Current law. In OBRA 1990, Congress enacted the following measures to expedite the fee approval process. Specifically, it provided that the Secretary shall (without requiring further justification) approve fees for claimants' representatives if:

- there is a written agreement between the claimant and representative prior to the Secretary's decision on the claimant's case before the Secretary;

- the agreed upon fee is not more than the lesser of $4,000 or 25 percent of past-due benefits; and

---

29. The source for this section (except for current law) is: Social Security Administration, Office of Hearings and Appeals, *Report to Congress: Attorney Fees Under Title II of the Social Security Act*, July 1988.

- the Secretary's decision is favorable to the claimant.

As under prior law, if the claim is for OASDI benefits and the representative is an attorney, then the law provides for SSA to pay the fee directly to the attorney out of past-due benefits. If the representative is not an attorney, or if the claim is for SSI benefits, any fee that is charged must still be approved by SSA, but the manner of payment is between the representative and the claimant.

Claimants' Representatives

There clearly has been significant growth in the size and sophistication of the "Social Security bar" over the last 15-20 years. For example, the National Organization of Social Security Claimants Representatives was first organized in 1979. Its purpose is to enhance the skills and knowledge of its members to enable them to represent their clients vigorously and well. Its 2,500 members across the country include attorneys in private practice, as well as legal services attorneys or other public or non-profit representatives of low-income persons seeking their rights to DI or SSI benefits. For some attorneys, Social Security cases are their entire practice, but for most, Social Security cases are part of a practice which includes workers' compensation and personal injury litigation. Most of their Social Security work is in disability claims.

The organization publishes a monthly newsletter which updates members on developments in Social Security policy and litigation. Two national forums are held each year to update members on successful methods of pursuing Social Security disability claims.[30]

Third Party Interests

In recent years there has been an increase in so-called "third party interest" in Social Security or SSI disability claims. They include groups other than the claimant, or the claimant's representative, that have a direct interest in having DI or SSI claims allowed to certain individuals.

- One is employers or private LTDI carriers and workers' compensation (WC) carriers in states that have "reverse offset" provisions. (Under these provisions, WC payments are reduced by the amount of Social Security disability benefits that are paid.) They have an interest in having claimants under their systems gain entitlement to DI benefits because the benefits they pay are offset dollar for dollar by Social Security benefits. Private disability insurance benefits are designed to supplement DI. Consequently, premiums and reserves of these plans are based on that assumption. Employers or insurers often employ experts to assist their claimants to apply for DI benefits and to pursue the claims through appeals, if necessary.

  In such cases, the claimant may also benefit from a shift from private or WC benefits to DI benefits. While the immediate cash benefits may be no higher, entitlement to DI does have other advantages for the claimant: DI provides cost of living increases in future benefits (which many private or WC plans may not); establishing a "disability freeze" protects the individual's future retirement benefits; and Medicare coverage becomes available under DI. While the shift to DI has some advantages to the worker, the immediate and direct benefit is a reduction in the cost of benefits to the insurer, or the employer that the insurer represents.

- A second category of third party interests, is state or county assistance programs which provide welfare benefits conditioned on the recipients filing a claim for SSI benefits. Here, the individual will benefit from establishing entitlement to SSI because the monthly benefit rate is more than the state's rate. Also, the state has an interest since the interim assistance provided to the individual is generally conditioned on the individual's agreeing to allow the state to recover its benefit costs from any past-due SSI benefits that are payable.

---

30. Nancy Shor, Executive director of the National Organization of Social Security Claimants' Representatives.

Table 6-4. 1993 ALJ Dispositions: Percent with Attorney or Other Representative by Type of Claim and Outcome, Fiscal Years 1977 and 1993

Type of case	Total	Favorable	Unfavorable	Dismissed
Title II (DI) only				
1993				
Number of dispositions (thousands)	122.1	89.5	22.6	10.0
Percent represented—total	72	73	82	38
Attorney	63	65	71	33
Other	9	8	11	5
1977				
Number of dispositions (thousands)	95.4	46.3	38.1	10.9
Percent represented—total	41	51	39	11
Attorney	34	43	31	9
Other	7	8	8	2
Concurrent (DI and SSI)				
1993				
Number of dispositions (thousands)	121.2	84.0	26.3	10.9
Percent represented—total	74	77	81	34
Attorney	60	62	65	27
Other	14	15	16	7
1977				
Number of dispositions (thousands)	45.4	21.1	18.7	5.6
Percent represented—total	37	48	34	12
Attorney	26	34	23	8
Other	11	14	11	4
Title XVI (SSI) only				
1993				
Number of dispositions (thousands)	106.6	62.6	30.7	13.4
Percent represented—total	65	71	69	28
Attorney	46	51	48	19
Other	19	20	21	9
1977				
Number of dispositions (thousands)	37.6	17.2	15.0	5.6
Percent represented—total	31	41	27	12
Attorney	16	22	14	5
Other	15	19	13	7

Abbreviations: ALJ = administrative law judge, DI = Social Security disability insurance, SSI = Supplemental Security Income.
Source: Social Security Administration, Office of Hearings and Appeals.

Others who may have a direct interest in helping people establish eligibility for SSI, and therefore Medicaid in most states, are hospitals, rehabilitation facilities or other providers of health care and related services. Without Medicaid coverage for their low-income patients, the care they provide is likely to be uncompensated.

Effect of Representation on Outcomes

Table 6-4 summarizes the growth in claimant representation between 1977 and 1993 in disability appeals before administrative law judges. Between 1977 and 1993:

- the proportion of DI or concurrent claimants represented by attorneys increased from about 30 percent to about 60 percent; and

- the proportion of SSI only claimants represented by attorneys increased from 16 percent to 46 percent.

Prior to 1992-1993, claimants who were successful in their claims before ALJs were much more likely to be represented by attorneys than were those whose claims were denied by an ALJ. In 1992 and 1993, those with favorable decisions are no more likely than those with unfavorable decisions to have been represented.

Chapter 7 Preliminary Findings

In its first year, the Disability Policy Panel has engaged in fact-finding and information gathering with regard to disability policy and the broad environment in which that policy operates. In its remaining work, the Panel is focusing on specific issues concerning disability income policy and, in particular, on ways to assist persons with disabilities to maximize their work capacity.

For purposes of its continuing study and final report and recommendations, the Panel has divided the world of disability policy analysis into nine necessarily overlapping categories:

- the definition of disability for Social Security disability insurance (DI) and Supplemental Security Income (SSI) eligibility, and its assessment in functional, medical and vocational terms;

- work and other incentives/disincentives for DI and SSI applicants and beneficiaries;

- prospects for vocational rehabilitation and job placement for persons with significant work disabilities;

- the coordination of health care and cash benefits for persons with disabilities;

- provisions for personal assistance services and assistive devices for persons with significant functional limitations;

- the coordination of short-term and long-term disability income protection;

- implementing and administering cash benefits and services for persons with disabilities;

- the relationship of disability and retirement policy, particularly in light of scheduled increases in the Social Security retirement age; and

- the special concerns of subgroups of persons with disabilities, including children and persons with severe mental illness.

In each area, we propose to develop what we believe to be the appropriate objectives of disability policy, to analyze the degree to which current programs and processes accomplish those objectives and to make recommendations, where necessary, to make policy and administration more consistent with the objectives as defined. As our work proceeds, we may decide that some of these categories require further disaggregation or that others are so interconnected that separate recommendations on those topics are unnecessary or unwarranted.

Although we are less than half way through our study period, the Panel has concluded that certain findings should be reported in this preliminary status report. In its proceedings to date, the Panel has been struck by the continuous reemergence of three issues related to current disability programs:

first is the critical importance of health care to persons with disabilities and the concerns they report about losing health care that is linked to DI or SSI if they should work; second are problems resulting from inadequate resources allocated to administering the DI and SSI programs; and third are major gaps in research about the population of persons with disabilities and about how disability benefit programs affect their well being. The ubiquity and importance of these issues has led us to identify them for treatment in this report.

DISABILITY BENEFITS AND HEALTH CARE

Health care is important for all Americans. Comprehensive health care is particularly important for persons with disabilities because they often have special health care needs, many are at risk of very high health care costs, and they often cannot gain adequate coverage in the private insurance market. In the absence of universal health care coverage, public programs — such as Medicare or, for people in financial need, Medicaid — are critical to people with disabilities. But access to these programs is linked to establishing entitlement to DI or SSI cash benefits, which are designed to provide income only to those who are severely limited in their ability to work. The Panel has heard repeatedly from persons with disabilities and those who represent them, that gaining access to and remaining eligible for the health care they need in order to function are overriding concerns in dealing with the DI and SSI programs. For example:

- Persons with disabilities may find that the only feasible way to gain access to the health care they need is to prove that they are unable to work in order to qualify for DI or SSI, which brings access to Medicare or Medicaid.

- In addition, because DI beneficiaries must wait a full 29 months after the onset of their disabling condition to be covered by Medicare, needed medical intervention may not be available during the critical early months following the onset of a potentially disabling disease or trauma. Delays in gaining access to Medicare may also discourage attempts to return to work before Medicare coverage begins.

- DI or SSI beneficiaries often fear losing Medicare or Medicaid if they demonstrate too much ability to work. Both DI and SSI have complex "work incentive provisions" that allow beneficiaries to receive Medicare or Medicaid after they return to work, as long as they are not found to have medically recovered. A finding of "medical recovery," however, causes an immediate end to Medicare or Medicaid. Because for most persons with disabilities, recovery is never complete and they remain at high risk of recurrence or relapse, the risk of being found "medically recovered" is a great source of uncertainty and anxiety.

- Some individuals with disabilities need costly prescription medications or long-term services to control or accommodate their disabling conditions so that they can function in everyday life and in the world of work. Outpatient medications and long-term services are not generally covered by Medicare; they are covered to some degree by Medicaid in most states. The need for help paying for costly medications or services places pressure on people with disabilities to demonstrate they are poor enough to qualify for SSI, and therefore Medicaid.

The Panel has heard directly from individuals with disabilities that the fear of losing health care and related services is, for many, the major barrier that keeps them from maximizing their earning capacity. Many have said that the risk of losing Medicare or Medicaid coverage is a far greater work disincentive than is the loss of cash benefits. Earnings from work can compensate for the loss of cash benefits. But earnings, alone, cannot buy health care coverage when affordable coverage is simply not available to people with severe chronic conditions.

The Panel finds that ensuring universal protection against health care costs would present a major breakthrough in national policy with regard to disability income and work. Such a guarantee of necessary health care — independent of work, disability, health or cash benefit status — would be a significant gain in:

- *alleviating fear and insecurity among the nation's citizens with disabilities who now rely on Medicaid and Medicare for the health care they need and who risk losing that coverage if they are found able to work;*

- *enabling people with disabilities to maximize their independence by remaining in or returning to the paid work force as well as participating in other productive activities; and*

- *fostering cash benefit policies that provide security, while encouraging work among people with disabilities who have the capacity to do so.*

Universal health care would also foster early intervention to prevent diseases or impairments from becoming permanent work disabilities. Improved access to uniform health care information will also improve the decision-making process for cash disability programs.

The Panel also emphasizes that certain health care benefits are particularly important for people with disabilities, including children. These features include coverage for prescription drugs, durable medical equipment, personal assistance services and devices and rehabilitation services for congenital or chronic conditions, including mental illness.

The Panel is not prepared to take a position on the merits of particular health care reform proposals. There are many factors to be considered as that debate proceeds and they are not our primary focus. Nor do we, as a Panel, take the position that only a universal health care scheme can address the particular concerns that are the subject of our work. Rather, our purpose is to highlight that secure appropriate health care for people with disabilities is an important underpinning for developing sound disability benefit policies that facilitate entry or return to paid employment for those with the capacity to do so.

EFFECTIVE ADMINISTRATION

In order for DI and SSI to fulfill the purposes for which they were intended, it is essential that adequate resources be allocated to administer the programs effectively. Individuals in the disability community and their advocates and representatives, as well as those responsible for administering the programs at the national and local level, have told the Panel about critical problems in administering these programs. The Panel recognizes that the Social Security Administration is committed to remedying problems in administering the disability programs and is actively engaged in reengineering its disability claims process to ensure that available resources are used as efficiently as possible. Nonetheless, in the wake of agency downsizing in the 1980s and unprecedented growth in disability claims and appeals since 1989, needed services are now being delayed or denied to both applicants and beneficiaries.

Between 1985 and 1989, staff resources for administering the Social Security and SSI programs were cut by 20 percent — from about 80,000 to 63,000 employees. Since then, the number of initial claims doubled — from about 1.5 million in fiscal year 1989 to about 3.0 million anticipated in fiscal year 1994 — and the number of appeals pending before administrative law judges has soared.

The growing workloads and staff reductions bring unacceptable delays in getting decisions to claimants. At the same time, under pressure to process claims, agency resources are not available for conducting continuing disability reviews and providing needed individualized services to disability beneficiaries.

The Panel believes that the effective administration of DI and SSI disability programs must include at least the following activities: fair, accurate and prompt decisions on disability claims; individualized services to disability beneficiaries that are required under the law, as well as clear and accurate answers to individuals' questions about their rights and responsibilities with regard to DI and SSI; and timely, predictable and complete reviews of the continuing eligibility of those receiving disability benefits. Each of these areas is discussed below.

Deciding Claims

The backlog of cases pending in state disability determination services was 712,000 in September 1993. The large backlog translates into long delays for applicants — 100 days is now about the average waiting time for initial disability decisions. Waiting times far in excess of this average are fairly common. Such delays clearly are unacceptable.

Disability insurance is a social insurance program that is financed by deductions from workers' earnings matched by employers. With those tax payments, Americans are buying, not only the right to benefits provided under the law, but also the right to fair, correct and prompt decisions on their benefit claims. SSI, as the program of last resort for low-income individuals with disabilities, also has a special obligation to provide prompt service to the nation's most vulnerable individuals. To put administrative costs in perspective: administrative costs for DI amount to about 2.8 percent of revenues to (or benefits paid from) the DI trust fund. Private disability insurance plans spend far more than this for deciding and managing disability claims.

Individualized Service for Disability Beneficiaries

Persons with disabilities often need a broad range of services in addition to cash benefits. The Social Security Administration is not expected to provide all needed services directly, but it is expected to provide appropriate referral to other sources of income and services, including rehabilitation. It is required under the law to provide specific services that are directly related to cash benefits, such as: determining whether representative payees are needed by severely disabled beneficiaries, and, if so, to assign a payee and monitor the payee's activities; determining changes in SSI benefit amounts when beneficiaries' circumstances change to avoid large overpayment or underpayment; and ensuring that beneficiaries understand their rights and responsibilities with regard to cash benefits.

The Panel's charge is to focus particularly on ways to assist disability beneficiaries to maximize their work capacity. An essential first step is simply to ensure that individuals who are willing and able to attempt to work can receive clear and accurate answers to their questions about how a particular change in their work effort will affect their cash benefits and their access to Medicare or Medicaid. Many of the existing work incentives in the law require individualized attention by staff in local Social Security offices. These include, for example: explaining how individuals' particular work plans will affect their SSI benefits and Medicaid under the 1619 work incentive provisions; developing and approving plans for achieving self support (PASS) for SSI recipients; reviewing and approving exclusions from countable resources of property essential for self support for SSI recipients; explaining how work activities affect DI benefits and Medicare coverage under the trial work period, extended period of eligibility, Medicare continuation, and options to purchase Medicare coverage; and reviewing and approving allowable impairment related work expenses that can be disregarded in determining whether an individual is engaging in substantial gainful activity for purposes of eligibility for either DI or SSI. Field offices are not in a position to promote use of these work incentives when they lack the resources to explain and administer them. In its remaining work, the Panel will consider ways to enhance work incentives. In the meantime, it is clear that existing work incentives can only succeed if beneficiaries know about them and can obtain clear and accurate answers about how their own particular work efforts will affect their benefits.

It is clear that agency resources are not adequate to both process initial benefit claims and provide disability beneficiaries with the all the individualized services that are contemplated under current provisions of the law.

Continuing Disability Reviews

The 1980 amendments to the Social Security law call for the Social Security Administration to conduct continuing disability reviews (CDRs) for each disability beneficiary every three years unless the individual is judged to be permanently disabled. These reviews generally are not being done. Instead, first priority is given to deciding initial claims. While it is difficult to fault that priority, the failure to conduct the continuing disability reviews has long-term negative consequences.

First, failure to conduct the reviews undermines public confidence in the integrity of the disability benefit programs. The experience of the past two decades highlights the risk of overreaction and adverse consequences that resulted from widespread belief that ineligible persons were receiving benefits. As has been recounted elsewhere in this report:

- In the mid-1970s, a severe economic recession coincided with new responsibilities for the Social Security Administration (SSA) to implement the SSI program. The number of disability claims and allowances grew at an unprecedented rate. In order to work within a government-wide limitation on staffing, SSA diverted resources from conducting continuing disability reviews to processing new claims.

- In the later 1970s, concerns were raised in Congress that a significant fraction of beneficiaries on the DI rolls no longer met the eligibility criteria. In 1980, Congress enacted the requirement that SSA conduct reviews every three years of all persons on the rolls whose disabilities were not permanent.

- In the early 1980s, with the statutory mandate from Congress and an expectation that the cost of disability benefits could be significantly reduced by administrative initiatives, the new Reagan administration accelerated the reviews and terminated benefits to those who did not meet a very restrictive interpretation of the eligibility requirements. There were widespread cases of severe hardship among those whose benefits were terminated, and many whose benefits were terminated later won reinstatement on appeal through the courts.

- In 1984, Congress enacted legislation that limited the conditions under which beneficiaries could be dropped from the rolls and required SSA to develop new criteria for deciding disability in the case of mental impairments.

In the 1990s, staff resources are again inadequate to both process new claims and conduct regular CDRs. At this time, it is important to learn from the tumultuous experience of the last two decades rather than to repeat it. Adequate resources are essential to stable administration of the programs.

In addition, failure to conduct the reviews can be costly. As indicated earlier in this report, the proportion of DI beneficiaries leaving the rolls because of recovery is at an all-time low — with fewer than 0.5 percent estimated to leave the disabled-worker benefit rolls for that reason in 1993. In March of 1993, the failure to conduct the reviews was estimated to cost the DI trust fund $1.4 billion over the period through 1997.[1]

The Panel finds that staff and related resources are not now adequate to administer the DI and SSI programs. It believes that such resources must be set at a level that ensures stable, effective management of the disability programs. Specifically, resources must be adequate to: provide fair, accurate and prompt decisions on disability claims; provide the individualized service to disability beneficiaries that are contemplated under current law, including clear and accurate answers to individuals' questions about how changes in their work effort will affect their benefits; and conduct timely and predictable review of the continuing eligibility of those receiving disability benefits.

---

1. Testimony by Jane L. Ross, Associate Director, Income Security Issues, U.S. General Accounting Office, before the U.S. House of Representatives, Committee on Ways and Means, Subcommittee on Social Security, March 25, 1993.

LONG-TERM RESEARCH

A fundamental question in projecting the future size and cost of disability benefits as well as in assessing policy options is — "How many people would meet the current eligibility criteria if they were not working?" In retirement income policy, a great deal of research has been done to estimate the present and future size of the elderly population and the behavioral response of older workers to various changes in retirement benefit policy. The most basic data to undertake comparable research for disability income policy are lacking. Basic data are not available to estimate the size of the potentially eligible population — that is, people with disabilities who might meet the existing or alternative medical, functional and vocational criteria for becoming eligible for benefits. In the absence of that basic information, little is known about what might distinguish those with disabilities who are successfully integrated into the work force from those who are unable to work because of their disabilities. Furthermore, estimates of the cost and consequences of policy changes are highly uncertain without this basic information.

Another important gap in knowledge concerns the prospects for current beneficiaries to return to work. First, it would be extremely useful to have more complete trend data about the circumstances under which beneficiaries leave the rolls (either voluntarily or involuntarily) because of recovery, as well as about those who return to work and ultimately leave the benefit rolls without having medically recovered. Second, there have been no rigorous experiments to assess the consequences of benefit changes or service interventions that would facilitate return to work. Legislation in 1980 authorized demonstration projects to test the effects of various partial benefit offset provisions in the disability insurance program, but they were not done. Similarly, rigorous controlled experiments to test other types of interventions to foster return to work have not been done. In the absence of such research, anecdotal evidence is used to support widely divergent views about the number of beneficiaries who might successfully return to work with appropriate supports.

There has been a dearth of rigorous research on the disability benefit programs over the last 10-15 years. In the 1960s and 1970s, the Social Security Administration conducted periodic comprehensive surveys to measure the prevalence of work disability in the general population and to assess the role of the disability income programs in meeting the needs of people with work disabilities. No comparable data have been collected since 1978. The lack of adequate data for disability policy development was noted by the 1988 Disability Advisory Council. In its 1988 report, it concluded:

> The Council believes that the DI and SSI programs should be restructured so as to assign a higher priority to encouraging beneficiaries to work than to declaring them unable to work...During our discussion of possible recommendations, however, we were frustrated by the lack of data that are essential to the formulation of sound policy.

A number of new research initiatives are underway to remedy some of the most basic gaps in knowledge. For example, a medical exam study is being undertaken as a first step in estimating the size of the potentially eligible population. That study seeks to estimate the number and attributes of people who have disabilities that would meet medical criteria for benefit eligibility, but who are working. Project NetWork, which seeks to assess the effect of individualized services on work outcomes for DI and SSI beneficiaries, could, with a rigorous evaluation of its results, provide useful information about the willingness, capacity and success of beneficiaries' work efforts when special individualized services are provided. Other new research initiatives include short-range studies to improve understanding about the recent growth in disability claims and allowances and longer-range projects, including a major survey of adults and children with disabilities that is planned for 1994-1995.

A comprehensive program of long-range research is needed in order to provide basic information about the populations being served and the changing environment in which disability programs operate. The Panel is encouraged to find that thoughtful new research initiatives are planned and underway to rectify major gaps in information that is needed to evaluate and forecast disability income programs. Multi-year funding commitments are needed for long-range research. The Panel strongly supports the continued investment in such research initiatives.

Appendix A Letter of Request

COMMITTEE ON WAYS AND MEANS

U.S. HOUSE OF REPRESENTATIVES
WASHINGTON, DC 20515

June 12, 1991

Mr. Robert M. Ball, Chair
National Academy of Social Insurance
505 Capitol Court, N.E., Suite 300
Washington, D.C. 20002

Dear Mr. Ball:

We are writing to ask for assistance from the National Academy of Social Insurance in conducting a comprehensive review of the social security disability program.

The disability program has now been in existence for more than three decades. While the Committee on Ways and Means has periodically reviewed and amended its provisions over this period, it has not undertaken a comprehensive review of the program since the late 1950s. As we enter the 1990s, we wish to undertake a second comprehensive evaluation.

We are particularly interested in the Academy's assessment of the relationship between disability insurance and labor force participation by disabled Americans. Given projected labor shortages later in this decade, it seems appropriate to reexamine disability policy to determine how best to encourage economic contributions by all who can work.

Is it correct, as some critics assert, that disabled Americans now confront strong incentives to emphasize their impairment as a means of securing and maintaining benefits? If so, are there changes that would encourage beneficiaries to use their residual work capacity rather than emphasizing their incapacity? Can an emphasis on rehabilitation and work be incorporated into the program without greatly expanding its costs or weakening the right to benefits of those who cannot work? Finally, how might the Committee increase protection for the large numbers of claimants who are denied benefits but still do not find employment?

While these questions are at the heart of our concerns, we do not intend to make them your exclusive focus. Rather, we would encourage the Academy to identify other important issues

Mr. Robert M. Ball,
June 12, 1991
Page 2

in the disability program; to conduct relevant, comparative analysis of other disability programs, such as those operating in the private sector and in Europe; and, where appropriate, to offer additional recommendations.

We are aware that a thorough reappraisal for the disability program will take a considerable amount of time. Thus, we are hopeful that the Academy can move quickly.

Thank you for your consideration of our request. We look forward to your response.

Sincerely,

Andy Jacobs, Jr.
Chairman
Subcommittee on Social Security

Dan Rostenkowski
Chairman

Appendix B: Legislative Development of the Disability Insurance Program

Background: 1930s and 1940s

The **1935 Committee on Economic Security** made a number of observations and, in the Public Health Service area, recommendations dealing with problems of illness and incapacity but did not include any recommendation regarding social insurance cash benefits in this area. They considered the need for compulsory health insurance but did not recommend such a plan in their January 1935 report. They suggested that the federal government should assume primary responsibility for providing work for those able and willing to work and they suggested that responsibility for "residual relief" "for the genuine unemployables — or near unemployables" should rest with the states.

The **1938 Advisory Council on Social Security** agreed in principle on the social desirability of providing benefits to insured persons who become permanently and totally disabled, but they disagreed as to timing. Some members favored providing such benefits right away while others thought that, because of concern about potential costs and administrative difficulties, the issue should be studied further. There was also concern whether disability insurance should be delayed pending more nearly universal Social Security coverage of the work force and pending further consideration of health insurance issues.

Throughout the **1940s**, the Social Security Board (and its successor, the Social Security Administration) recommended in its annual reports the payment of social insurance benefits to permanently and totally disabled persons. Some of the specific proposals made to implement this recommendation were:

- Benefits should be payable only after a six-month waiting period and then only if the disabled person had been in covered employment within a reasonably recent period, for a reasonably substantial time, and with reasonably substantial income.

- Benefits should be paid to dependents of disabled workers.

- Vocational rehabilitation for beneficiaries should be financed from the trust fund.

As for the definition of disability, the Board said that for "permanent" disability to imply a concept of lifetime disability, requiring a medical prognosis of permanency, was socially and administratively unsatisfactory. Instead, benefits should be paid for loss of earnings after a suitable waiting period (six months) and for the duration of total incapacity for substantial gainful work.

The **1948 Advisory Council on Social Security**, appointed by the Senate Finance Committee in 1947, following a hiatus in social legislation during the World War II years, recommended providing disability insurance benefits for the permanently and totally disabled, through the old-age and survivors insurance system. Under the Council's recommendations, benefits would be provided to insured persons who were "unable, by reason of a disability medically demonstrable by objective tests, to perform any substantially gainful activity" over an "indefinite period."

The 1948 Council also recommended establishing a non-categorical federal-state matching public assistance program. Such a program would include (but not be limited to) needy persons with disabilities. The Council also reviewed existing state programs of temporary disability insurance (TDI) — New Jersey, Rhode Island, and California — and the federal TDI program which was part of the program for railroad workers. Although the report contains a discussion of the issues, the Council felt it had "been unable to devote the time necessary for making policy decisions in the field of temporary disability."

Program Beginnings: Early 1950s

In line with the recommendations of the 1948 Advisory Council on Social Security, the Truman administration recommended, in 1949, provisions for both a federal/state General Assistance program and benefits under the Old-Age and Survivors Insurance program (Social Security) for extended disability. The Administration also recommended a federal temporary disability insurance program. However, the only related legislation included in the Social Security Act Amendments of 1950 was a program of federal/state public assistance payments for Aid to the Permanently and Totally Disabled.

In 1952, the Congress adopted a proposal (which never took effect) to "freeze" the Social Security work records of disabled persons so that periods of inability to work due to severe disability would not adversely affect any future retirement or survivors benefits that might be payable on account of the worker's covered employment.

A modified version of the "disability freeze" was enacted in 1954 and took effect in 1955. To a large degree, the work requirements, the definition of disability, the nature of the disability determinations, and the emphasis on rehabilitation that were later used in the Social Security disability insurance benefits program were initially established in this 1954 freeze legislation. The requirements for the freeze included:

Strict Work Requirements. To qualify for the disability freeze, a person had to meet both the "currently insured" work requirements needed for young survivors benefits and a special "disability insured" test of substantial recent covered work. To meet this "disability insured" test, a worker must have credit for at least 5 years of covered employment in the 10 years immediately preceding the onset of disability. (In addition, when cash benefits were provided under the 1956 legislation, the worker had also to meet a "fully insured" work requirements analogous to the fully insured for retirement benefits. At that time, for "fully insured" status, a worker needed covered work over a period equivalent to about one half the time elapsing after 1950 (or age 21 if later) and up to the onset of disability (or retirement), but not more than 10 nor less than 1.5 years' work.)

Definition of Disability. The concept of permanent and total disability was defined in the law as "inability to engage in any substantial gainful activity by reason of any medically determinable physical or mental impairment which can be expected to result in death or to be of long-continued and indefinite duration, or blindness; and the term 'blindness' means central visual acuity of 5/200 or less in the better eye with the use of a correcting lens. An individual shall not be considered to be under a disability unless he furnishes such proof of the existence thereof as may be required." A disability freeze could not be established until the disability had lasted at least six months.

Administrative Structure and Role of State Agencies. The law provided for the Secretary to enter into agreements for disability determinations to be made by the state agency that was responsible for administering the state plan approved under the Vocational Rehabilitation Act, or any other appropriate state agency. The Secretary was authorized to review and reverse state agency determinations that individuals were disabled, or that the disability began later, but could not reverse state agency denials or set an earlier onset date. (This restriction was removed in 1980.) The Secretary was authorized to make disability determinations for persons not covered by state agreements.

The law also provided that any individual who was dissatisfied with a determination, whether by the state agency or by the Secretary, had the right to a hearing and to judicial review.

Rehabilitation. The law also provided that all applicants for the disability freeze should be promptly referred to the appropriate state agency responsible for the state's vocational rehabilitation (VR) program and stated the congressional intent as follows:

> It is hereby declared to be the policy of the Congress ... that disabled individuals applying for a determination of disability shall be promptly referred to the state agency or agencies administering or supervising the administration of the state plan approved under the Vocational Rehabilitation Act for necessary vocational rehabilitation services, to the end that the maximum number of disabled individuals may be restored to productive activity.

Similar language, with appropriate modifications as the program has been amended over the years, still appears in the disability insurance (DI) part of the Social Security Act.

The First Decade: 1956-1965

Under the **1956 amendments**, monthly cash benefits were provided after a six-month waiting period to disabled workers aged 50-64 and to the adult children of retired or deceased workers, where the children had been disabled since childhood (before age 18). The disabled worker's benefit was calculated like a retirement benefit, as though the worker had reached age 65 when he became disabled. Benefits for disabled adult children were calculated like benefits for non-disabled children in the Old-Age and Survivors Insurance part of the program—50 percent of the worker's benefit if the worker was alive and 75 percent if the worker was deceased.

The benefits and administrative costs were to be financed from a separate Federal Disability Insurance Trust Fund, to which a specified portion of the Social Security tax was allocated.

Benefits were to be withheld from beneficiaries who, without good cause, refused to accept available vocational rehabilitation services. Beneficiaries receiving VR services who returned to work were not to be regarded as able to engage in substantial gainful activity (SGA) for at least one year after the work began—the beginning of the "trial work" concept. Also, the Secretary was authorized to suspend a person's DI benefits, pending a determination of continuing disability, if he had reason to believe the disability no longer existed.

The law also provided that any Social Security disability insurance benefit would be offset $1-for-$1 by any workers' compensation benefit the individual might be entitled to or any other federal benefit (including service-connected veterans benefits) based on his/her disability. (These provisions were soon repealed; other offset provisions were adopted later.)

In 1958, the law was amended to provided benefits to disabled workers' dependents — spouses over age 62, children and young spouses caring for entitled children. The 1958 legislation also eliminated the "currently insured" work requirement so that workers no longer needed to have credit for at least six quarters of work in the 13-quarter period ending with the onset of disability.

The 1958 legislation also repealed the offset for workers' compensation and other federal disability benefits; the offset for service-connected veterans' compensation had been repealed in 1957. The rationale for the 1958 repeal of the offset, as stated by the Ways and Means Committee, was that "the danger that duplication of benefits might produce undesirable results is not of sufficient importance to justify reduction of the social security disability benefits."

In 1960, the age 50 requirement for disabled worker benefits was eliminated and the second 6-month waiting period was eliminated for workers who become disabled again within 5 years of termination of prior entitlement to DI benefits. Also **in 1960 and 1961**, the general insured status requirements were modified making it somewhat easier for all workers, including disabled workers, to qualify for benefits.

The 1960 legislation also modified the trial work provisions to make them applicable to all disabled beneficiaries (including adult children) and to specify that if, after 9 months (not necessarily consecutive) of trial work, the beneficiary has demonstrated the ability to engage in substantial gainful employment (SGA), he will receive benefits for an additional 3 months.

The 1960 amendments provided further that any beneficiary — whether or not there was a work effort — whose disability ceased would receive an additional three months benefits prior to termination. Although there is no statutory reference to "medical improvement," the Ways and Means Committee report describes this provision as:

> a continuation of benefits for three months for any person, irrespective of attempts to work, whose medical condition improves to the extent that he is no longer disabled within the meaning of the law. A person who recovers from his disability, especially if he has spent a long period in a hospital or sanitarium, may require benefits for a brief interval during which he is becoming self-supporting.

The Senate Finance Committee Report contained similar language.

In 1965, the definition of disability was amended to eliminate the requirement that a worker's disability must be expected to be of long-continued and indefinite duration. Under the amended definition the disability must be expected to result in death or must have lasted, or be expected to last, for a continuous period of not less than 12 months.

The 1965 changes also provided an occupational definition of blindness in the case of blind workers age 55 and older ("inability by reason of such blindness to engage in substantial gainful activity requiring skills or abilities comparable to those of any gainful activity in which he has previously engaged with some regularity and over a substantial period of time") and modified the disability insured status requirements to make it easier for blind persons under age 31 to meet the test of substantial recent work.

The 1965 legislation provided for the use of DI trust fund monies to pay for certain rehabilitation costs: amounts up to 1 percent of the prior year's DI benefit payments could be used to reimburse vocational rehabilitation agencies for services furnished to disabled beneficiaries.

Also, a provision was included for offsetting DI benefits of workers under age 62 on account of receipt of workers' compensation payments. (The original provision for such an offset had been repealed in 1958.) Under the offset, total monthly payments to a worker and family could not exceed 80 percent of the worker's average earnings, with periodic adjustment in the average to reflect changing economic conditions.

Actual program costs in the very early years of the disability program had been lower than expected. Thus, the previously enacted liberalizations were financed without any modification in the tax revenues allocated to the DI program. By 1965, however, the program was projected to have a long-range deficit and the allocation was increased to cover these costs and the cost of the 1965 legislation.

The 1965 amendments, which provided for Medicare for Old-Age, Survivors, and Disability Insurance (OASDI) beneficiaries aged 65 and older (and for Medicaid for persons in financial need), did not extend Medicare coverage to DI beneficiaries. Major considerations at the time related to costs and to the method of financing the Supplementary Medical Insurance (Part B) of Medicare for the disabled without charging excessive premiums to the disabled and or requiring extensive subsidy from aged enrollees or from federal general revenues. Thus, the 1965 legislation provided for a special Advisory Council on Health Insurance for the Disabled to consider this issue and to submit its report by 1968.

The Second Decade: 1967-1977

The **1967 legislation** introduced several further changes:

- the alternative disability insured status provisions for persons under age 31 that were made applicable to the blind under the 1965 law were extended to all disabled persons;

- the definition of "blindness" was liberalized;

- the calculation of the worker's average earnings for purposes of the workers' compensation offset was modified to include earnings in excess of amounts counted for Social Security taxes and benefits;

- reduced benefits were made available (under the survivors part of the Social Security program) to disabled widows and widowers aged 50 or older; and

- as discussed further below, the basic definition of disability was clarified in response to erosion by recent court decisions.

Also, the allocation of Social Security taxes to the disability program was increased to meet program costs.

With regard to the definition of disability, the basic definition was restated in the 1967 amendments without change:

"inability to engage in any substantial gainful activity by reason of any medically determinable physical or mental impairment which can be expected to result in death or which has lasted or can be expected to last for a continuous period of not less than 12 months."

However, new guidelines for making disability determinations were provided in the law. (The statutory definition of disability before and after the 1967 amendments, and under current law, is shown in the attachment at the end of this appendix.) For persons other than disabled widow(er)s, disability would be found only if the individual was unable to engage in any kind of substantial gainful work that exists in the national economy, even though such work does not exist in the general area in which the individual lives.

Further, as discussed in the Conference Committee Report on the 1967 amendments, "work which exists in the national economy" is defined in the law to mean "work that exists in significant numbers in the region in which the individual lives or in several regions in the country." The Conference Committee Report further states that "The purpose of so defining the phrase is to preclude from the disability determination consideration of a type or types of jobs that exist only in very limited number or in relatively few geographic locations in order to assure that an individual is not denied benefits on the basis of the presence in the economy of isolated jobs that he could do."

This provision was expected to offset, in part, the effects of court decisions which tended to erode the strict definition of disability the Congress had intended. In its report on the 1967 amendments, the Ways and Means Committee stated that one court had found that "once a claimant has shown inability to perform his usual vocation, the burden falls on the Secretary to show the (reasonable) availability of suitable positions." The Committee further quotes a court which summarized its interpretation of the statute and case law as follows:

> "The standard which emerges from these decisions in our circuit and elsewhere is a practical one: whether there is a reasonably firm basis for thinking that this particular claimant can obtain a job within a reasonably circumscribed labor market."

A disabled widow(er) could be found to be disabled only if unable to engage in any gainful work, rather than substantial gainful work. The more strict test for widow(er)s may have reflected concern about applying the work-based definition of disability to persons with little or no history of gainful employment.

Also, legislation enacted in **1967, 1969, 1971 and 1972**, provided general benefit increases (of 13, 15, 10, and 20 percent, respectively) such that benefits more than kept pace with inflation and there was some real increase in benefit levels for both current and future beneficiaries. In several of these acts, there were also increases in the amount of a worker's annual earnings that could be taxed and credited for Social Security purposes (the "contribution and benefit base.") As a result, even greater increases in real benefit levels were possible for newly disabled workers, particularly younger workers, who had been high earners.

The Social Security **Amendments of 1972** significantly affected the DI program both directly, in the form of program amendments, and indirectly, through the extension of Medicare to DI beneficiaries, enactment of the Supplemental Security Income (SSI) program, and provisions for automatic adjustment of the OASDI program to changes in the economy.

- **DI program changes**. These changes included reducing the DI waiting period from 6 to 5 months, eliminating the disability insured work requirement for the blind, and increasing from 18 to 22 the age before which a "childhood disability" must have begun. The 1972 legislation also increased the portion of DI trust funds that could be used to reimburse state VR agencies for services to beneficiaries from 1 percent of the prior year's benefit payments to 1.25 percent of that amount for 1973 and 1.5 percent beginning in 1974.

- **Medicare for Disability Beneficiaries**. Medicare coverage was made available to persons who had been receiving disability benefits for 24 consecutive months. While such an extension of Medicare had been recommended by the 1968 Advisory Council on Health Insurance (appointed under the 1965 amendments), that council had recommended financing all of Medicare for the aged and the disabled on the basis of Social Security payroll taxes, covering the disabled after a waiting period of only 3 months and including older workers on the basis of less severe disability than was required for DI benefits. The final provision, with a 24-month waiting period, presumably reflects a compromise between the recognized need of DI beneficiaries for Medicare protection and the costs of providing such coverage.

- **Impact of SSI**. The numbers of disabled persons receiving public assistance (APTD) had been growing rapidly (by about 100,000 per year) prior to the SSI program. There were further increases in the numbers of persons receiving assistance based on disability (or blindness), when SSI took effect in 1974, due to such factors as the federal income guarantee being higher than the prior assistance levels in some states and added publicity and state outreach efforts. With common definitions of disability and common administration for the two programs, and considering the requirement that persons applying for SSI should also apply for DI, if potentially eligible, there was some growth in applications for, and allowances of, benefits under the DI program.

- **Impact of general provisions and automatic adjustments**. The provisions for automatically adjusting both individual and family benefits to changes in the economy that were adopted in 1972 were highly sensitive to the interaction of wage and price growth in the economy. With the unforseen economic developments of the mid 1970s, including high inflation, it was quickly apparent that the automatic adjustments would produce higher than expected benefits, especially for future beneficiaries. Projections made after the 1972 legislation, taking account of developing economic trends, showed that potential replacement rates — initial benefits as a percent of pre-retirement earnings — would rise much faster than wage levels generally. These effects were particularly marked in the case of benefits for younger disabled workers since such workers were most apt to have young families and had their earnings, for benefit computation purposes, averaged over a shorter, more recent period than was the case for older workers.

The Social Security **Amendments of 1977** instituted a new method of calculating initial benefits, so as to maintain relatively stable replacement rates, and a revised system for automatic cost of living adjustments in benefits for persons on the rolls. As noted above, the effect on the disability program was primarily to greatly reduce the potential advantage of a relatively short computation period, to offset some of the unintended benefit growth since 1972, and to prevent further unintended escalation in initial benefit levels. The 1977 legislation also included a provision specifying that the dollar figure taken to represent SGA in the case of blind beneficiaries should be increased to the level of the retirement earnings text exempt amount for retirees aged 65 and older, and adjusted as that amount is automatically adjusted to increases in average wage levels generally.

The 1977 legislation also provided for significant increases in the schedule of Social Security tax allocations to the DI trust fund to assure program solvency both in the near term and over the long range future. This schedule (modified in 1983) provided in effect that, ultimately, beginning in 1990, of 1.1 percent of the total OASDI tax of 6.2 percent for employers and employees, each, would be allocated to the DI program. Although the Chairman of the Ways and Means Subcommittee on Social Security, among others, introduced major DI bills in 1976-77, it was understood that the Congress would deal first with the benefit structure issues in the 1977 legislation before revisiting the DI program.

A Period of Reform: 1978-1984

The Social Security **Amendments of 1980** were the product of a number of years work in the Congress. There had been growing concern during the 1970s about growth in the DI rolls both as a result of higher than expected applications and awards (attributed variously to the advent of SSI, the economic downturn, the higher relative benefit levels, and/or other causes) and because relatively few beneficiaries were being rehabilitated and returning to work. There was also concern, as reflected in an internal SSA study, and in a General Accounting Office (GAO) report based on that study, that there were substantial numbers of persons on the rolls who were not disabled.

Finally, in the 1980 amendments and subsequent legislation, there were many amendments relating to the administration of disability benefits and work incentives that applied both to the DI program and to the SSI program. These provisions are generally included in this legislative history, and are not discussed in detail in the SSI legislative history (appendix C).

The 1980 legislation provided for further limiting disability benefit levels by:

- relating the number of years of low earnings that could be dropped in computing average earnings to the length of time the person could be expected to have worked under the program; and

- setting special limits on family benefits in disability cases.

The 1980 amendments also included provisions for tightening administration of the DI and SSI programs through:

- pre-effectuation review of up to 65 percent of state agency allowances. Although the statutory requirement applies only to the DI program, committee report language suggested that SSA conduct similar reviews in SSI cases;

- provisions authorizing the Secretary to reverse state agency denials as well as allowances in both DI and SSI;

- periodic (triennial) reviews of continuing disability (CDRs) among disabled DI and SSI beneficiaries whose disabilities may not be permanent. Where a finding is made that an individual's disability is permanent, review of the beneficiary's condition may be made at such times as the Secretary considers appropriate; and

- performance standards and procedures for the state disability determination process to be established by regulations rather than agreements with the states. The law specified that the new regulations may cover matters such as administrative structure, accuracy and timeliness of determinations, fiscal control procedures and the like. The law also included provisions governing potential federal takeover of disability determinations. These provisions were temporarily superseded, through 1987, by changes enacted in 1984 amendments.

Additional administrative and procedural amendments affecting both DI and SSI included: reactivation of existing authority for Secretarial review of ALJ decisions; a prohibition on the introduction of new evidence after an ALJ hearing; limitation on certain court remands of OASDI and SSI cases; a requirement that notices to denied disability applicants be in understandable language and include a discussion of the specific evidence and reason for the denial of the claim; provision for federal reimbursement for the costs of providing medical evidence for DI purposes, similar to preexisting authority in the SSI program; and permanent authority to pay for certain travel expenses incident to SSA-required medical examinations and expenses incurred by a claimant and his/her representative and/or witnesses in travelling to hearings or face-to-face reconsiderations.

The 1980 amendments also included a number of provisions intended to enhance rehabilitation and work incentives by:

- Extending the nine-month trial work period, previously available to disabled workers and adult children under OASDI, to disabled widow(er)s.

- Extending disability status for DI and SSI purposes for 15 months after completion of trial work period, as long as there is no medical recovery. DI benefits are not generally payable for months of SGA during this "Extended Period of Eligibility." (The 15 month period was increased to 36 months in 1987 and the applicability of this provision in SSI was superseded in 1986, when the "Section 1619" incentives provisions were made permanent.)

- Deducting the amount of impairment-related work expenses (IRWE), such as medical devices and attendant care, from earnings in determining whether a DI or SSI claimant or beneficiary is engaging in SGA. (IRWEs were also disregarded in calculating SSI payment amounts, but not in counting income for purposes of determining initial eligibility; this was corrected in legislation in 1990.)

- Continuing benefits for DI or disabled SSI beneficiaries who medically recover while in an approved vocational rehabilitation program.

- Extending Medicare coverage for up to 36 months beyond the month DI cash benefits terminate for beneficiaries who have returned to work but have not medically recovered. In describing this provision, the House Ways and Means Committee Report refers to the fear that disabled persons have that if they work they may lose Medicare and may not be able to get any other "public or private medical care coverage...this provision removes the potential loss of medicare coverage as a deterrent to work effort for this substantial period." The Senate Finance Committee expressed their purpose in including this provision somewhat differently: "...to encourage disabled workers to attempt employment as well as to remove the possibility that incurring higher health insurance premiums might discourage employers from hiring the disabled..."

- Eliminating the second Medicare waiting period for workers whose DI benefits had terminated and who became re-entitled to DI benefits within 5 years (7 years for disabled widow(er)s). In 1987, these time limits were eliminated and Medicare was available without a second waiting period for persons whose subsequent disability was based on essentially the same impairment(s) as the prior disability.

Additional provisions relating only to the SSI program (including counting sheltered workshop income as earned rather than unearned income) are included in the SSI legislative history.

The 1980 legislation also provided temporary demonstration authority in several significant areas:

- **DI and SSI Waiver Demonstration Authority.** The law provided temporary authority to waive provisions of the law to conduct studies of potential work incentive provisions, including in the DI area, a study of the effect a partial offset of benefits as earnings rise, rather than the all-or-nothing effect of the present application of SGA rules. The provision for SSI projects was made a permanent part of the law in 1986 (the 1985 COBRA). The DI provision — often referred to as section 505 demonstrations — was modified and extended several times; it expired in 1993.

- **The 1619 Program.** This SSI work incentive program began as a 3-year demonstration to provide special cash benefits, Medicaid, and social services to disabled recipients who had completed the trial work period and continued to have earnings in excess of the SGA level ($300 in 1980). Special cash payments would continue until countable income reached the "breakeven" level. Medicaid and social services could continue after countable income precluded payment of cash benefits. This provision was extended and ultimately, with modifications, made a permanent part of the SSI program in 1986.

- **Optional Social Services Demonstrations.** The law authorized, for a 3-year period, a program of grants to states, at state option, for demonstrations and experiments involving the provision of medical assistance and social services to severely disabled individuals with earnings in excess of SGA and who would not otherwise qualify for DI, SSI, Medicaid, or social services and who need such services to continue working.

There was also consideration, in the context of the 1980 disability bill, of alternative methods of financing vocational rehabilitation (VR) for SSI and DI beneficiaries. The House of Representatives had passed a provision that would have repealed authority of trust fund financing of VR services and that would have paid the states, from federal general revenues amounts equal to twice the state share of the costs of VR services for DI and SSI beneficiaries where those services led to the performance of SGA over a period of 12 consecutive months. However, while this legislation was pending, the administration initiated plans for an alternative system of "incentive reimbursement" under which the reimbursement funds would be allocated to states on the basis of the relative number of successful rehabilitations, with success measured in terms of two months earnings at the SGA level. (Initially, in 1979, "successful rehabilitation" was measured in terms of achievement, for at least two months, of the individual's rehabilitation goals.)

Finally, **subsequent legislation in 1980** contained provisions limiting the payment of DI benefits to incarcerated felons (SSI benefits are not generally payable to institutionalized individuals) and reallocating tax revenues from the DI program to the Old-Age and Survivors Insurance (OASI) part of the program, for which significant short-term cash flow difficulties were then projected.

In 1981, the Omnibus Budget Reconciliation Act (OBRA) included a number of provisions affecting disability benefits under DI and SSI. With regard to the DI program the amendments provided a "mega cap" which called for reducing DI benefits whenever total disability benefits from OASDI and any other public sources not based on covered earnings (such as earnings in non-covered federal, state, or local governmental employment) exceeded 80 percent of the workers' prior earnings. This provision responded to concerns about potentially excessive combined disability benefits from OASDI and other public programs not coordinated with OASDI.

In addition, the workers' compensation offset provision was made applicable to workers age 62-64. Also the prior provision, under which the federal offset would not apply if the state workers' compensation plan provided a comparable offset, was limited to apply only with respect to those states with such an offset as of February 1981.

Also, the provisions for financing VR from the DI trust fund were amended to allow for trust fund reimbursement only if the disabled beneficiary successfully engaged in SGA for 9 continuous months and if the VR services contributed to the successful return to work.

In 1982 (PL 97-455, signed 1/12/83), the Congress adopted several largely administrative changes in the DI program in response to concerns arising from the implementation of the 1980 provision relating to the continuing disability review of persons receiving disability benefits. The 1982 legislation provided that:

- on a temporary basis, persons appealing decisions that their disability had ceased could elect to have benefits and Medicare coverage continued pending review by an administrative law judge (ALJ). (This provision was later extended several times and made permanent in 1990.);

- the Secretary must provide an opportunity for a face-to-face evidentiary hearing at the reconsideration level of appeal of any decision that disability has ceased; and

- the Secretary must submit semiannual (now annual) reports to the Congress on the results of continuing disability reviews.

The first two of these provisions were not applicable to SSI since there was pre-existing authority under the Supreme Court decision in *Goldberg v. Kelly* for continued payment of SSI benefits during appeal to the ALJ level and the "reconsideration" level of appeal did not apply in these SSI cases. However, in view of the importance attached to the opportunity for a face-to-face evidentiary hearing at the reconsideration level, SSA extended this provision to SSI. In 1984, the Congress provided explicit, permanent, statutory authority for continued payment of SSI benefits in such cases during appeal to an ALJ.

The Social Security **Amendments of 1983** included numerous provisions to restore the financial soundness of the OASDI program. Provisions specifically affecting benefits based on disability included the elimination of the reduction below 71.5 percent of the deceased worker's benefit for disabled widow(er)s aged 50-60 and the continuation of benefits for certain disabled widow(er)s who remarry.

There were changes in the allocation of tax revenues between DI and OASI and a temporary provision for inter-fund borrowing under which the OASI trust fund borrowed, and later repaid, some $5 billion from the DI trust fund. Within the "ultimate" 6.2 percent OASDI tax rate for employers and employers, each, effective for 1990 and thereafter, the portion allocated to DI was reduced from 1.1 percent (set in 1977) to 0.6 percent for 1990-99 and 0.71 percent thereafter.

One 1983 provision of potentially great significance for the DI program is the gradual increase, from 65 to 67, in the age at which full retirement benefits are available, and the related increase in the amount of early retirement benefit reduction for workers claiming benefits before age 67. When the provision is fully effective, in the mid 2020s, the amount payable at age 62 will be 70 percent of the amount the worker would receive at age 67 (rather than 80 percent of the age-65 benefit, as is the case today).

Thus, not only will workers remain on the DI rolls for an additional 2 years before automatically being "converted" to the retirement rolls, there may be more older workers applying for, and becoming entitled to, disability benefits because of the change in the retirement age provisions.

In 1984, the Congress again considered disability issues and enacted a number of changes affecting interpretations of "disability" and the way in which the DI and SSI programs are administered:

- **Medical improvement standard.** Under new standards of review to be promulgated by the Secretary, DI or SSI benefits based on disability may be terminated on the basis that the impairment has ceased, no longer exists or is not disabling, only if: the individual has medically improved and is able to engage in SGA; new medical evidence and a new assessment of residual functional capacity demonstrate that, although there may be no medical improvement, the person has benefitted from advances in medical or vocational therapy or technology and is now able to perform SGA; on the basis of new or improved diagnostic techniques or evaluations the individual's impairment is not as disabling as it was considered to be at the time of the most recent disability determination and therefore the individual is able to engage in SGA; or on the basis of evidence on the record at the time of a previous determination, the earlier determination was in error.

- **Combined effect of all impairments.** In determining whether a person's impairment(s) are of such medical severity as to prevent SGA, the Secretary must consider the combined effect of all impairments, without regard to whether any one impairment, considered separately, would be considered "severe."

- **Moratorium and revision of mental impairment listings** (based on an administrative initiative announced by the Secretary on June 7, 1983). Provided for deferral of periodic reviews of mentally impaired individuals until criteria for evaluating mental disorders are revised to realistically evaluate the ability of a mentally impaired person to engage in SGA in a competitive workplace. Generally applicable to DI and SSI cases in which an initial CDR decision had not been made as of the date of enactment (October 9, 1984), cases appealed on or after June 7, 1983. While new initial determinations could be made under the old criteria, any unfavorable decisions would have to be reviewed under the new criteria. Persons with mental impairments who had unfavorable initial or CDR decisions as far back as March 1, 1981, when the CDRs mandated under the 1980 legislation began, and who reapplied within a year after enactment would retain rights to a period of disability based on their earlier status.

- **Evaluation of pain.** Provided, through 1986, for a statutory standard for evaluating cases involving pain or certain other symptoms. The statutory provision reflected current SSA policy and was intended to allow time under current practices for deliberate consideration of the issue. The law also provided for the appointment of a 12-member expert Commission on the Evaluation of Pain to study the evaluation of pain in determining whether or not a person is disabled under the DI and SSI programs and to report by the end of 1985. (The Pain Commission recommended a number of follow-up studies; the statutory provision for evaluation of pain expired and has not been replaced.)

- **Notification of CDRs and face-to-face demonstrations.** This provision requires the Secretary to provide advance notice to DI or SSI beneficiaries whose cases are selected for CDRs, including information on the nature of the review, the potential for benefit termination, and the individual's right to provide medical information for use in the review. It also provides for demonstration projects involving a personal appearance before a decision-maker prior to a decision that disability has ended.

- **Involvement of psychologist or psychiatrist.** The Secretary must make reasonable efforts to involve psychiatrists or psychologists in DI and SSI cases involving mental impairments.

- **Consultative examinations and medical evidence.** The Secretary is required to publish regulations covering standards for deciding when a consultative examination (CE) should be obtained, standards for CE referrals, and monitoring procedures. Also requires the Secretary to seek medical evidence from the treating physician before evaluating evidence from a CE and requires that a complete medical history covering at least 12 months be developed prior to a cessation determination.

- **Uniform Standards.** The Secretary is required to publish regulations setting forth uniform standards of DI and SSI disability determinations which will be binding at all levels of adjudication. (Some of the relevant materials were in the Program Operations Manual or other administrative instructions which were not necessarily binding at all levels of adjudication.)

- **Frequency of CDRs.** The Secretary is required to issue regulations establishing standards to be used in determining the frequency of CDRs. This provision was intended to facilitate scheduling of CDRs where an individual was recently found eligible after a lengthy appeal, where an individual was classified as permanently disabled, and where recovery was expected in less than 3 years. (Following court challenges and a build-up of CDR-related backlogs in 1982 and 1983, the Secretary had announced (4/14/84) a complete moratorium on CDRs, which lasted until late 1985.)

- **DDS compliance with federal law.** This provision, effective through 1987, required the Secretary to take over the functions of a state disability determination service (DDS) within 6 months of finding that the state was substantially failing to follow federal law and SSA guidelines in making disability determinations. The provision included authority for the Secretary to exceed federal personnel ceilings and waive hiring restrictions, as necessary; it also authorized preferential hiring of former DDS employees and provided for protection, to the extent feasible, of the rights of DDS employees not hired by the Secretary.

- **Vocational rehabilitation.** Modified and clarified vocational rehabilitation reimbursement provisions to provide that states will be reimbursed for cases where the individual medically recovers while in a rehabilitation program or drops out of VR without good cause and states will not be reimbursed for VR that occurs after the individual has engaged in SGA for nine months or after entitlement to DI benefits ends, whichever occurs first.

Recent Legislation: 1985-1990

Since 1984 there have been numerous, but individually relative minor, legislative changes in the OASDI disability insurance program. As noted above, several provisions enacted earlier on a temporary basis were extended and ultimately made permanent. Also, as described below, the Congress has acted on a number of technical adjustments and administrative matters affecting the DI program and on health care coverage issues affecting disabled beneficiaries.

The **Consolidated Omnibus Budget Reconciliation Act of 1985 (COBRA)**, enacted in April, 1986, included minor modifications or clarifications in the DI program to: assure that a second re-entitlement period would be available to a re-entitled disabled child on the same basis that it was available to other re-entitled disability beneficiaries; modified treatment of family benefits in cases where a non-disabled person receiving benefits on the basis of family relationship to a disabled worker beneficiary has substantial earnings that cause benefits to be withheld; and technical amendments to the 1981 offset provisions.

SSI and related Medicaid changes in the 1985 COBRA are described in the SSI legislative history.

The **1986 OBRA** included several Medicaid provisions that are described in appendix C, and the following provision for employment based health insurance:

Employer-provided health coverage. Large employers — those with 100 or more employees — must offer to any employee who is, or has a family member who is, a Medicare disabled beneficiary the same group health insurance protection that is offered to other employees. As under prior law, Medicare coverage in such a case would be secondary to the employment-based group health plan.

The **Medicare Catastrophic Coverage Act of 1988**, most of which was later repealed, included the following provision for DI and Medicare beneficiaries that remains in effect. State Medicaid programs were required to pay Medicare premiums, deductibles, and coinsurance for aged and disabled Medicare beneficiaries with incomes below the poverty level and resources at or below 200 percent of the SSI resources limits. SSI and Medicaid provisions of this Act are described in appendix C.

Other legislation **in 1988**, provided for the payment of "interim" disability benefits where the outcome of an Appeals Council review of an ALJ decision to allow benefits was delayed for more than 110 days.

The **1989 OBRA** included a provision allowing former DI beneficiaries to "buy-in" for Medicare coverage. Persons who are no longer entitled to DI benefits and regular Medicare coverage because they engage in SGA despite their continuing impairment(s) may purchase Medicare coverage during specified enrollment periods. The premiums are the same as those charged to uninsured aged persons. State Medicaid programs were required to pay, on a sliding scale, the Hospital Insurance (Medicare - Part A) premiums for eligible disabled individuals with incomes equal to 200 percent of poverty or less and resources not in excess of 200 percent of the SSI resources limits.

The **1990 OBRA** included a number of relatively minor disability insurance amendments, the more significant of which:

- made the definition of disability for disabled widow(er)s (see 1967) the same as that for disabled workers;

- modified the trial work period (TWP) to provide for disregarding trial work months that occurred before a rolling 5-year period and to make the TWP available to a disabled worker who became re-entitled to benefits;

- modified the pre-effectuation review provisions to reduce the number of mandatory reviews of favorable decisions and require some reviews of other decisions, with annual reports to Congress;

- provided for benefit continuation for disabled DI or SSI beneficiaries who recover while participating in a non-state VR program, comparable to the existing provision for those who recover while in a state VR program; and

- required the Secretary to conduct demonstration projects permitting disabled beneficiaries to select a qualified public or private rehabilitation provider to furnish them with rehabilitation services.

The 1990 OBRA also include relevant amendments in the Medicare and Medicaid programs. These amendments:

- Required the Secretary to provide information, counseling, and assistance for potentially eligible persons concerning the Medicare and Medicaid programs, Medicare supplemental (Medigap) policies, and other health insurance matters. The law also required the establishment of a national toll-free telephone information service regarding Medicare and Medigap plans and experimentation with regard to a similar state-wide service for the Medicaid, Medicare, and Medigap programs.

- Accelerated the schedule for requiring state Medicaid plans to pay Medicare premiums, deductibles, and coinsurance for Qualified Medicare Beneficiaries (QMBs), including disabled beneficiaries, with income below 100 percent of poverty and extended the provision in the future to persons with incomes of 120 percent of poverty or less.

Additional provisions in the 1990 legislation related exclusively to the SSI disability program and are described further in the SSI legislative history.

ATTACHMENT TO APPENDIX B
Definition of Disability in the Social Security Act

Before the 1967 Amendments
Section 223.
(c)(2) The term "disability" means—

(A) inability to engage in any substantial gainful activity by reason of any medically determinable physical or mental impairment which can be expected to result in death or which has lasted or can be expected to last for a continuous period of not less than 12 months; or

(B) in the case of an individual who has attained the age of 55 and is blind (within the meaning of "blindness" as defined in section 216(i)(1)), inability by reason of such blindness to engage in substantial gainful activity requiring skills or abilities comparable to those of any gainful activity in which he has previously engaged with some regularity and over a substantial period of time.

An individual shall not be considered to be under a disability unless he furnishes such proof of the existence thereof as may be required.

After the 1967 Amendments
Section 223.
(d)(1) The term "disability" means—

(A) inability to engage in any substantial gainful activity by reason of any medically determinable physical or mental impairment which can be expected to result in death or which has lasted or can be expected to last for a continuous period of not less than 12 months; or

(B) in the case of an individual who has attained the age of 55 and is blind (within the meaning of "blindness" as defined in section 216(i)(1)), inability by reason of such blindness to engage in substantial gainful activity requiring skills or abilities comparable to those of any gainful activity in which he has previously engaged with some regularity and over a substantial period of time.

(2) For purposes of paragraph (1)(A)—

(A) an individual (except a widow, surviving divorced wife, or widower for purposes of section 202(e) or (f)) shall be determined to be under a disability only if his physical or mental impairment or impairments are of such severity that he is not only unable to do his previous work but cannot, considering his age, education, and work experience, engage in any other kind of substantial gainful work which exists in the national economy, regardless of whether such work exists in the immediate area in which he lives, or whether a specific job vacancy exists for him, or whether he would be hired of he applied for work. For purposes of the preceding sentence (with respect to any individual), "work which exists in the national economy" means work which exists in significant numbers either in the region where such individual lives or in several regions of the country.

(B) A widow, surviving divorced wife, or widower shall not be determined to be under a disability (for purposes of section 202 (e) or (f)) unless his or her physical or mental impairment or impairments are of a level of severity which under regulations prescribed by the Secretary is deemed to be sufficient to preclude an individual from engaging in any gainful activity.

(3) For purposes of this subsection, a "physical or mental impairment" is an impairment that results from anatomical, physiological, or psychological abnormalities which are demonstrable by medically acceptable clinical and laboratory diagnostic techniques

(4) The Secretary shall by regulations prescribe the criteria for determining when services performed or earnings derived from services demonstrate an individual's ability to engage in substantial gainful activity. Notwithstanding the provisions of paragraph (2), an individual whose services or earnings meet such criteria shall, except for purposes of section 222(c), be found not to be disabled.

(5) An individual shall not be considered to be under a disability unless he furnishes such medical and other evidence of the existence thereof as the Secretary may require.

Current Definition of Disability

Section 223.
(d)(1) The term "disability" means—

(A) inability to engage in any substantial gainful activity be reason of any medically determinable physical or mental impairment which can be expected to result in death or which has lasted or can be expected to last for a continuous period of not less that 12 months; or

(B) in the case of an individual who has attained the age of 55 and is blind (within the meaning of "blindness" as defined in section 216 (i)(1)), inability by reason of such blindness to engage in substantial gainful activity requiring skills or abilities comparable to those of any gainful activity in which he has previously engaged with some regularity and over a substantial period of time.

(2) For purposes of paragraph (1)(A)—

(A) An individual shall be determined to be under a disability only of his physical or mental impairment or impairments are of such severity that he is not only unable to do his previous work but cannot, considering his age, education, and work experience, engage in any other kind of substantial gainful work which exists in the national economy, regardless of whether such work exists in the immediate area in which he lives, or whether a specific job vacancy exists for him, or whether he would be hired of he applied for work. For purposes of the preceding sentence (with respect to any individual), "work which exists in the national economy" means work which exists in significant numbers either in the region where such individual lives or in several regions of the country.

(B) In determining whether an individual's physical or mental impairment or impairments could be the basis of eligibility under this section, the Secretary shall consider the combined effect of all of the individual's impairments without regard to whether any such impairment, if considered separately, would be of such severity. If the Secretary does find a medically severe combination of impairments, the combined impact of the impairments shall be considered throughout the disability determination process.

(3) For purposes of this subsection, a "physical or mental impairment" is an impairment that results from anatomical, physiological, or psychological abnormalities which are demonstrable by medically acceptable clinical and laboratory diagnostic techniques.

(4) The Secretary shall by regulations prescribe the criteria for determining when services demonstrate an individual's ability to engage in substantial gainful activity. No individual who is blind shall be regarded as having demonstrated an ability to engage in substantial gainful activity on the basis of earnings that do not exceed the exempt amount under section 203(f)(8) which is applicable to individuals described in subparagraph (D) thereof. Notwithstanding the provisions of paragraph (2), an individual whose services or earnings meet such criteria shall, except for purposes of section 222(c) be found not to be disabled. In determining whether an individual is able to engage in substantial gainful activity by reason of his earnings where his disability is sufficiently severely to result in a functional limitation requiring assistance in order for him to work, there shall be excluded from such earnings an amount equal to the cost (to such individual) of any attendant care services, medical devices, equipment, prostheses, and similar items and services (not including routine drugs or routine medical services unless such drugs or services are necessary for the control of the disabling condition) which are necessary (as determined by the Secretary in regulations) for that purpose, whether or not such assistance is also needed to enable him to carry out his normal daily functions; except that the amounts to be excluded shall be subject to such reasonable limits as the Secretary may prescribe.

(5)(A) An individual shall not be considered to be under a disability unless he furnishes such medical and other evidence of the existence thereof as the Secretary may require. An individual's statement as to pain or other symptoms shall not alone be conclusive evidence of disability as defined in this section; there must be medical signs and findings, established by medically acceptable clinical or laboratory diagnostic techniques, which show the existence of a medical impairment that results from anatomical, physiological, or psychological abnormalities which could reasonably be expected to produce the pain or other symptoms alleged and which, when considered with all evidence required to be furnished under this paragraph (including statements of the individual or his physician as to as to the intensity and persistence of such pain or other symptoms which may reasonably be accepted as consistent with the medical signs and findings), would lead to a conclusion that the individual is under a disability. Any non-federal hospital, clinic, laboratory, or other provider of medical services, or physician not in the employ of the federal government, which supplies medical evidence required and requested by the Secretary under this paragraph shall be entitled to payment from the Secretary for the reasonable cost of providing such evidence.

(B) In making any determination with respect to whether an individual is under a disability or continues to be under a disability, the Secretary shall consider all evidence available in such individual's case record, and shall develop a complete medical history of at least the preceding twelve months for any case in which a determination is made that the individual is not under a disability. In making any determination the Secretary shall make every reasonable effort to obtain from the individual's treating physician (or other treating health care provider) all medical evidence, including diagnostic tests, necessary in order to properly make such determination, prior to evaluating medical evidence obtained from any other source on a consultative basis.

(6)(A) Notwithstanding any other provision of this title, any physical or mental impairment which arises in connection with the commission by an individual (after the date of enactment of this paragraph) of an offense which constitutes a felony under applicable law and for which such individual is subsequently convicted, or which is aggravated in connection with such an offense (but only to the extent so aggravated), shall not be considered in determining whether an individual is under a disability.

(B) Notwithstanding any other provision of this title, any physical or mental impairment which arises in connection with an individual's confinement in a jail, prison, or other penal institution or correctional facility pursuant to such individual's conviction of an offense (committed after the date of the enactment of this paragraph) constituting a felony under applicable law, or which is aggravated in connection with such a confinement (but only to the extent so aggravated), shall not be considered in determining whether such individual is under a disability for purposes of benefits payable for any month during which such individual is so confined.

Appendix C: Legislative Development of the Supplemental Security Income Program

Background and Early Federal Legislation: 1930s and 1940s

The **1935 Committee on Economic Security** made a number of observations and recommendations dealing with problems of poverty, unemployment, illness and incapacity, but did not include any recommendation regarding federal programs for cash assistance for working-age persons with disabilities. They recommended, and the Social Security Act of 1935 included, federal matching grant programs to assist the states in providing public assistance payments for needy persons age 65 and older and to fatherless children in financial need. The question of relief for persons with disabilities who were not able to work was addressed in the broader context of "residual relief" and relief for "unemployables."

The Committee suggested that the federal government should assume primary responsibility for providing work for those able and willing to work and they suggested that responsibility for "residual relief" should rest with the states. The 1935 report states: "As for the genuine unemployables, or near unemployables, we believe the sound policy is to return the responsibility for their care and guidance to the states." The notion of 'returning' responsibility presumably referred to the availability, in 1935, under the Federal Emergency Relief Act, of federal grants to help states meet the costs of their emergency relief programs. (For a more detailed discussion and rationale, see the excerpts from the Committee's report, attached at the end of this appendix.)

The **Social Security Act of 1935** included, in addition to the Old-Age and Survivors Insurance (OASI), old-age assistance programs and unemployment compensation, provisions for federal-state assistance programs of Aid to the Blind (AB) (with no federal age requirements) and Aid to Dependent Children (ADC), including a dependent child under age 16, who is deprived of parental support due to the physical or mental incapacity of a parent. The ADC population (the Aid to Families with Dependent Children (AFDC) population, after 1962) could and often did (prior to implementation of Supplemental Security Income (SSI) in 1974) include needy children with disabilities.

The original Social Security Act also included provisions for maternal and child health, disabled children's services, child welfare services, enhanced public health service programs, and vocational rehabilitation programs, which might be expected to be of particular value to children and adults with disabilities.

The **1938 Advisory Council on Social Security** focused almost entirely on modifications in OASI and ways to enhance that social insurance program. While it agreed in principle on the social desirability of providing social insurance benefits to insured persons who become permanently and totally disabled, it did not make any specific recommendation for such a program. It did not address, separately, the provision of public assistance to needy persons with disabilities.

The **Social Security Amendments of 1939** included several relevant provisions. First, funding for **vocational rehabilitation** was substantially increased (from $1.938 million to $3.5 million) and the program was extended to Puerto Rico. The Senate Finance Committee report, in discussing the need for this amendment, included several observations:

- An estimated 3 percent of the general population is disabled — nearly 4 million persons.

- Some 800,000 persons become physically disabled annually due to accidents or disease. According to vocational rehabilitation experience:

  - about two-thirds are able to make their own employment adjustment; and

  - about one-third (over 260,000) require rehabilitation services "to aid them to engage in remunerative employment."

- Disabled persons who require assistance in their employment adjustment include:

  - those who, with training and other rehabilitative services, can return to competitive employment (some 60,000 annually);

  - those who can be trained in small business enterprises or sheltered workshops (about 150,000 annually); and

  - those so severely disabled that, if they are to be employed at all, must be provided with suitable work in their homes.

The Committee suggested that the first group, those who could reenter competitive employment, constituted the most pressing problem and that virtually all of this group could and should be rehabilitated to complete self-support.

Second, the definition of dependent child for purposes of the ADC program was revised to include individuals aged 17-18, if regularly attending school. (The school attendance requirement was dropped in 1956.) Also, the term "needy" was added to the law characterizing recipients under the various federal-state assistance programs.

Third, administrative safeguards were added to the program of Aid to the Blind (and to the other assistance titles): to provide for merit personnel standards in the administering state agencies; to restrict disclosure of information about applicants for and recipients of aid; and to facilitate financial adjustments between the states and the federal government in situations where the state is able to recover assistance payments from a recipient or his/her estate.

Although there was no further major legislation in this area for a number of years, the question of additional federal assistance remained under consideration. For example, in 1941, the Federal Security Agency published a *Brief in Support of a Recommendation in Favor of a Category of General Public Assistance To Be Added to the Social Security Act*, a report of the Family Security Committee, a group of experts from within and outside the government that had been appointed to advise the Director of Defense Health and Welfare Services (the wartime title of Paul McNutt, Administrator of the Federal Security Agency, which had federal jurisdiction for the public assistance programs).

In support of a strong recommendation for a federal/state matching program of general assistance, the Committee cited, among other points: the non-inclusive character of the existing categorical assistance programs; the need for a comprehensive approach to public welfare; the fiscal and other difficulties of the states in meeting current assistance needs in the absence of additional federal financial participation; and administrative simplification and fairness.

Although various limited and temporary programs for special war-related relief were adopted during the war years, this was not generally a time for major public welfare initiatives or additional federal spending in this area. Following the war, in 1947, the Senate Finance Committee appointed a special

Advisory Council to consider Social Security and public assistance issues.

The **1948 Advisory Council on Social Security** recommended establishment of a non-categorical federal-state matching public assistance program. Such a program would include, but not be limited to, needy persons with disabilities. They also recommended federal financial participation in medical care for assistance recipients. In addition, this Council recommended disability insurance benefits for the permanently and totally disabled, through the OASI system and considered, but did not recommend, a federal program for temporary disability insurance (TDI).

Aid to the Permanently and Totally Disabled: The 1950s

In line with the recommendations of the 1948 Advisory Council on Social Security, the Truman administration recommended, in 1949, provisions for both a federal/state general assistance program and disability benefits under the OASI program (Social Security) for extended disability. The administration also recommended a federal temporary disability insurance program. However, the final Social Security legislation in 1950 did not include any of the recommendations relating to disability insurance.

The **Social Security Act Amendments of 1950** did, however, include provisions for: a program of federal-state public assistance payments for Aid to the Permanently and Totally Disabled (APTD); federal matching payments for medical vendor payments made on behalf of assistance recipients, including needy blind and disabled persons; federal matching funds for expenditures for assistance to aged, blind, and disabled persons in public medical institutions (other than institutions for mental illness and tuberculosis); and extended federal assistance for categorical aid to Puerto Rico and the Virgin Islands.

Under the original APTD program, federal matching payments were available for aid to persons aged 18 or older who were found by the state to be permanently and totally disabled, however, no definition of disability for this purpose was included in the federal law. The Social Security Administration (SSA) did, however, issue guidelines for the states to use in their APTD programs. It stated:

> Total disability did not have to mean complete incapacity but rather a substantial inability to engage in one's usual productive work, including homemaking. Permanent disability meant the likelihood rather than near-certainty that the individual would not be able to regain his or her ability to engage in productive work; medical procedures and vocational rehabilitation might be instrumental toward the latter end.

Under the law, "aid" for the purpose of the APTD program included: money payments to needy individuals; medical care on their behalf; or "any type of remedial care recognized under state law" on their behalf. The federal law specifically excluded from the definition of APTD payments to or care on behalf of: any person in a public institution (except as a patient in a medical institution); any person who is a patient in an institution for tuberculosis or mental illness; or any person who has been diagnosed as having tuberculosis or psychosis and is a patient in a medical institution as a result of that diagnosis.

The 1950 legislation also amended the AB program to provide for an optional disregard of up to $50 of earned income per month through June 1952, and a mandatory $50 earnings disregard for the blind thereafter. (In the case of the disabled, as had previously been the rule for the blind, states were required to take account of any other income and resources, without exceptions, in determining need.) The 1950 legislation also required states to use optometrists or physicians skilled in diseases of the eye in making determinations of blindness.

By June 30, 1951, 38 states had approved APTD plans in operation; by the end of 1959, 45 states were participating in the program. State general assistance caseloads declined in the early 1950s (from 866,000 in 1950 to 587,000 in 1952) as the APTD rolls grew. The APTD rolls grew steadily by 20,000 to 40,000 per year throughout the 1950s, reaching 369,000 in 1960. (The state general assistance rolls hovered in the 700,000 to 900,000 range during the mid-1950s, and rose sharply after 1957, to nearly 1.25 million in 1960.)

There were numerous amendments to the public assistance programs, including AB and APTD, during **the 1950s**, relating to incentives, social services, matching provisions, compliance issues, etc. The **1956 amendments** provided for separate federal (50-50) matching for medical vendor payments and encouraged the provision of services designed to help needy blind or disabled persons to attain self-support and self-care by specifying that federal matching for administrative expenses included state agency costs of furnishing such services. Legislation **in 1958** further strengthened federal financial participation in the categorical public assistance programs and extended the programs to Guam.

The 1960s

The **1960 legislation** established the Kerr-Mills program of medical assistance for the aged (MAA). This legislation increased federal funding for medical services (vendor payments) for persons getting Old-Age Assistance (OAA) and authorized federal matching for medical assistance for the aged who, though not eligible for cash assistance, were medically indigent. Although the 1960 provisions did not affect the blind and disabled, they were viewed as a first step in strengthening medical assistance for the needy. In 1962, the more favorable federal matching for assistance recipients became available to the blind and disabled under the new Title XVI assistance program for the aged, blind, and disabled.

Also in 1960, the program of Aid to the Blind (AB) was amended, effective in 1962, to increase the monthly earned income disregard from $50 to $85, and to provide for disregarding one-half of any earned income above that amount.

In 1962, the law was amended to give substantial new emphasis to the provision of services to assistance recipients and to make other program improvements. The 1962 provisions affecting the blind and disabled included the following changes:

- The federal matching rate was increased from 50 to 75 percent for: services to blind or disabled applicants or recipients to help them attain or retain capability for self-support and self-care; other services specified by the Secretary as likely to prevent or reduce dependency; specified services for persons who have been or are likely to become applicants for or recipients of aid as blind or disabled; and training for personnel of the state or local agency administering the program. (Specifically excluded from matching funds under this provision were the services of state vocational rehabilitation (VR) agencies which were funded and made available to the AB and APTD populations under the VR Act.)

- A new public assistance title, Title XVI, allowed state "adult" assistance programs to be administered on a combined basis. For the combined OAA, AB, and APTD programs under this new Title XVI, the provision of separate additional federal funds for vendor payments for medical care were extended to the blind and disabled, as well as to the aged. The provision for up to 42 days of medical care in a medical institution for persons with a diagnosis of tuberculosis or psychosis, previously available only to the aged, was extended to the blind and disabled under Title XVI.

- The aged, the blind and the disabled received a mandatory disregard of expenses attributable to the earning of income. For the blind, in addition to the earnings disregard (enacted in 1960, and mandatory after June 1962) of $85, plus 50 percent of any additional earnings, any income or resources necessary to fulfill a plan for achieving self-support (PASS) would be disregarded for up to one year. Applicants aged 65 or older, received an optional provision for disregarding up to $10 of the first $50 of earnings, as well as one half of any remainder.

- A waiver of state plan requirements was provided for demonstration projects (Section 1115 waiver demonstrations).

- States were allowed to disregard, in their AFDC programs (renamed in 1962), earnings or other income that is set aside for future identifiable needs of a dependent child, such as his or her education.

- Federal matching funds were allowed for aid to a second (incapacitated or unemployed) parent in an AFDC household.

The **Social Security Amendments of 1965** created the Medicaid program and made other significant changes in public assistance programs affecting needy blind and disabled persons.

Medicaid. The legislation provided for combining all of the medical assistance provisions for public assistance recipients in a new "Title XIX" and provided increased federal matching for medical assistance under this new Medicaid program. Prior medical assistance (MAA and vendor payments) would be phased out (by 1970) and medical assistance under the new Medicaid program would be available to all cash assistance recipients, and, with a state option, to the medically needy as well.

Under the new program (as under MAA) there was no dollar ceiling on federal matching. Also, the new law provided for modifications and flexibility in the income and resource determinations for Medicaid purposes.

Income Disregards. The legislation provided for: a permanent disregard in all the assistance titles of not more than $5 per person to accommodate the Social Security benefit increase (7 percent, but not less than $4); and an optional disregard of the retroactive amounts of the 1965 benefit increases. Also, optional earnings disregards for the aged were increased to $20 plus 50 percent of the next $60 of earnings; optional earnings disregards were provided for the disabled. In addition, for the disabled, any additional income and resources could be exempted as part of an approved plan to achieve self-support (PASS) during the period the person was undergoing vocational rehabilitation.

Other. Restrictions on federal matching for needy blind and disabled who had tuberculosis or psychosis and were treated in general medical institutions were removed.

The Supplemental Security Income Program: The 1970s

In 1974, the federal Supplemental Security Income program, with provision for supplementary payments by the states, replaced the former federal-state matching programs of aid to the aged, blind, and disabled in the 50 states and the District of Columbia. The SSI program with nationally uniform income and resources standards and other eligibility requirements, uses essentially the same definition of disability as that used in the Social Security disability insurance (DI) program. The federal SSI program is financed from federal general revenues, with any State supplementation funded entirely by the state.

SSI, unlike the DI program (and state APTD programs before it), provides benefits based on disability to persons under age 18. (Prior to SSI, needy disabled children were generally included in states' AFDC programs rather than the assistance programs for disabled persons. According to the Ways and Means Committee report on the original SSI legislation, blind and disabled children in low-income households were included in the SSI program because they were "certainly among the most disadvantaged of all Americans" and "deserved special assistance in order to help them become self-supporting members of our society."

The **1972 legislation** establishing the SSI program grew, in part from the Administration's recommendations, beginning in 1969, for a federal "Family Assistance Plan" to replace the AFDC program and to provide for the "working poor." As it became increasingly apparent that the administration's original recommendations were encountering serious hurdles in Congress, it became clear that there was growing support for federalization, under SSA, of the adult assistance programs of old-age assistance (OAA), AB and APTD. The populations served by these programs were seen to overlap significantly with those already served by SSA, these programs were considered to be more stable and less controversial than the programs of assistance for families with children, and there were not the same concerns about work requirements, child care, training programs, and so on.

The SSI program, as established under the Social Security Amendments of 1972 (and modified in 1973), took effect in 1974 replacing, in the 50 states and the District of Columbia, the state matching programs of assistance to needy aged, blind and disabled persons. As noted above, SSI also assumed responsibility for needy disabled children, many of whom were previously included in state AFDC programs. Under SSI, the federal government enforced new rules:

- There were nationally uniform rules regarding the amounts of income and resources a person (or couple) could have and still be eligible for benefits, and uniform disregards of income/earnings in calculating payments. While there had been some interest in assuring that an aged individual (or couple) with no other income (or with only Social Security, up to $20 of which could be disregarded under the general income disregard) would be at or above national poverty levels, this was not achieved under the federal benefit rate (FBR) established for the program. However, the legislation did require that where a recipient received a higher payment in December 1973 than he would receive under the federal SSI program, states would be required to supplement to maintain the individual's prior income level.

- Age 65 was established as the age requirement for benefits based on age.

- As under most prior state programs, regular SSI payments would not be made to persons who were inmates of public institutions. However, a special payment (up to $25 per month, later $30) was payable to otherwise eligible individuals in medical facilities covered by Medicaid.

- The definitions of blindness and disability that were used in the DI program were to be used in the SSI program for the blind and disabled. Congress recognized that there might be difficulties in applying the regular DI definition in the case of the young children who might be eligible for SSI benefits based on disability. Disability determinations were rarely, if ever, made for young children under the DI program. The new law extended the definition of disability to children with language providing, "in the case of a child under the age of 18, if he suffers from any medically determinable physical or mental impairment of comparable severity."

The SSI program, like many of the federal/state programs it replaced, also included provisions to encourage rehabilitation and work among blind and disabled beneficiaries. The nationally uniform provisions in the new SSI law included:

- Payment (from federal general revenues) for the full cost of Vocational Rehabilitation (VR) services for beneficiaries. Non-payment of benefits to blind or disabled persons who refused to accept such services or who refused appropriate treatment for alcohol or drug addiction.

- Disregard of grants, scholarships, fellowships, etc. that are used solely for paying tuition or fees as countable income. And, disregard of the earnings of children who were students, subject to limitation by the Secretary.

- Disregard of the first $60 per month of earnings and one-half of any additional earnings and exclusion from resources of certain property that was determined to be essential to income-producing activities.

- Disregard of earned income and certain resources of a blind or disabled recipient that were necessary for an approved plan for achieving self-support (PASS).

As the national assistance program of "last resort," income from virtually all other sources was counted in calculating individual benefits, and persons were required to apply for any benefits that they might be eligible for under other programs. In recognition of the inability of many applicants to withstand administrative delays in payment of benefits, the law also provided for: an advance payment of up to $100 against future benefits for which a person would likely become eligible; and up to three months' payments to applicants if a presumption could be made that their impairment(s) would meet the definition of blindness or disability and they were otherwise eligible.

The SSI program included provisions for state supplementation of the basic SSI payment. In general, states in which payment levels under the prior programs had exceeded those under the federal SSI program were required to maintain prior levels and special "hold-harmless" provisions were included to protect states from any possible cost increases as a result of the SSI program. The law also allowed for federal administration, at no cost to the states, of state supplements, where the state plan used roughly the same rules as the federal program.

The new program also addressed the question of relationships with other programs, such as Food Stamps and Medicaid. There was a lot of discussion during the legislative process of cashing out the food stamp program and it was initially anticipated that SSI recipients would not be eligible for Food Stamps. This provision was modified, however, in 1973, before the SSI program took effect. With respect to Medicaid, the law required states to provide coverage for the aged, blind and disabled using either SSI eligibility criteria or, at state option ("209(b)" states), more restrictive criteria used by the state in January 1972. For states using SSI criteria, SSA would make the eligibility determination on behalf of the state, if the state so desired.

A number of other changes were adopted **in 1973**. One related to the upcoming conversion of state APTD rolls to SSI. First, it may be worth noting that in the years immediately preceding 1974, the number of recipients of APTD grew annually by more than 100,000. Also, since it was recognized that some persons on the state APTD rolls might not meet the Social Security definition of disability in the federal SSI program, a special "grandfather" provision was included in the 1972 law to protect persons who had met the state definition of disability, but could not meet the federal definition. A concern developed in 1973, that some states were making extraordinary efforts to "load up" their APTD rolls in anticipation of the federal takeover. In response to this concern, the grandfather provision was amended in 1973 so that it would apply only to persons on the state rolls in December 1973 who had also been on the state assistance rolls in or before July 1973. The provisions for grand-fathering income and resources rules of the former state plans were restricted to persons who remained in the state and remained otherwise eligible for SSI.

Mid and Late 1970s

During this period, there were numerous relatively technical amendments to the SSI program. Many of these had to do with income disregards and with relationships with other programs. For example, provisions were included to exclude certain property held in trust for Indian tribes from resources, to disregard certain disaster assistance, and to exclude housing assistance from income.

Several of the changes in this period suggested that there were greater administrative difficulties in program implementation and operation than had been anticipated. For example, provision was made for reimbursement to the states for interim assistance that the state furnished while an SSI claim was pending. Also, provision was made for continuing payments to disabled persons who did not meet the conditions for the "grandfather" provision and for whom a new disability determination would be needed.

In 1973, the federal benefit rate was increased on an ad hoc basis to account for sudden sharp increases in the Consumer Price Index (CPI). In 1974, provisions for automatic cost-of-living adjustments (COLAs) were included in the SSI program to take effect in 1975.

Legislation in 1976 provided for referral of blind and disabled children under age 16 for rehabilitative services and for presumptive eligibility for the blind. Provision was also made to protect the Medicaid eligibility for persons who lost SSI eligibility because of Social Security COLAs and to require states to pass along federal SSI benefit increases to recipients of state supplements.

The 1980s

During the 1980s, major areas of legislative activity affecting the blind and disabled under SSI related to rehabilitation and work incentives and administrative matters regarding interpretation and implementation of the disability provisions. In many cases the issues and legislative solutions in SSI were essentially the same as those affecting the DI program. As is noted below, where legislative provisions were enacted that affected both the SSI and the DI programs, they are more fully discussed in the DI legislative history (appendix B).

The Social Security Disability **Amendments of 1980** included, on a 3-year demonstration basis, the SSI work incentive provisions that have come to be referred to as "Section 1619." This provision, which calls for continuing a person's SSI disability status, regardless of his/her demonstrated ability to engage in substantial gainful activity (SGA), was subsequently extended and, in 1986, modified and made a permanent part of the SSI program.

Over the preceding years there had been growing concern about work disincentives in the SSI program generally. Since the level of earnings that was considered substantial gainful activity, and therefore indicative of non-disability status was close to the federal SSI benefit rate and much less than the regular break-even level. It was difficult to justify terminating benefits for persons who so demonstrably could not be considered to be self-supporting. Regardless of the conceptual validity of a test of SGA in a program intended to pay benefits only to persons who are unable to work, such a test could not be sustained in a needs-based program of last resort when it meant terminating payments to persons who were obviously severely impaired and who had countable income below the cut-off levels for assistance based on financial need.

The essential elements of the 1619 provision are:

- extension of cash and Medicaid benefits to individuals whose earnings preclude regular eligibility for SSI (under the earnings disregards); and

- extension of Medicaid coverage to individuals whose earnings, although high enough to preclude eligibility for SSI or 1619(a) may not be enough to provide for medical care.

Additional provisions relating only to the SSI program included counting sheltered workshop income as earned rather than unearned income and ending parent-to-child deeming of income in the case of a disabled child aged 18-22 who is a student and lives with his/her parents. In general, parental income may be deemed available to a disabled son or daughter only if the son or daughter is under age 18 and lives with his/her parent. With enactment of this change, all disabled persons over age 18 are treated as adult individuals and parental deeming does not apply.

The 1980 amendments also included provisions for tightening administration of the both SSI and the DI programs and enhancing work incentives in both programs. These provisions are described in further detail in the DI legislative history. The major administrative provisions included: pre-effectuation review (PER) of up to 65 percent of state agency allowances; periodic (triennial) reviews of continuing disability (CDRs) among disabled beneficiaries whose disabilities may not be permanent; and performance standards and procedures for the state disability determination process to be established by regulations.

Provisions intended to enhance rehabilitation and work incentives included deducting the amount of impairment-related work expenses (IRWE), such as medical devices and attendant care, from earnings in determining whether a DI or SSI claimant or beneficiary is engaging in SGA, and continuing benefits for DI or SSI beneficiaries who medically recover while in an approved vocational rehabilitation program.

The 1980 legislation also provided temporary demonstration authority for SSI and DI studies. The law provided temporary authority to waive provisions in the law to conduct studies of potential work incentive provisions, including, in the DI area, a study of the effect of a partial offset of benefits as earnings rise, rather than the all-or-nothing effect of the present application of SGA rules. The provision for SSI projects was made a permanent part of the law in 1986 (COBRA 1985). The DI provision, often referred to as Section 505 demonstrations, was modified and extended several times; it expired in October 1993.

Numerous, individually minor, SSI amendments were adopted **in 1980-82**, including, in 1981, retrospective monthly accounting in place of a prospective quarterly accounting system for determining eligibility and benefit amounts.

Also, **in 1981**, the provisions for general revenue reimbursement to states for VR for SSI recipients were amended to allow for such reimbursement only if the disabled person successfully engaged in SGA for nine continuous months and if the VR services contributed to the successful return to work.

Another SSI provision in 1981 changed the way the break even level would be figured for purposes of the Section 1619(b) part of the 3-year demonstration program. The change, which presumably conformed to separate provisions for funding Title XX social services through a block grant to the states, was to exclude from countable income the value of benefits under Title XX in determining whether an individual had sufficient income to meet his health care needs without Medicaid.

In 1982, the Congress adopted several largely administrative changes in the DI program in response to concerns arising from the implementation of the 1980 provision relating to the continuing disability review of persons getting disability benefits. This 1982 legislation provided, among other changes discussed further in the DI legislative history, that first, on a temporary basis, persons appealing decisions that their disability had ceased could elect to have DI benefits and Medicare coverage continued pending review by an administrative law judge (ALJ) and second, the Secretary must provide an opportunity for a face-to-face evidentiary hearing at the reconsideration level of appeal of any decision that disability has ceased. These provisions were not technically applicable to SSI since there was pre-existing authority under the Supreme Court decision in *Goldberg* v. *Kelly* for continued payment of SSI benefits pending appeal to the ALJ level and the "reconsideration" level of appeal did not apply in these SSI cases. However, in view of the importance attached to the opportunity for a face-to-face evidentiary hearing at the reconsideration level, SSA extended this provision to SSI. In 1984, the Congress provided explicit, permanent, authority for continued payment of SSI benefits in such cases during appeal to an ALJ.

In 1983, the July 1983 COLA was replaced by a special $20 increase in the FBR ($30 for couples); future COLAs were scheduled on a January-to-January basis, instead of the previous July-to-July schedule. This legislation included provision for up to three months payments to otherwise eligible persons residing temporarily in public emergency shelters for the homeless and for the exclusion from income of in-kind, needs-based assistance provided by private, non-profit organizations.

The 1983 amendments also contained a provision requiring the Secretary to notify all elderly Social Security beneficiaries who might be eligible for SSI of the availability of SSI benefits and to notify all beneficiaries under age 65 of the availability of SSI at the same time they are notified with respect to potential eligibility for Supplementary Medical Insurance (Part B of Medicare).

The **1984 disability amendments** included a number of changes affecting interpretations of "disability" and the way in which the DI and SSI programs are administered. These provisions, which are described more fully in the DI legislative history, included:

- New "medical improvement" standards of review, to be promulgated by the Secretary, to be used in determining when DI or SSI benefits based on disability may be terminated on the basis that the impairment has ceased, no longer exists or is not disabling.

- A requirement that the Secretary must consider the combined effect of all impairments, without regard to whether any one impairment, considered separately, would be considered "severe."

- Instructions to the Secretary regarding revision of mental impairment listings and a moratorium on denials or terminations based on existing listings. Requirements for the involvement of psychologists or psychiatrists in DI and SSI cases involving mental impairments.

- Modification in vocational rehabilitation provisions to provide that states will be reimbursed for cases where the individual medically recovers while in a rehabilitation program or drops out of VR without good cause.

In separate 1984 legislation, a schedule of increases in SSI resource limits was adopted so that by 1989 the limits would be $2,000 for individuals and $3,000 for couples, as they are today.

The **Consolidated Omnibus Budget Reconciliation Act of 1985 (COBRA)**, enacted in April 1986, included modifications to protect the Medicaid status of certain disabled widow(er)s who lost SSI eligibility because of entitlement to higher Social Security benefits and authorize SSA to administer state supplementary payments provided to residents of Medicaid facilities in cases in which the federal payment was limited to $25 (sometimes referred to as a personal needs allowance).

The 1985 COBRA also included a Medicaid provision dealing with the issue of trust income. It provided, essentially, that for purposes of determining Medicaid eligibility for persons not eligible for SSI, the entire amount of the trust that could be distributed to the beneficiary would count as income or resources, except where undue hardship would result.

The **1986 Employment Opportunities for Disabled Americans Act** (P.L. 99-643) included numerous significant changes in the SSI program. The 1619 work incentives program was made permanent, and numerous related incentive provisions were included. Those provisions:

Modification of 1619 program. The provisions for a trial work period and for an "extended period of eligibility" would no longer apply to the SSI program. Barriers to movement between regular SSI status and status under sections 1619(a) and 1619(b) were removed. A CDR would be required within 12 months of an individual's becoming eligible under 1619. An individual could be reinstated to regular SSI benefits or benefits under 1619 if, within the previous 12 months he had become ineligible for 1619 benefits because of a nonmedical reason. In considering whether a persons earnings could provide the equivalent of his/her publicly funded disability and health benefits, the value of publicly funded attendant care would be considered and IRWE and PASS would be disregarded.

Eligibility of blind and disabled persons while institutionalized. A blind or disabled person receiving benefits under section 1619 may remain eligible for SSI benefits based on the full FBR for the first 2 months in which he is in a medical or psychiatric institution, but only if the institution agrees that the individual will not be required to use such benefits to help pay for the cost of care. The purpose of the provision was to permit persons who have been working to continue to receive their SSI benefits during short periods of hospitalization.

Medicaid eligibility. This provision assures that persons getting benefits under section 1619(a) will continue to have Medicaid coverage in those "209(b)" states which base Medicaid eligibility on

December 1972 rules and which did not previously provide Medicaid to 1619 recipients. The 1986 OBRA extended comparable protection for persons in 1619(b) states.

Other provisions. Other provisions of this law include: a requirement for notification to potentially eligible applicants and recipients of the provisions of section 1619; protection of the Medicaid status of certain persons who lost SSI eligibility because of entitlement to higher benefits as disabled adult children under DI; and modification of the treatment of certain couples in medical institutions.

The **1986 OBRA** included a number of relevant health care provisions. Those provisions:

New (optional) Medicaid category. The legislation provided for a new optional categorically needy group, for Medicaid purposes, consisting of persons age 65 and older or disabled (as defined for SSI purposes) whose incomes (after SSI exclusions including IRWE but not including other costs of medical or remedial care) do not exceed levels to be established by states, but not in excess of the non-farm poverty level. States which establish such a Medicaid category must provide persons in this category the same package of benefits offered to other categorically needy Medicaid recipients.

Medicaid coverage of certain working disabled. This provisions requires states to provide Medicaid coverage for persons who work despite severe impairments and who previously received SSI benefits based on disability or blindness, state supplementary payments, or special SSI payments under Section 1619(a) and who meet certain other requirements.

Effect of certain trusts on certain persons with mental impairments. The 1985 COBRA had specified that, for purposes of determining Medicaid eligibility for persons who were not categorically eligible (i.e., automatically eligible for Medicaid because they were eligible for cash assistance such as SSI) the states would count as income or resources amounts that could be distributed from a "Medicaid qualifying trust," whether or not such amounts were actually distributed, except where undue hardship would result. (A Medicaid qualifying trust is a trust established by an individual or his spouse with himself as a beneficiary and with a trustee who has discretion in making payments to the individual.) The 1986 OBRA excluded from this provision trusts that were established prior to April 7, 1986 in the case of residents of intermediate care facilities for the mentally retarded (ICF/MR).

The **1993 OBRA** made three further exceptions to the Medicaid qualifying trust provision. Excluded are trusts containing a disabled individual's (under age 65) assets: set up by a parent, grandparent, legal guardian or court; managed by a nonprofit agency; or those for any individual if the trust is composed only of the individual's pension, Social Security and other income. Any amounts remaining in the excluded trust after the individual's death are to be used to reimburse the state for medical assistance provided the individual.

Also, the **immigration reform legislation of 1986** included provisions affecting SSI, by increasing the potentially eligible population that might be expected to apply for benefits. The legislation made it possible for various categories of aliens (certain persons who had been present in the United States for a period of time and certain agricultural workers) to achieve "lawful temporary resident" status and eventually "lawful permanent resident" status. And although the law general limited federal/state assistance in the case of those granted temporary status, this limitation did not apply to SSI and Medicaid benefits. As a practical matter, however, no immediate upsurge in applications materialized as a result of this legislation.

The **1987 OBRA** included several provisions affecting blind and disabled persons under SSI. Those provisions:

- Increased the maximum emergency advance SSI payment from $100 to the amount of the FBR.

- Applied interim assistance reimbursement arrangements with the states in cases involving SSI benefit suspensions and terminations as well as initial eligibility determinations, as under prior law.

- Established special procedures governing notifications to blind applicants and recipients, including, depending on the individual's preference, sending all notices affecting his rights under the SSI program by certified mail, or with a telephone call follow up, or using such other arrangements as might be worked out with the beneficiary. (Although SSA already had special procedures for communicating with blind applicants and recipients there was some concern that the procedures were not effective.)

- Increased from six to nine the number of months a person living in a public shelter for the homeless can be eligible for SSI benefits.

- Permitted continued payment of SSI based on the full FBR to individuals who are institutionalized in a medical facility if the expected period of institutionalization is not likely to exceed three months and if the continued receipt of benefits is needed to maintain living arrangements to which the person may return.

- Protected Medicaid eligibility of disabled SSI recipients who may lose SSI when they qualify for Social Security benefits as non-disabled widow(er)s at ages 60-64.

- Authorized demonstration programs to be carried out by the states to ensure that homeless individuals are aware of the availability of SSI and other programs under the Social Security Act. The provision, which was never fully implemented, was designed to test the effectiveness of outreach teams made up of case workers from state adult social services agencies, consultative medical examiners from the DDS, and SSA claims representatives.

- Increased the SSI benefit rate for individuals in medical institutions, where Medicaid pays at least half the cost of their care, from $25 to $30 per month and required that states that supplement this "personal needs allowance" pass through the increase to the individuals.

- Provided that, for purposes of the Medicaid plan option to cover in-home services for children age 18 or younger, if the cost of doing so would be less than caring for the child in a hospital or skilled nursing intermediate care facility, the child need only be eligible for Medicaid if he or she was in an institution, rather than having to be eligible for SSI or state supplementary payment if institutionalized.

In addition, the 1987 McKinney Homeless Assistance Act included a provision which required organizations that operate facilities under the Emergency Assistance for the Homeless and Chronically Mentally Ill Individuals Block Grant program to assist the homeless in applying for aid from programs such as SSI and Food Stamps and requires such organizations to serve, at the request of the Secretary of Health and Human Services, as representative payees for SSI recipients.

The **Medicare Catastrophic Coverage Act of 1988,** most of which was later repealed, included some relevant provisions that remained in effect. Those provisions:

- Required state Medicaid programs to pay Medicare premiums, deductibles, and coinsurance for aged and disabled Medicare beneficiaries with incomes below the poverty level and resources at or below 200 percent of the SSI resources limits.

- Repealed SSI transfer of asset provisions and revised comparable provisions for Medicaid.

- Protected income and resources of a "community spouse" by requiring state Medicaid programs to allow the non-institutionalized spouse to retain a certain proportion of the institutionalized spouse's income and resources.

Also, the 1988 McKinney Homeless Assistance amendments provided for a new Department of Labor program of Jobs for Employable Dependent Individuals (JEDI) which included an incentive bonus system for states for successful job placement of recipients of means-tested benefits, including SSI.

Additional legislation in 1988 provided for the payment of "interim" disability benefits under both DI and SSI where the outcome of an Appeals Council review of an ALJ decision to allow benefits was delayed for more than 110 days and called for reports to Congress concerning DI and SSI claims involving AIDS and AIDS-related complex.

The **1989 OBRA** included a number of provisions relating exclusively to the SSI program:

Outreach to children. The Secretary was required to establish an ongoing program of outreach to children who are potentially eligible for SSI on the basis of disability or blindness. In so doing the Secretary is to work with agencies and organizations, including school systems, that focus on the needs of children and have knowledge of potential SSI recipients.

Children of persons in the armed forces stationed overseas. Provided for continuing SSI eligibility for children of military personnel who live with their parents who are on permanent duty assignment outside the United States. (Further legislation, in 1993, made comparable provision for military personnel stationed in Puerto Rico.)

"Kalleigh Mulligan" deeming waiver. Provides that the deeming of parental income to be available to a child who lives with his/her parents will not apply in certain cases where a disabled child who, if institutionalized, would be eligible for the SSI personal needs allowance receives medical care at home under a Medicaid state home care plan. If the application of the usual provisions for deeming parental income and resources to be available to the child would cause such a child to lose SSI eligibility, then the child receive benefits based on the $30 personal needs allowance, regardless of the parents' income and resources.

Gifts of tickets for domestic travel. Provided for excluding from countable income for SSI purposes tickets that are actually used for travel, regardless of whether they could have been converted to cash. Previously, such tickets were counted as income if they could have been converted to cash.

Income producing property. Eliminated Secretarial authority to establish limits on the value of property used in a trade or business or by a worker that can be excluded as essential to self support. Previously, regulations required that in order to be excluded, income producing property could not have an equity value of more than $6,000 and would have to provide a return of at least 6 percent of the equity value. This rule was regarded as too restrictive, particularly as it affected farm families.

The 1989 OBRA also included a provision allowing former DI beneficiaries to "buy-in" for Medicare coverage. Persons who are no longer entitled to DI benefits and regular Medicare coverage because they engage in SGA despite their continuing impairment(s) may purchase Medicare coverage during specified enrollment periods. The premiums are the same as those charged to uninsured aged persons. State Medicaid programs were required to pay, on a sliding scale, the hospital insurance (Part A) premiums for eligible disabled individuals with incomes up to 200 percent of poverty or less and resources not in excess of 200 percent of the SSI resources limits.

The **1990 OBRA** included a number of disability-related amendments. Provisions affecting the DI program only and those affecting both DI and SSI are described in the DI legislative history. One of these changes provided for benefit continuation for disabled DI or SSI beneficiaries who recover while participation in a non-state VR program, comparable to the existing provision for those who recover while in a state VR program.

The OBRA 1990 provisions affecting the SSI program only:

- Excluded victims compensation payments from countable income and specified that (as under existing administrative practices) refusal to accept victims compensation could not be a basis for denial of SSI eligibility.

- Eliminated age 65 as a termination point for Medicaid protection under the 1619(b) program.

- Eliminated the requirement that, in order to become initially eligible for SSI on the basis of disability, a person had to meet the basic income test with out application of the provision for disregarding impairment-related work expenses.

- Required that the Secretary make reasonable efforts to ensure that a qualified pediatrician or appropriate specialist evaluate the cases of persons under age 18 in making disability determinations.

- Authorized VR reimbursement for months in which a person was in 1619(b) status or otherwise temporarily not in receipt of federal SSI payments.

- Extended the period for which SSI eligibility could be based on presumptive blindness or disability from three to six months.

- Precluded the possibility that continuing blindness or disability reviews could occur more than once a year under 1619 provisions. (This change confirmed existing SSA policy not to conduct such reviews more often than once a year.)

- Required that the Secretary, in complying with court-ordered notification to individuals potentially eligible for retroactive benefits under the Zebley decision, provide written notices which would clearly explain: that retroactive SSI payments are excluded from resources under SSI for only 6 months; the potential effects on future SSI eligibility of retroactive payments; the possibility of establishing a trust account that would not be considered as income or resources under SSI; and that legal assistance in establishing such a trust may be available form various legal referral services.

The 1990 OBRA also included relevant amendments in the Medicare and Medicaid programs. These amendments:

- Required the Secretary to provide information, counseling, and assistance for potentially eligible persons concerning the Medicare and Medicaid programs, Medicare supplemental (Medigap) policies, and other health insurance matters. The law also required the establishment of a national toll-free telephone information service regarding Medicare and Medigap plans and experimentation with regard to a similar state-wide service for the Medicaid, Medicare, and Medigap programs.

- Accelerated the schedule for requiring state Medicaid plans to pay Medicare premiums, deductibles, and coinsurance for Qualified Medicare Beneficiaries, including disabled beneficiaries, with income below 100 percent of poverty and extends the provision in the future to persons with incomes of 120 percent of poverty or less.

- Provided for phasing in mandatory Medicaid coverage of children age 7-18 where family income does not exceed 100 percent of poverty. (No change was made in the prior law provision which made Medicaid coverage mandatory for children age six and under where family income does not exceed 133 percent of poverty.)

- Clarified authority for states to make their own determinations of blindness or disability, using SSI standards, for Medicaid eligibility purposes. (State determinations are effective until final determinations are made by SSA.)

ATTACHMENT TO APPENDIX C
Excerpts of the Committee on Economic Security, 1935

Residual Relief

The measures we suggest all seek to segregate clearly distinguishable large groups among those now on relief or on the verge of relief and to apply such differentiated treatment to each group as will give it the greatest practical degree of economic security. We believe that if these measures are adopted, the residual relief problem will have diminished to a point where it will be possible to return primary responsibility for the care of people who cannot work to the state and local governments.

To prevent such a step form resulting in less humane and less intelligent treatment of unfortunate fellow citizens, we strongly recommend that the states substitute for their ancient, outmoded poor laws modernized public-assistance laws, and replace their traditional poor-law administrations by unified and efficient state and local public welfare departments, such as exist in some states and for which there is a nucleus in all states in the federal emergency relief organizations.

Unemployment has become an agglomeration of many problems. In the measures here proposed we are attempting to segregate and provide for distinguishable groups in practical ways.

One of these large groups is often referred to as the "unemployables." This, a vague term, the exact meaning of which varies with the person making the classification. Employability is a matter of degree; it involves not merely willingness and ability to work, but also the capacity to secure and hold a job suited to the individual. Relatively few people regard themselves as unemployables, and, outside of the oldest age groups, the sick, the widowed, and deserted mothers, most adults would, in highly prosperous times, have some employment.

The fact remains that even before the depression, there were large numbers of people who worked only intermittently, who might be described as being on the verge of unemployability—many of them practically dependent on private or public charity. These people are now all on relief lists, plus many others who, before the depression, were steady workers, but who have now been unemployed so long that they are considered substandard from the point of view of employability.

There are also large numbers of young people who have not worked or have worked but little in private employment since they left school, primarily because they came into the industrial group during the years of depression. Then there are the physically handicapped, among whom unemployment has been particularly severe. Included on the relief lists also are an estimated total of 100,000 families in "stranded industrial communities," where they have little likelihood of ever again having steady employment. There are 300,000 impoverished farm families whose entire background is rural and whose best chance of again becoming self-supporting lies on the farm.

Policies which we believe well calculated to rehabilitate many of these groups are now being pursued by the Government. These clearly need to be carried through and will require considerable time for fruition. This is especially true of the program for rural rehabilitation and the special work and educational programs for the unemployed young people. There are other serious problems, among them those of populations attached to declining overmanned industries. Only through the active participation of the Federal Government can these problems be solved and the many hundreds of thousands of individuals involved be salvaged.

As for the genuine unemployables, or near unemployables, we believe the sound policy is to return the responsibility for their care and guidance to the states. In making this recommendation, we are not unmindful of the fact that the states differ greatly as regards wealth and income. We recognize that it would impose an impossible financial burden on many state and local governments if they were forced to assume the entire present relief costs. That, however, is not what we propose. We suggest that the Federal Government shall assume the primary responsibility for providing work for those able and willing to work; also that it aid the states in giving pensions to the dependent aged and to families without breadwinners. We, likewise, contemplate the continued interest of the Federal Government for a considerable time to come in rural rehabilitation and other special problems beyond the capacity of any single state. With the Federal Government carrying so much of the burden for pure unemployment, the state and local governments we believe should resume responsibility for relief. The families that have always been partially or wholly dependent on others for support can best be assisted through the tried procedures of social case work, with its individualized treatment.

We are anxious, however, that the people who will continue to need relief shall be given humane and intelligent care. Under the stimulus of federal grants, the administration of relief has been modernized throughout the country. In this worst depression of all time, human suffering has been alleviated much more adequately than ever before. It is not too much to say that this is the only great depression in which a majority of the people in need have really received relief. It would be tragic if these gains were to be lost.

There is some danger that this may occur. While the standards of relief and administration have been so greatly improved in these last years of stress and strain, the old poor laws remain on the statute books of nearly all states. When relief is turned back to the states, it should be administered on a much higher plane than that of the old poor laws.

The states should substitute modernized public assistance laws for the ancient, outmoded poor laws. They should replace uncentralized poor-law administrations with unified, efficient state and local public-welfare departments such as already exist in some states and for which all states have a nucleus in their State Emergency Relief Administrations. The Federal Government should insist as a condition of any grants in aid that standard relief practice shall be used and that the states who receive federal moneys preserve the gains that have been made, in the care and treatment of the "unemployables." Informed public opinion can also do much and we rely upon it to thus safeguard the welfare of these unfortunate human beings and fellow citizens.

Appendix D: Federal Programs Affecting Persons with Disabilities

This is an update to the *"List of Federal Programs Affecting Persons With Disabilities,"* found in *Toward Independence: An Assessment of Federal Laws and Programs Affecting Persons With Disabilities - With Legislative Recommendations,* by the National Council on Disability, February 1986. Updates were obtained mainly from the *1993 Catalog of Federal Domestic Assistance* (CFDA), published by U.S. Government Printing Office. Other updates were obtained from the U.S. House of Representatives, Committee on Ways and Means, *Overview of Entitlement Programs (1993 Green Book),* WMCP 103-18 (Washington, DC: U.S. Government Printing Office, 1993).

Medicare

Authorization:
　42 U.S.C. 1395 et seq.; 42 U.S.C. 1305 Note
Administered by:
　Health Care Financing Administration
Expenditures - FY 1993:
　$143.1 billion (total); 17.0 billion for disabled
Served:
　31.3 million elderly and 3.7 million disabled (Hospital Insurance - Part A); 30.8 million elderly and 3.4 million disabled (Supplementary Medical Insurance - Part B)

The Medicare program provides hospital and medical insurance protection for the elderly and for disabled individuals under 65 years of age who have qualified for DI benefits for 24 months or for railroad retirement benefits based on disability for 29 consecutive months; in addition, persons under age 65 with chronic kidney disease are eligible. [CFDA 93.773 (HI) and 93.774 (SMI), HCFA]

Medicaid

Authorization:
　42 U.S.C. 1396 et seq.
Administered by:
　Health Care Financing Administration
Expenditures - FY 1993:
　$80.3 billion (total)
Served:
　32,765,000 (total)

Medicaid provides federal funds to states to pay for health care for persons who are poor. Disabled individuals generally qualify if they are eligible for Supplemental Security Income (SSI). In FY 1991, blind disabled persons were 14 percent of all Medicaid recipients and accounted for 37 percent of Medicaid expenditures. [CFDA 93.778, Green Book, p.1651,1654]

Social Security Disability Insurance (SSDI)

Authorization:
　42 U.S.C. 401, 420-425
Administered by:
　Social Security Administration
Expenditures - FY 1993:
　$33.7 billion

Served:
    3.468 million disabled workers; 1.422 million dependents of disabled workers

The SSDI program is intended to replace part of the earnings lost because of a physical or mental impairment severe enough to prevent a person from working. All disabled recipients are under 65 years of age. The average monthly benefit for disabled workers at the end of FY 1993 was $625. [CFDA 93.802, Green Book, p.52]

Supplemental Security Income (SSI)

Authorization:
    42 U.S.C. 1381-1383c
Administered by:
    Social Security Administration
Expenditures - FY 1993:
    $21.0 billion (total); ages 18-64: $12.0 billion
Served:
    3,060,544 (blind and disabled between ages 18-65)

SSI provides a minimum guaranteed income for the elderly and for blind or disabled individuals under age 65 who meet a means test and who are unable to engage in substantial gainful activity. Monthly payments range to a maximum of $434; $652 for an eligible couple. The average monthly benefit for an individual in 1992 was $196. Many states provide supplementary benefits. [CFDA 93.807, *Green Book,* p.813, 852]

Veterans' Compensation for Service—Connected Disabilities

Authorization:
    38 U.S.C. 1110, 1131
Administered by:
    Department of Veterans' Affairs
Expenditures - FY 1993:
    $10.2 billion
Served:
    2,172,506

Veterans' compensation provides direct payments to veterans who became disabled while on active duty. Regular monthly benefits range from $83 for a 10 percent disability, to $1,730 for 100 percent disability. Veterans with service-connected disabilities are entitled to free medical services in VA hospitals and are given priority over veterans with non-service connected disabilities, and the general public. [CFDA 64.109]

Social Insurance for Railroad Workers

Authorization:
    45 U.S.C. 351-367; 45 U.S.C 231-231u
Administered by:
    Railroad Retirement Board
Expenditures - FY 1993:
    $8.0 billion
Served:
    33,400 disabled; 862,200 dependents and survivors

This insurance program includes disability benefits for railroad workers who retire due to disability or who are sick or injured and unable to work and for their dependents, pursuant to the Railroad Retirement Act and the Railroad Unemployment Insurance Act. The maximum monthly benefit for disabled retired beneficiaries is about $2,016, with the average being $1010; for disabled, unemployed and sick workers, the maximum is $1,484 per month and the average is $996 per month. Significant amendments have been made to the Act to keep the fund solvent. [CFDA 57.001]

Special Education—
State Grants (Part B Individuals with Disabilities Education Act)

Authorization:
    20 U.S.C. 1401-14-19
Administered by:
    Department of Education
Expenditures - FY 1993:
    $2.4 billion

This program provides formula grants to states to assist them in providing a "free, appropriate, public education" for children with disabilities, including preschool students. The average state grant was over $26.5 million. All program participants are disabled and under age 21. [CFDA 84.027]

Veterans' Pension for Non-Service Connected Disabilities

Authorization:
   38 U.S.C. 1511,1512,1521
Administered by:
   Department of Veterans' Affairs
Expenditures - FY 1993:
   $2.3 billion
Served:
   516,270 disabled and elderly

This program provides means-tested pensions to low-income aged or disabled veterans who have had wartime service whose disabilities are not service-connected. The annual pension was $7,818 as of December 1, 1993, reduced by countable income, for an individual; $10,240 for a veteran with one dependent; and $1,330 for each additional dependent. If the veteran is in need of personal attendant care, the pension may increase to $12,504 for Aid and Attendant care for an individual or $9,556 for a housebound veteran and $14,927 for Aid and Attendant care for a veteran with one dependent or $11,977 for a housebound veteran with one dependent. [CFDA 64.104]

Rehabilitation Services—Basic Support

Authorization:
   29 U.S.C. 720-724, 730-731
Administered by:
   Department of Education
Expenditures - FY 1993:
   $1.9 billion
Served:
   941,771 (1992), estimated 1,045,600 (1993)

This program provides grants to states to enable them to deliver counseling and related services to disabled persons. Approximately 194,200 persons are "rehabilitated" to gainful employment annually. Five of the last six years have shown a decline in the number of those "rehabilitated." In 1993, 68.9 percent of those "rehabilitated" had severe disabilities, which is the highest percent in 18 years. [CFDA 84.126]

Federal Transit Capital Improvement Grants

Authorization:
   49 U.S.C. 1601 et seq.
Administered by:
   Department of Transportation
Expenditures - FY 1993:
   $1.6 billion
Served:
   Information Unavailable

This program includes a 1% set aside of federal gasoline tax revenues to be used to support transportation projects and programs benefiting disabled persons. [CFDA 20.500]

Supportive Housing for the Elderly (Section 202)

Authorization:
   P.L. 101-507; 42 USC 12701
Administered by:
   Department of Housing and Urban Development
Expenditures - FY 1993:
   $1.4 billion
Served:
   Information Unavailable

This program is designed to expand the supply of housing with supportive services for the elderly. Residents also received Section 8 rental assistance. [CFDA 14.157]

Specialized Benefits for Disabled Coal Miners

Authorization:
   30 U.S.C. 901-945
Administered by:
   Social Security Administration
Expenditures - FY 1993:
   $568 million (including dependents and survivors)
Served:
   43,723 (Part C), 38,095 (Part B)

This "black lung" program provides direct payments to coal miners who become disabled with pneumoconiosis or other chronic lung disease and to their widows and dependents. No new applications have been accepted since 1973 for Part B, except survivors. Part C covers coal miners and their widows and dependents after June 30, 1973. Part C is administered through the Department of Labor, is authorized by P.L. 97-119, and is titled, "Coal Mine Workers' Compensation." The basic monthly payments for Part B and C are $418.20, with a maximum of $836.40 as of January 1993. [CFDA 93.806]

Low Income Housing Assistance (Section 8)

Authorization:
   42 U.S.C. 1401-1435, 1437
Administered by:
   Department of Housing and Urban Development
Expenditures - FY 1993:
   $400 million
Served:
   100,000

Section 8 rent subsidies are paid to building owners to help defray rental costs; the beneficiaries pay 30 percent of adjusted income for rent. [CFDA 14.152, 14.182, and 14.856]

Vocational Rehabilitation for Disabled Veterans

Authorization:
   38 U.S.C. 1502
Administered by:
   Department of Veterans' Affairs
Expenditures - FY 1993:
   $209.4 million (benefits); $1.8 million (loans)
Served:
   36,652 (benefits); 5,500 (loans)

This program provides payment for education expenses, including full tuition, books, and fees and supplies, as well as monthly allowances. The monthly payment ranges to a maximum of $330 for a single veteran and $486 for a veteran with two dependents (plus $35 for each additional dependent). Non-interest-bearing loans are also available, for up to $666 per enrollment period. All recipients are disabled or hospitalized. [CFDA 64.116]

Veterans' Prosthetic Appliances

Authorization:
   38 U.S.C. 362 et al.
Administered by:
   Department of Veterans' Affairs
Expenditures - FY 1993:
   $195.6 million (value and repair)
Served:
   1,500,000 (devices purchased or repaired)

This program purchases aids and devices for disabled veterans. Medical equipment, hearing aids, orthopedic shoes, prosthetic devices and other appliances are provided. The range of purchase and/or repair expenditures is from about $10 to $25,000, with an average per aid of $114. [CFDA 64.013]

Education of Children with Disabilities in State-operated or State-supported Schools (Chapter 1 of the Elementary and Secondary Education Act)

Authorization:
   20 USC 2791
Administered by:
   Department of Education
Expenditures - FY 1993:
   $127.3 million
Served:
   247,000

This program helps states to improve services for students with disabilities in state-operated or state-supported schools and institutions. Children with disabilities through age 20 whose education is the state's responsibility may be served. [CFDA 84.009]

Developmental Disabilities— Basic Support and Advocacy Grants

Authorization:
   42 USC 6042-6043
Administered by:
   Department of Health and Human Services; Administration for Children and Families

Expenditures - FY 1993:
   $89.9 million

This program assists states to develop plans to coordinate services (which require a 10-25 percent matching state funds) and a support system (which requires no matching funds) that protects legal and human rights of persons with severe disabilities occurring prior to age 22. All beneficiaries are disabled. Most funds are used for advocacy activities rather than for direct services. [CFDA 93.630]

National Institute on Disability and Rehabilitation Research (NIDRR)

Authorization:
   Public Laws 98-221, 93-112, 95-102, 99-506, 100-630, and 102-569
Administered by:
   Department of Education
Expenditures - FY 1993:
   $67.2 million
Served:
   Information Unavailable

NIDRR conducts research and demonstration projects and disseminates research findings. [CFDA 84.133]

Books for the Blind and Disabled

Authorization:
   2 U.S.C. 135, 9, a-1b
Administered by:
   Library of Congress
FY 1993:
   $43.1 million
Served:
   776,000

This program provides books on cassette, disc, and in Braille as well as machines to read them. A total of 56 regional and 88 subregional libraries are supported. [CFDA 42.001]

Centers for Independent Living

Authorization:
   29 U.S.C. 796e
Administer by:
   Department of Education
Expenditures - FY 1993:
   $31.4 million
Served:
   26,566

This program provides grants to states or nonprofit organizations to establish and operate independent living centers serving severely disabled individuals. [CFDA 84.132]

Rehabilitation Services—Service Projects

Authorization:
   29 U.S.C. 750, 777a(a)(1), 777b, 777f, 795g
Administered by:
   Department of Education
Expenditures - FY 1993:
   $29.3 million (grants)
Served:
   Information Unavailable

This program provides demonstration grant monies to states and nonprofit organizations to improve rehabilitation services to disabled persons. Funds provide for 44 projects for 1992, of which 27 are continuations and 17 are new. Grants for particular supports include: $1.2 million for migratory farm workers, $2.6 for special recreation, and $10.6 for supported employment. [CFDA 84.128]

Early Education for Children with Disabilities (Early Education Program)

Authorization:
   20 U.S.C. 1423
Administered by:
   Department of Education
Expenditures - FY 1993:
   $25.2 million (grants)
Service:
   38 new projects planned

This program supports demonstration and dissemination projects for children with disabilities below eight years of age. [CFDA 84.024]

Secondary Education and Transitional Services for Youth with Disabilities

Authorization:
  P.L. 98-199
Administered by:
  Department of Education
Expenditures - FY 1993:
  $22.0 million (grants)
Served:
  Information Unavailable

This program made 22 grants in FY 1993 for projects on secondary and post-secondary education of youth with disabilities. [CFDA 84.158]

Automobiles and Adaptive Equipment for Certain Disabled Veterans and Members of the Armed Forces

Authorization:
  39 U.S.C. Chapter 39
Administered by:
  Department of Veterans' Affairs
Expenditures - FY 1993:
  $21.6 million
Served:
  843 cars purchased (estimate)

This program provides financial assistance toward the purchase price of an automobile and additional funds for adaptive equipment such as lifts or hand controls. Service-connected disabilities affecting upper or lower limbs or certain vision impairments to a prescribed degree. Up to $5,500 may be provided for an automobile or van. There is no maximum for adaptive equipment. [CFDA 64.100]

Special Education—Innovation and Development

Authorization:
  20 U.S.C. 1441-1442
Administered by:
  Department of Education
Expenditures - FY 1993:
  $20.6 million
Served:
  Information Unavailable

This program supports research and demonstration projects to improve education for children and youth with disabilities. Emphasis is upon model programs and instructional interventions. [CFDA 84.023]

Media and Captioning for Individuals with Disabilities

Authorization:
  20 U.S.C. 1451-1452
Administered by:
  Department of Education
Expenditures - FY 1993:
  $17.9 million
Service:
  54 new awards planned

This program supports grants for demonstrating innovative ways of using technology to assist disabled persons, captioning of films and of television programs, and training of teachers and parents. It maintains free loan service of captioned instructional materials. [CFDA 84.026]

Developmental Disabilities— University Affiliated Programs

Authorization:
  42 USC 6061-6077
Administered by:
  Department of Health and Human Services
Expenditures - FY 1993:
  $16.1 million
Served:
  Information Unavailable

These grants defray operating costs for programs that provide training and deliver services for persons with developmental disabilities. Core support grants were awarded to 516 University Affiliated Programs (1992). [CFDA 93.632]

Blind Veterans Rehabilitation Centers and Clinics

Authorization:
  38 U.S.C. 610

Administered by:
    Department of Veterans' Affairs
Expenditures - FY 1993:
    $14.6 million
Served:
    887 (1992)

This program supports VA hospital programs serving blinded veterans in personal and social adjustment programs. [CFDA 64.007]

Specially Adapted Housing for Disabled Veterans

Authorization:
    38 U.S.C. 2101-2106
Administered by:
    Department of Veterans' Affairs
Expenditures - FY 1993:
    $14.8 million
Served:
    464 (estimate)

This program provides up to 50% of the cost of housing, land, and other allowable expenses, to a maximum of $38,000, for disabled veterans and up to $6,500 for adaptations to the veteran's residence. [CFDA 64.106]

Services for Deaf-blind Children and Youth

Authorization:
    20 U.S.C. 1422
Administered by:
    Department of Education
Expenditures - FY 1993:
    $12.8 million
Served:
    5,440 (1992 estimate)

This program provides technical assistance to teachers and professionals who work with deaf-blind persons. Grants, usually for one year, are offered to schools and other education agencies. Four new awards are planned for 1993. [CFDA 84.025]

Assistance Loans for the Disabled

Authorization:
    Small Business Act of 1953, as amended
Administered by:
    Small Business Administration
Expenditures - FY 1993:
    $11.7 million
Served:
    Information Unavailable

One hundred eight direct loans were approved for $11.6 million in FY 1992, estimates for 1993 are unavailable. [CFDA 59.021]

Special Education—Programs for Children with Severe Disabilities

Authorization:
    20 U.S.C. 1424
Administered by:
    Department of Education
Expenditures - FY 1993:
    $9.3 million (grants)
Served:
    Information Unavailable

This program offers contracts to improve educational or training services for children and youth with severe disabilities. [CFDA 84.086]

Rehabilitation Services— Client Assistance Program (CAP)

Authorization:
    29 U.S.C. 732
Administered by:
    Department of Education
FY 1993:
    $9,296,000 (formula grants); $160,368 average
Served:
    68,166 (estimate)

This program supports state agency assistance for clients of state rehabilitation agencies. By law, the state governor selects the agency to administer the CAP program. The program provides funds to advise clients on their rights under the Rehabilitation Act and helps clients apply for and receive services. [CFDA 84.161]

Post-secondary Education Programs for Persons with Disabilities

Authorization:
  20 USC 1424a
Administered by:
  Department of Education
Expenditures - FY 1993:
  $8.8 million

This program provides demonstration grant monies to support interpreting, reading, note taking, tutoring, counseling, and related services for post-secondary students with disabilities. A total of 13 projects are planned in FY 1993. [CFDA 84.078]

Special Education Regional Resource and Federal Centers

Authorization:
  20 U.S.C. 1421
Administered by:
  Department of Education
Expenditures - FY 1993:
  $7.2 million
Served:
  Information Unavailable

Provides grants to establish and operate resource centers assisting school districts and teachers. [CFDA 84.028]

Employment Promotion of People with Disabilities

Authorization:
  Executive Order 12640
Administered by:
  President's Commission on Employment of People with Disabilities
Expenditures - FY 1993:
  $4.3 million
Served:
  Information Unavailable

The Commission sponsors an Annual Meeting and selected other conferences and issues publications to enhance employment of youths and adults with disabilities. [CFDA 53.001]

Longshore and Harbor Workers Compensation

Authorization:
  36 DC Code 501; 33 USC 901-952; 42 U.S.C. 1651, 1701; 43 U.S.C. 1333; and 5 U.S.C. 8171
Administered by:
  Department of Labor
Expenditures - FY 1993:
  $4.0 million
Served:
  Information Unavailable

This program makes direct payments to longshore workers, harbor workers, and certain other employees to compensate for total or partial disability. About two-thirds of base pay is provided. Number of workers or survivors being compensated are estimated at 18,500 per month. Compensation is also paid to survivors. [CFDA 17.302]

Disabled—Special Studies and Evaluations

Authorization:
  20 USC 1488
Administered by:
  Department of Education
Expenditures - FY 1993:
  $3.9 million
Served:
  Information Unavailable

This program supports data collection and impact studies of program effectiveness in the area of education for disabled persons. It assesses the impact of programs under the Individuals with Disabilities Act (IDEA), develops and publishes an annual report and assists state effectiveness for disabled persons. [CFDA 84.159]

Developmental Disabilities—Projects of National Significance

Authorization:
    42 USC 6081-6083
Administered by:
    Department of Health and Human Services
Expenditures - FY 1993:
    $3.0 million (grants)
Served:
    Information Unavailable

In FY 1993, grant awards focus on home ownership, personal assistance services through leadership and advocacy, ongoing data collection, federal interagency initiatives, technical assistance, and funding FY 1992 continuation grant awards. [CFDA 93.631]

Architectural and Transportation Barriers Compliance Board

Authorization:
    42 U.S.C. 4151 et seq.
Administered by:
    Architectural and Transportation Barriers Compliance Board
Expenditures - FY 1993:
    $2.9 million
Served:
    Information Unavailable

The Board enforces the Architectural Barriers Act of 1968, issues minimum requirements for four standard-setting federal agencies, and provides technical assistance on removal of barriers facing physically disabled persons. [CFDA 88.001]

President's Committee on Mental Retardation

Authorization:
    Executive Order 11776 (1985), 12610 (1987), 11776 (1991)
Administered by:
    Department of Health and Human Services
Expenditures - FY 1993:
    $655,269 (salaries and expenses)
Served:
    Information Unavailable

The President's Committee conducts public information and advisory activities. [CFDA 93.613]

National Council on Disability

Authorization:
    29 U.S.C. 780-785
Administered by:
    National Council on Disability
Expenditures - FY 1993:
    $355,000 (estimate)
Served:
    Information Unavailable

The Council advises the Congress and the President on public policies concerning persons with disabilities. [CFDA 92.001]

Disability Policy Panel Biographies

Jerry L. Mashaw, Chair, is Sterling Professor of Law at Yale Law School and a Professor at the Institute of Social Policy Studies at Yale University. He is a leading scholar in administrative law and has written widely on social insurance and social welfare issues, including disability policy. His works related to disability policy include: *Social Security Hearings and Appeals* (1978); *Bureaucratic Justice: Managing Social Security Disability Claims* (1983); *Social Security: Beyond the Rhetoric of Crisis* (1988); and *America's Misunderstood Welfare State* (1990). He received his LL.B. from Tulane University and his Ph.D. in European governmental studies from the University of Edinburgh.

Monroe Berkowitz is Professor of Economics, Emeritus at Rutgers University and Director of Disability and Health Economics in the Bureau of Economic Research. He is also the Director of Research at Rehabilitation International. He is a leading authority on the economics of disability and rehabilitation in both public programs (Social Security disability insurance and workers' compensation), private disability insurance and public and private rehabilitation systems. Professor Berkowitz has also conducted extensive comparative analyses of foreign systems. His publications include: *Disability and the Labor Market* (1986), winner of the Book of the Year Award from the President's Committee on the Employment of People with Disabilities; and *Measuring the Efficiency of Public Programs,* (1988). He received his Ph.D. in economics from Columbia University.

Richard V. Burkhauser is a Professor of Economics and Associate Director for the Aging Studies Program at the Center for Policy Research, part of the Maxwell School of Citizenship and Public Affairs, at Syracuse University. He has published widely on social insurance issues, particularly in disability policy. He has also conducted several comparative analyses of foreign systems. His works include: *Disability and Work: The Economics of American Policy* (1982); *Public Policy Toward Disabled Workers: A Cross-National Analysis of Economic Impacts* (1984) and *Passing the Torch: The Influence of Economic Incentives on Work and Retirement* (1990). He received his Ph.D. in economics from the University of Chicago.

Gerben DeJong is Director of the National Rehabilitation Hospital Research Center in Washington, DC, and Professor in the Department of Family Medicine at Georgetown University's School of Medicine. He has written extensively on health, disability and income policy issues. He has experience in state income assistance programs and has conducted numerous studies on health and disability issues over the last 20 years. His works include: "Physical Disability and Public Policy" (in *Scientific American,* 1983); *Economics and Independent Living* (1985); and "America's Neglected Health Minority: Working Age Persons with Disabilities" (in *Milbank Quarterly,* 1989). In 1985, he received the Licht Award for Excellence in Scientific Writing from the American Congress of Rehabilitation Medicine. He received his Ph.D. in public policy studies from Brandeis University.

James Ellenberger is Assistant Director of the Department of Occupational Safety and Health for the AFL-CIO. He represents the federation on disability issues and workers' compensation. He co-chairs the Labor-Management Discussion Group on Workers' Compensation. He has written on a wide variety of subjects for various publications, including articles on disability policy, social insurance, health reform, and international labor and management issues. Mr. Ellenberger received his bachelor's degree from San Francisco State University and is a Certified Employee Benefit Specialist.

Lex Frieden is Senior Vice President of the Institute for Rehabilitation and Research and Professor of Physical Medicine and Rehabilitation at Baylor College of Medicine in Houston. He also currently serves as Vice President for North America for Rehabilitation International. From 1989-1993, he served as Chair of the Advisory Board for the National Center for Medical Rehabilitation Research at the National Institutes of Health. As Executive Director of the National Council on Disability from 1984-1988, Mr. Frieden was instrumental in developing the analyses and advocacy leading to the Americans with Disabilities Act of 1990. Working in the independent living movement for people with severe disabilities since the early 1970s, Mr. Frieden has published several books and papers on independent living. He has received two Presidential Citations for his work in the field of disability. Mr. Frieden received his M.A. in social psychology from the University of Houston.

Howard Goldman, M.D. is a Professor of Psychiatry at the Institute of Psychiatry and Human Behavior at the University of Maryland School of Medicine. He has extensive research publications on issues in public health, mental illness, and disability policy. He served on the American Psychiatric Association Work Group on the Diagnostic and Statistical Manual (DSM) IV (1988-93), the President's Task Force on Health Care Reform (1993), and the Social Security Administration's expert panel to update the mental impairment listings (1985). Among his many publications are: *Long-term Care for the Chronically Mentally Ill* (1983); "Cycles of Institutional Reform" in *Mental Illness and Social Policy* (1984); and *Inching Forward: A Report on Progress Made in Federal Mental Health Policy in the 1980's* (1992). He received his M.D. from Harvard University and his Ph.D. in social welfare research from Brandeis University.

Arthur E. Hess is a consultant in public administration, health care, and social policy. He has led a distinguished career in public service in the Social Security Administration, were he served as the Acting Commissioner of Social Security (1973-74) and the Deputy Commissioner of Social Security beginning in 1967. Mr. Hess was also the first Director of Health Insurance (Medicare, 1965-1967). As the first Director of Disability Insurance (1954-65), he developed the administrative structure for linking federal Social Security offices with state agencies for making disability determinations. He has consulted widely and received numerous citations for distinguished service, including a President's Award for Distinguished Federal Civilian Service. Mr. Hess received his A.B. from Princeton University and his LL.B. from the University of Maryland.

Thomas C. Joe is a social policy analyst focusing on the organization and delivery of human services, social insurance programs and income maintenance. He is the founder and Director of the Center for the Study of Social Policy. Mr. Joe served on the first National Council for the Handicapped in 1982, was instrumental in developing the nation's SSI program and helped two administrations draft welfare reform plans for families in poverty. He served as Special Assistant to the Undersecretary of the Department of Health, Education and Welfare, and subsequently served as consultant to the White House Domestic Policy Council. Mr. Joe received his M.A. in political science from the University of California, Berkeley.

Mitchell P. LaPlante is Associate Adjunct Professor in the Department of Social and Behavioral Sciences, and the Institute for Health and Aging at the University of California, San Francisco. He is also Director of the National Disability Statistics Rehabilitation Research and Training Center. He has written extensively on conceptual and definitional issues in disability, the demography and epidemiology of disability, and disability policy. Among his publications are: *Data on Disability from the National Health Interview Survey, 1983-85* (1988); contributor in *Disability in America: Toward A National Agenda for Prevention* (1991); "The Demographics of Disability" (in *Milbank Quarterly,* 1991); and *Disability in the United States: Prevalence and Causes, 1992* (1996). Professor LaPlante received his Ph.D. in sociology from Stanford University.

Douglas A. Martin is Special Assistant to the Chancellor at the University of California, Los Angeles, and as one of the original national pioneers of the independent living movement, co-founded the Westside Center for Independent Living in Los Angeles. His extensive knowledge of the Americans with Disabilities Act and the work incentive provisions of the Social Security disability insurance and Supplemental Security Income programs distinguish him as a leading scholar in disability studies. He is a founding member of the Society for Disability Studies and helped develop the research agenda for the National Institute on Disability and Rehabilitation Research, under the U.S. Department of Education. He was instrumental in the creation of a host of Social Security work incentive amendments including the SSI Section 1619 legislation. Mr. Martin received Ph.D. in urban studies from the University of California, Los Angeles.

David Mechanic is Director of the Institute for Health, Health Care Policy, and Aging Research and the René Dubos Professor of Behavioral Sciences at Rutgers University. He is also the Director of the NIMH Center for the Organization and Financing of Care for the Seriously Mentally Ill. As a recognized expert in mental health issues, he served as Coordinator of the Panel on Problems, Scope and Boundaries for the President's Commission on Mental Health and as vice chair of the Institute of Medicine's Committee for Pain, Disability, and Chronic Illness Behavior. Among the books he has written are: *Future Issues in Health Care: Social Policy and the Rationing of Medical Services* (1979); *From Advocacy to Allocation: The Evolving American Health Care System* (1986); *Mental Health and Social Policy* (3rd Edition, 1989); and *Inescapable Decisions: The Imperatives of Health Reform* (1994). Professor Mechanic received his Ph.D. in sociology from Stanford University.

Patricia M. Owens is President of Integrated Disability Management at UNUM America. She is responsible for developing new linkages of disability, health and workers' compensation programs and for overseeing research on disability issues at UNUM, and she coordinates an ongoing study of the full employer-related costs of disability to identify better risk sharing and risk management solutions. She has consulted with numerous employers assisting in compliance with the Americans with Disabilities Act and improved management of psychiatric disabilities. She served as Associate Commissioner for Disability of the Social Security Administration (1982-86), and was awarded the Health and Human Services Distinguished Leadership Award and a Social Security Commissioner's Public Service Citation for management of the disability program. Ms. Owens received her M.P.A. from the University of Missouri.

James Perrin, M.D. is Associate Professor of Pediatrics at Harvard Medical School, and Director of Ambulatory Care Programs and General Pediatrics, Pediatric Service, at the Massachusetts General Hospital. He serves as chair of the Committee on Children with Disabilities of the American Academy of Pediatrics and served on the expert panel for the Social Security Administration to establish eligibility criteria for the SSI childhood disability program to comply with the Supreme Court decision in *Sullivan v. Zebley.* He also served on the congressionally mandated National Commission on Childhood Disability (1995). A recognized expert in the field of pediatrics and chronic conditions, Dr. Perrin has published widely on the issues of chronic illnesses and public policies affecting children and disability. Some of his works include: "Reinterpreting Disability: Changes in SSI for Children" (in *Pediatrics,*

1991); *Home and Community Care for Chronically Ill Children* (1993); and "Health Care Reform and the Special Needs of Children" (in *Pediatrics,* 1994). He received his M.D. from Case Western Reserve University.

Donald L. Shumway is co-director of "Self-Determination for Persons with Developmental Disabilities," the Robert Wood Johnson Foundation Project at the Institute on Disability at the University of New Hampshire. A leading advocate for people with developmental disabilities and those with mental illness, Mr. Shumway is managing a nationwide grant-giving and technical assistance program involving health care and long-term care needs in a managed care environment. Formerly, he was Director of the Division of Mental Health and Developmental Services in New Hampshire, and was appointed by the governor to assume overall responsibility for the division's statewide system of institutions and community services for persons who have mental illnesses, developmental disabilities, or are homeless. New Hampshire became the first state to completely close its institutional levels of care and develop an integrated system of community supports. Mr. Shumway received his M.S.S. from Bryn Mawr College.

Susan S. Suter is the President of the World Institute on Disability. Ms. Suter has held several leading positions in the rehabilitation field including Commissioner of the Rehabilitation Services Administration, U.S. Department of Education (1988); Director of the Illinois Department of Rehabilitation Services (1984-88); Director of the Illinois Department of Public Aid (1988-89); and Director of the Illinois Department of Children and Family Services (1991-92). A distinguished and active expert in the disability community, she consults widely on issues involving the Americans with Disabilities Act, human resources and other employment issues. Ms. Suter received her M.A. in clinical psychology from Eastern Illinois University.

Eileen P. Sweeney is Director of Government Affairs at the Children's Defense Fund. Previously, she was a staff attorney with the National Senior Citizens Law Center, where she specialized in Social Security and SSI, and at the Legal Assistance Foundation of Chicago. She is a recognized expert in the field of administrative law, particularly the Social Security programs where she served as co-counsel on several cases. She is an effective advocate for children, the elderly, people with disabilities, and those in poverty. She also served as a member of the SSI Modernization Panel (1992), which was charged to examine the fundamental structure and purpose of the SSI program. Ms. Sweeney received her J.D. from Northwestern University.

Jerry Thomas is the President of the National Council of Disability Determination Directors. He is also the Director of Adjudicative Services for the state of Georgia. He has spent over 20 years in the state disability adjudication agency in various positions. He is a member of the Social Security Administration's Disability Redesign Advisory Council, a member of SSA's National Disability Issues Group, and has represented state disability agencies on many national panels and work-groups. He received his M.S. in political science from Florida State University. Mr. Thomas replaced Charles Jones on the Panel in July of 1994.

List of Abbreviations

AB	Aid to the Blind	FY	fiscal year
ADA	Americans with Disabilities Act	GAO	U.S. General Accounting Office
ADC	Aid to Dependent Children	GDP	gross domestic product
ADL	activities of daily living	HHS	U.S. Department of Health and Human Services
AFDC	Aid to Families with Dependent Children	HI	Hospital Insurance; Medicare Part A
AIDS	acquired immune deficiency syndrome	HIV	human immunodeficiency virus
AIME	average indexed monthly earnings	IADL	instrumental activities of daily living
ALJ	administrative law judge	IDEA	Individuals with Disabilities Education Act
APTD	Aid to the Permanently and Totally Disabled	ICF/MR	intermediate care facility for the mentally retarded
CAP	Client Assistance Program	IFA	individualized functional assessment
CDR	continuing disability review	IRWE	impairment related work expense
CE	consultative examination	JEDI	Jobs for Employable Dependent Individuals
CETA	Comprehensive Employment and Training Act	JTPA	Job Training and Partnership Act
CFDA	Catalog of Federal Domestic Assistance	LTDI	long-term disability insurance
COBRA	Consolidated Omnibus Budget Reconciliation Act	MAA	Medical Assistance for the Aged
COLA	cost-of-living adjustment	NHIS	National Health Interview System
CPI	Consumer Price Index	NIDRR	National Institute on Disability and Rehabilitation Research
DB	defined benefit		
DC	defined contribution	NOSSCR	National Organization of Social Security Claimants Representatives
DDS	disability determination service		
DI	Social Security disability insurance	OAA	Old-Age Assistance
DoL	U.S. Department of Labor	OASDI	Old-Age, Survivors, and Disability Insurance
DVA	U.S. Department of Veterans' Affairs		
EBRI	Employee Benefit Research Institute	OASI	Old-Age and Survivors Insurance
EPE	extended period of eligibility	OBRA	Omnibus Budget Reconciliation Act
FAP	Family Assistance Plan	PASS	Plan for Achieving Self-Support
FBR	federal benefit rate	PER	pre-effectuation review
FICA	Federal Insurance Contributions Act	PES	Property Essential for Self-Support

QMB	Qualified Medicare Beneficiaries	STDI	short-term disability insurance
RFC	residual functional capacity	TDI	temporary disability insurance
SECA	Self-Employment Contributions Act	TJTC	Targeted Jobs Tax Credit
SGA	substantial gainful activity	TWP	trial work period
SMI	Supplementary Medical Insurance; Medicare Part B	VC	Veterans' Compensation
		VR	vocational rehabilitation
SSA	Social Security Administration	WC	workers' compensation
SSI	Supplemental Security Income		